THE LIBRARY OF HOLOCAUST TESTIMONIES

Hasag-Leipzig Slave Labour Camp for Women

The Struggle for Survival, Told by the Women and their Poetry

The Library of Holocaust Testimonies

Editors: Antony Polonsky, Sir Martin Gilbert CBE, Aubrey Newman, Raphael F. Scharf, Ben Helfgott MBE

Under the auspices of the Yad Vashem Committee of the Board of Deputies of British Jews and the Centre for Holocaust Studies, University of Leicester

My Lost World by Sara Rosen
From Dachau to Dunkirk by Fred Pelican
Breathe Deeply, My Son by Henry Wermuth
My Private War by Jacob Gerstenfeld-Maltiel
A Cat Called Adolf by Trude Levi
An End to Childhood by Miriam Akavia
A Child Alone by Martha Blend
The Children Accuse by Maria Hochberg-Marianska and Noe Gruss
I Light a Candle by Gena Turgel
My Heart in a Suitcase by Anne L. Fox
Memoirs from Occupied Warsaw, 1942–1945
by Helena Szereszewska
Have You Seen My Little Sister? by Janina Fischler-Martinho
Surviving the Nazis, Exile and Siberia by Edith Sekules
Out of the Ghetto by Jack Klajman with Ed Klajman
From Thessaloniki to Auschwitz and Back
by Erika Myriam Kounio Amariglio
Translated by Theresa Sundt
I Was No. 20832 at Auschwitz by Eva Tichauer
Translated by Colette Lévy and Nicki Rensten
My Child is Back! by Ursula Pawel
Wartime Experiences in Lithuania by Rivka Lozansky Bogomolnaya
Translated by Miriam Beckerman
Who Are You, Mr Grymek? by Natan Gross
Translated by William Brand
A Life Sentence of Memories by Issy Hahn,
Foreword by Theo Richmond
An Englishman at Auschwitz by Leon Greenman
For Love of Life by Leah Iglinski-Goodman
No Place to Run: A True Story by Tim Shortridge and
Michael D. Frounfelter
A Little House on Mount Carmel by Alexandre Blumstein
From Germany to England Via the Kindertransports by Peter Prager
By a Twist of History: The Three Lives of a Polish Jew by Mietek Sieradzki
The Jews of Poznań by Zbigniew Pakula
Lessons in Fear by Henryk Vogler

Hasag-Leipzig Slave Labour Camp for Women

The Struggle for Survival,
Told by the Women and their Poetry

FELICJA KARAY

translated by Sara Kitai

VALLENTINE MITCHELL
LONDON • PORTLAND, OR

First Published in 2002 in Great Britain by
VALLENTINE MITCHELL
Crown House, 47 Chase Side
Southgate, London N14 5BP

and in the United States of America by
VALLENTINE MITCHELL
c/o ISBS, 5824 N. E. Hassalo Street
Portland, Oregon 97213-3644

Website: http://www.vmbooks.com

British Library Cataloguing in Publication Data

Karay, Felicja
  Hasag-Leipzig slave labour camp for women: the struggle
  for survival, told by the women and their poetry. – (The
  library of Holocaust testimonies)
  1. Karay, Felicja 2. Women concentration camp inmates –
  Germany – Leipzig – Biography 3. World War, 1939–1945 –
  Concentration camps – Germany – Leipzig
  I. Title
  940.5'31743212'092

ISBN 0-85303-447-8 (paper)
ISSN 1363-3759

Library of Congress Cataloging-in-Publication Data

A catalog record for this book is available from the Library of Congress

Typeset in 11 on 13pt Palatino by FiSH Books, London WC1
Printed in Great Britain by MPG Books Ltd, Victoria Square, Bodmin, Cornwall

To my sisters.
With them, and thanks to them,
I survived the atrocities of the Holocaust

Contents

List of Illustrations

List of Tables

Abbreviations and Glossary

AGK (Archiwum Głównej Komisji Badania Zbrodni przeciwko Narodowi Polskiemu, Instytut Pamięci Narodowej, Warszawa): Archive of the Central Commission for Research of Crimes Against the Polish Nation, National Memorial Institute, Warsaw.

Anklageschrift (Kamienna Prozess): indictment (Kamienna trial).

APMM (Archiwum Państwowego Muzeum na Majdanku): Archive of the National Museum at Majdanek

BA Bundesarchiv Koblenz.

BGKBZHwP (Biuletyn GKBZHwP): *Bulletin of Main Commission for Investigation of Nazi Crimes in Poland.*

'Bunkerkommando' Performing arts troupe, organized by the Polish women in Hasag-Leipzig Camp.

DAW (Deutsche Ausrüstungswerke): German equipment works, a WVHA enterprise.

Doc. occup. Documenta occupationis teutonicae.

Erntefest Campaign 4–8 November 1943 in which 42,000 Jews in three camps, Majdanek, Poniatowa and Trawniki, were slaughtered by special SS units.

GG Generalgouvernement.

HSSuPF (Höherer SS und Polizeiführer): Higher SS and Police Leader.

IMT International Military Tribunal, Nuremberg.

ITS International Tracing Service, Arolsen.

KL (Konzentrationslager): concentration camp.

NMG (Archiv der Mahn und Gedenkstätte Buchenwald): Archive of the Buchenwald and Commeration Site.

Nur. doc. Nuremberg documents.

Odezwa proclamation.

Oświadczenie declaration.

RmfRüK (Reichsminister für Rüstung und Kriegsproduktion): Ministry of Armaments and War Production.

RSHA (Reichssicherheitshauptamt): Reich main security office.

Rü-Betrieb (Rüstungsbetrieb): Munitions plant.

Rü In (Rüstungsinspektion): Armament Inspectorate.

RüKdo (Rüstungskommando): Armament Command.

SSuPF (SS und Polizeiführer): SS and Police Leader.

SS-WVHA (SS-Wirtschaftsverwaltungshauptamt): SS economic and administrative main office.

sygn. (sygnatura): signature.

StAL (Sächsisches Staatsarchiv Leipzig–Saxony): state archives, Leipzig.

SWK (Sąd Wojewódzki Kielce): District Court of Justice at Kielce.

Tagebuch Hans Frank Diary.

ThHSA (Thüringisches Hauptstaatsarchiv, Weimar): Thüringen Central State Archive, Weimar.

WVHA See SS-WVHA.

YV Yad Vashem Archives, Jerusalem.

ŻIH (Żydowski Instytut Historyczny): Jewish Historical Institute, Warsaw.

Acknowledgements

This study was originally written in Hebrew, under the auspices of the Tel Aviv University Diaspora Research Institute, as another chapter in the history of 'the Hasag slaves' – the Polish Jews in the Hasag camps in the Generalgouvernement and the Third Reich during World War II. It was published in 1997 by 'Moreshet' and Yad Vashem and I am grateful to Professor Israel Gutman, and to Professor Yehuda Bauer, the academic advisers of Yad Vashem for recommending it for publication.

Thanks are due to all those who had a hand in perpetuating the memory of the Hasag-Leipzig camp, especially the former prisoners who supplied me with invaluable testimony, including Rina Fradkin, Eda Jewin, Luna Kaufman, Maria Lewinger, Ester Necer, Maryla Reich, Felicja Shahar, Sara Shalem, Helena Zorski, and others. Sadly, some I could no longer thank personally for their testimony, such as the late Henryka and Ilona Karmel, Malka Hottner and Genia Reiser. In addition, all my Polish friends were of great help in supplying me with invaluable material on camp life.

This study is based largely on material in the Yad Vashem Archives in Jerusalem, and I am grateful to all members of its staff. I would also like to thank the following individuals and institutions for making important documentary material available to me: Dr Irmgard Seidel of the Nationale Mahn und Gedenkstaette Buchenwald Archives (NMG); the staff of the Archives of Main Commission for Investigation of Crimes Against Polish People (AGK) in Warsaw; and the staff of the Sächsisches Staatsarchiv Leipzig (StAL). The English translation of this book was made possible by a grant from the 'Conference on Jewish Material Claims Against Germany, Inc.', and I am exceedingly grateful to Mr Saul Kagan, Special Consultant to the Claims Conference, and to Ms Sara Kitai, for her fine translation of both the text and the poems. And special thanks to Mr Rafael F. Scharf and Mr Ben Helfgott for their assistence.

Finally, thanks must go to my husband, Hayim Karay, for the excellent and meticulous design of the book's format. His assistance and infinite patience gave final form to this project.

The Library of Holocaust Testimonies

It is greatly to the credit of Frank Cass that this series of survivors' testimonies is being published in Britain. The need for such a series has been long apparent, where many survivors made their homes.

Since the end of the war in 1945 the terrible events of the Nazi destruction of European Jewry have cast a pall over our time. Six million Jews were murdered within a short period; the few survivors have had to carry in their memories whatever remains of the knowledge of Jewish life in more than a dozen countries, in several thousand towns, in tens of thousands of villages, and in innumerable families. The precious gift of recollection has been the sole memorial for millions of people whose lives were suddenly and brutally cut off.

For many years, individual survivors have published their testimonies. But many more have been reluctant to do so, often because they could not believe that they would find a publisher for their efforts.

In my own work over the past two decades I have been approached by many survivors who had set down their memories in writing, but who did not know how to have them published. I also realized, as I read many dozens of such accounts, how important each account was, in its own way, in recounting aspects of the story that had not been told before, and adding to our understanding of the wide range of human suffering, struggle and aspiration.

With so many people and so many places involved, including many hundreds of camps, it was inevitable that the historians and students of the Holocaust should find it difficult at times to grasp the scale and range of events. The publication of memoirs is therefore an indispensable part of the extension of knowledge, and of public awareness of the crimes that had been committed against a whole people.

Sir Martin Gilbert
Merton College, Oxford

Prologue

I cannot now remember when, where, or from whom, I heard
this story:

It happened one night in Auschwitz, when we were lying
exhausted on our bunks, totally drained, barely alive.
Suddenly we heard singing. It was Sala, a Jew from Vienna,
as emaciated and ashen as the rest of us. But when she
opened her mouth to sing, out came a Schubert serenade.
Sala's extraordinary soprano filled the miserable barracks,
the beautiful melody transporting us to another world, far
away, whose existence we have long ago forgotten... We
were so intent on the music that not one of us gave a
thought to the SS officer who had quietly entered the
barracks. He stood by the door with an expression of
amazement on his face, listening... We didn't have time to
warn Sala. All of a sudden, as if awakening from a dream,
he strode over to Sala's bunk, pulled her down to the floor,
and began beating her, shouting: '*Du verfluchte Jüdin!* – You
damnable Jew, you don't have the right to sing that song!'

Introduction

I wrote this journal on factory work-sheets using a pencil I stole from the foreman. I wrote on Sundays when we had a day off, at night, in the corner under the light on my breaks during the night shift at the plant, in the bunker during an air raid, wanting, hoping to be able to hold on to it, to hand it over to those who would live to witness the defeat of Hitler. To the prisoners of the camps at Bergen-Belsen, Ravensbrück, Gross Rosen, Stutthof, Mauthausen, what we underwent may not seem so horrible. They were in the death camps, unashamedly named *Vernichtungslager* – extermination camps.

Our concentration camp was actually a labour camp. We were needed to work in the munitions plant, one of the largest in Germany, and we came into contact with the civilian population, so it was necessary to maintain a veneer of humane treatment. And yet the terror was still there. There were hundreds of camps just like it attached to factories and mines throughout wartime Germany. They must never be forgotten either.

These words were written by Felicja Bannet-Schäftler, a prisoner of the Hasag camp at Leipzig-Schönefeld in Germany. It was a multinational women's camp, an 'outside squad' (*Aussen-kommando*) of Buchenwald, one of seven attached to the munitions plants owned by Hugo Schneider Aktiengesellschaft – Hasag-Leipzig. The same concern also maintained six Jewish forced labour camps in the Generalgouvernement (GG). To date, a study of only one of these, Skarżysko-Kamienna, has been published.[1] It was dismantled in the summer of 1944 and the inmates transferred to other Hasag camps. The present study focuses on the fate of 1,200 Jewish women transported from Skarżysko-Kamienna to Hasag-Leipzig.

1

The historical background of the Hasag-Leipzig camp was different to that of the labour camps in the Generalgouvernement. By the summer of 1944 it was abundantly clear that the defeat of Nazi Germany was imminent. This fact had implications for the relationship between Hasag and the Armaments Ministry on the one hand, and the SS economic and administrative main office (SS–WVHA) on the other. In the Generalgouvernement, Hasag had held a monopoly in munitions production, earning it a privileged status. In Germany the concern was only one of many, raising the question of whether it continued to enjoy an advantage over other weapons manufacturers.

A further question concerns the nature of financial connections between Hasag and the leading German banks. Investigation of this issue may help provide information as to the real owners of Hasag. Of no less interest are the relations between the Buchenwald camp administrators and the Hasag owners, who, until the very last minute, derived enormous financial benefits from prisoner labour. The first chapter of this study deals with these questions. It introduces the General Manager of Hasag, Paul Budin, the link between the company's camps in the Generalgouvernement and the new camps erected on his initiative in Germany.

Chapter 2 relates to the establishment and organization of the Leipzig camp. Although it was one of the many auxiliary camps of Buchenwald, as Oswald Pohl, the head of the WVHA, stated, no two camps were identical.[2] Despite the existence of uniform procedures for the administration of concentration camps, implementation varied in response to several factors:

1. the type of work for which the prisoners were needed;
2. the type and specific purpose of the camp;
3. the personality and influence of the camp commandant;
4. the composition of the prisoner population;
5. the composition of the prisoner functionaries (*Lagerver-waltung*).

In respect of the last two items, it should be noted that Ravensbrück was the only concentration camp designed exclusively for women, and has been the subject of countless studies and memoirs. It is less well known that Buchenwald, holding male prisoners alone, maintained 27 auxiliary camps for women. So far only one of these has been investigated.[3] The history of the others remains totally unknown. Interest in these camps has been growing of late, and this book represents the first attempt to investigate the subject.

The first two chapters of this book thus serve as the background for the main section devoted to a description of the internal life of the Leipzig camp. Chapters 3–8 paint a broad picture of the diverse prisoner population composed of some 18 national groups, with the Jewish women constituting one of the largest. The multinational nature of the camp makes it possible to consider relations on several levels: between the German staff and the prisoners in the factory; between the internal administration of the camp and the rank-and-file inmates; and between the various national groups. Special attention is paid to the issue of the attitude toward the Jews on all levels, and the question of whether it changed in any way in response to developments in the world political situation

There is, in addition, the basic question of whether Hasag-Leipzig, like all Nazi camps, was designed to serve as a 'laboratory' in which the German authorities conducted experiments on the bodies and minds of the prisoners under conditions of extreme terror. In order to survive, every individual, man or woman, who was thrust into this world was made to discard the accepted values of normal society and adjust to a new reality. Under such circumstances, did they have any chance of preserving their inner spirit and upholding basic moral, social and national values, even if only to the most minor degree?

In an attempt to address this issue, a description of social and cultural life in the camp is offered here, with emphasis on the Jewish prisoners. Along with the facts, their interpretation, and scenes of daily life, the book contains numerous poems written in the camp. In contrast to conventional practice in similar studies, here they do not appear in a separate chapter on cultural life,[4] but are integrated into the various chapters. This seemed to me to be the best way of enabling the reader to imagine what camp life was like, and to enter, albeit very peripherally, the prisoner's mental world.

It might be claimed that the large number of poems detracts from the objective character of this study. I would reply that they are not a mere addendum to the testimony – they are the testimony itself. The camp at Leipzig was fortunate not only to count among its population several talented women who organized extensive cultural activities, but also to have had a considerable number of poems survive, particularly those of Henryka and Ilona Karmel. This is not, however, a study devoted to their large, multifaceted opus. It is a study of the Leipzig camp containing only those works that relate directly to situations and events in the annals of the camp. The same criterion was applied to the work of other writers. In addition to recording the 'camp chronicles', these poems contain insight into social behaviour, 'international' relations, and the 'prominents.' They give expression to the individual and collective emotional reaction to events past and present, as well as to hopes for the future. Even those whose literary value might be questioned were written invariably in response to public demand and were immediately 'presented to the masses,' who awaited them eagerly, and this is the essence of their significance.

The study also contains a briefer description of other national groups, including their cultural activities, and a comparison between them and the efforts of the Jewish prisoners in terms of content and form. Nevertheless, it must be stated from the outset that the book is written from the perspective of the Jewish sector.

The sources employed in this study are of three types: German documents directly related to the history of Hasag and the camp; court records; and material written by the prisoners themselves. Unfortunately, the Hasag general archives have yet to be discovered, and it was only by chance that a few documents were found relating to the development and financial status of the concern, the relations between Hasag and Armaments Minister Speer, and negotiations between Hasag and the WVHA. The composition of the prisoner population in terms of national origin was reconstructed on the basis of lists belonging to the political department of Buchenwald that the camp commanders did not have time to destroy. A small number of sources concerning the make-up of the German staff in the camp have also survived. Regrettably, it was impossible for me to view certain documents, such as those in the ITS archives in Arolsen.

References to Hasag employees and the functionaries of the internal administration of the camp were found in trial transcripts. Material concerning Hasag's policy toward slave labourers was derived from the management's directives.

The description of the internal life of the Leipzig inmates and their work conditions in the factory rely on extant writings of the prisoners themselves, including:

1. sources written in the camp, among them:
    *   journals, the most important being that of Felicja Bannet-Schäftler;
    *   poems and prose excerpts;
    *   incidental verses and couplets;
    *   writings for the stage (sketches, plays and other 'recital pieces');
2. later sources:
    *   the testimony of former prisoners written after liberation;
    *   the testimony of former prisoners, both Jewish and Polish, obtained by request of the author;
    *   oral interviews;
    *   autobiographical memoirs published after the war by former Jewish, Russian, Polish and French prisoners. (Unfortunately, I was unable to establish contact with former prisoners of other nationalities.)

Every historian must deal with the problem of the relative credibility of testimony with regard to a variety of facts and figures, such as names, dates and numbers. Existing German documents make it possible to correct certain inaccuracies (for example, all testimonies report the size of the prisoner population to be larger than the actual camp figures). In other cases the consistency of information over a number of testimonies served as evidence of its validity.

There was also a subjective motivation for my decision to undertake this study: I too was a prisoner at Leipzig. It has been claimed that research by Holocaust survivors is problematic, incurring the risk that the authors may lose sight of the boundaries between personal experience and objective scientific observation. I can only repeat the words of the Holocaust researcher Professor Israel Gutman: some studies can only be written by the people who underwent the experience themselves. The readers must decide for themselves whether or not this study belongs to that category.

Notes

1. Felicja Karay, *Death Comes in Yellow: Skarżysko-Kamienna Slave Labour Camp* (Amsterdam: Harwood Academic Publishers, 1996).
2. International Military Tribunal (IMT), Vol. XXXVIII, doc. R 129.
3. Dieter Vaupel, *Das Aussenkommando Hess. Lichtenau des Konzentrationslager Buchenwald 1944/45,* (Kassel: Gesamthochschule Kassel, 1984) p. 75.
4. Cf. Bella Gutterman, *With Death a Toast to Life: The Tale of Janowska Concentration Camp, 1941–1943* (Hebrew), (Tel Aviv: Tel Aviv University, 1993), p. 135.

1   The Masters

Hasag & Co. – the face behind the mask

October 1943 marked a turning point in the war, as fighting ceased in the main arena, on the Eastern Front. According to the German press, it was the brilliant strategy of the *Wehrmacht* that brought this about. In Italy, the Allies advanced northward at a snail's pace, and the bombing of German towns eased off. Yet despite the lull, all of Europe was on tenterhooks waiting for the results of the Allied conference set for mid-October. Each party was pinning its hopes on the outcome. The Germans hoped for a worsening of relations among the Allies, quoting the British *Observer* that had warned against the far-reaching territorial demands of Soviet Russia. The occupied countries were desperately waiting for the opening of a second front, with the word 'October' appearing overnight in huge letters on the walls of Warsaw as a warning to their occupiers.[1]

The change came on 8 October. Contrary to expectations, Radio Moscow reported that the Red Army had launched a new offensive along the River Dnieper. The following day, there were again massive air attacks on northern Germany. But still there was no second front. The battle slipped back into its former routine, and October 1943 became the month of unfulfilled hopes.

In southeast Germany people still entertained the delusion that they were immune from heavy Allied bombing. In Leipzig, the capital of Saxony, life seemed to be going on as ever. With a sense of 'business as usual', the Hasag Concern shareholders gathered on 11 October at company headquarters on Hugo Schneider Street for a general meeting convened to approve the firm's financial statement of 1942.

The meeting was conducted by Dr Ernst Schön von

Wildenegg, chairman of the board (*Aufsichtsrat*) and a legal expert. It was attended by four men representing 31 shareholders who together held 80 per cent of the company's stock: Curt Pretzsch, director of the Allgemeine Deutsche Credit-Anstalt (ADCA) in Leipzig; Eduard Pendorf, manager of the local Deutsche Bank branch; Karl Geithe, representing the Commerzbank in Leipzig; and Georg Kaiser, the local agent for the Dresdner Bank.[2]

What kind of status did Hasag enjoy that its shareholders included the financial elite of Leipzig? The annals of the company in the Third Reich have been documented only in part thus far,[3] with new sources uncovered when the dissolution of East Germany enabled access to its archives. The *Handbuch der deutschen Aktiengesellschaften* (Handbook of Public German Companies) of 1943, for example, provides some intriguing information.[4]

From the section on the structure and history of the firm, we learn that Hasag-Leipzig was one of the oldest industrial plants in the Saxony capital. It began as a modest lamp-making workshop, growing into an impressive factory when it was taken over by the merchant Hugo Schneider in 1863. The 60 workers employed in 1870 had swelled to 200 by 1880. With Schneider's death in 1888, his eldest son, Johann Schneider-Dörfell, assumed management of the plant, joined by his younger brother Martin Schneider in 1894.

The unification of Germany in 1870 led to an economic boom from which Hasag, too, benefited. The factory was converted from lamp production to the manufacture of a special type of burner. At a later stage, the owners added a copper-working plant near the Leipzig-Schönefeld railway station, which soon became a leading enterprise in its field. The need for new production floors convinced the managers to transfer the factory bit by bit to a large complex in Schönefeld. In 1899 the partnership went public. The directors appear to have succeeded in steering the company ship through the difficult time of the Weimar Republic. In the crash brought about by the revaluation of the German mark and resulting deflation, a large number of firms were forced into bankruptcy. Hasag's habitually cautious financial policy, however, enabled it to amass capital which it could then use to buy out companies that had collapsed. Thus, for example, Hasag acquired all the stock in Otto Müller AG of Berlin, which was merged with the parent company in 1931.

Since there were as yet no signs of an end to the economic crisis, on 4 July 1932 a general meeting of Hasag shareholders decided to take steps to recoup the losses incurred by the drop in the value of the firm's assets. As a result, together with the liquidation of a 587,000-mark reserve fund, the founder capital of the company was depreciated by a ratio of 10:7, from 6 million marks to 4,200,000, effective retroactively from the 1931 balance sheet. All this was done with one goal in mind: to preserve the integrity and financial security of the company in face of future political developments, still shrouded in mist.

The year 1932 marked a momentous change in the history of Hasag when, at the recommendation of the engineer Dr Richard Koch, a member of the board of directors, Paul Budin, an SS functionary from Berlin, was appointed to the post of general manager. Without a doubt, Budin, born in 1892, must have been experienced in financial management, since at this time his SS connections alone would not have carried enough weight to earn him such a responsible position in this distinguished and well-established firm. The new manager deftly planned his strategy to adapt to the changes in the political constellation. When Hitler rose to power, the Hasag plants were converted in part to the production of munitions and other military *matériel*, and at the same time, its connections with the army's armaments office were tightened. In 1939 the Hasag Metalworks (Hasag Metallwerke G.m.b.H. Leipzig) were founded, and in 1940 merged with the parent company, Hugo Schneider AG (see the factory card, Figure 1.1). The war spurred the rapid development of Hasag, which, by the late 1930s, had become virtually a munitions plant (*Rüstungsbetrieb*) specializing in a variety of armaments, from bullets for infantry rifles to rocket shells for combat planes. By the end of 1939 the concern could boast ten plants:[5]

1. Werk Leipzig-Paunsdorf
2. Werk Berlin-Köpenick
3. Betriebstätte Altenburg
4. Betriebstätte Meuselwitz

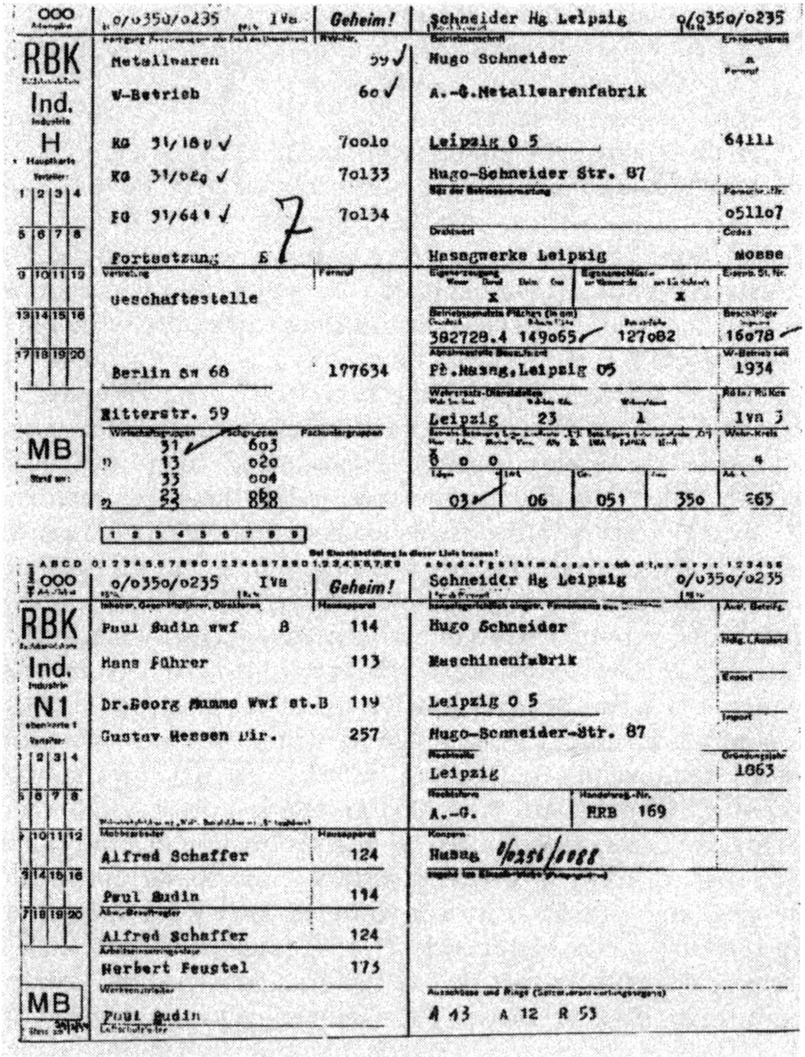
RBK
Ind.
H
o/o350/o235 IVa Geheim!
Metallwaren 59
W-Betrieb 60
RG 31/18 7oolo
RG 31/02 7o133
RG 31/64 7o134
Fortsetzung 7
Geschäftsstelle
Berlin SW 68 177634
Ritterstr. 59
31 6o3
13 o2o
33 oo4
23 868
Schneider Hg Leipzig o/o35o/o235
Hugo Schneider
A.-G. Metallwarenfabrik
Leipzig O 5 64111
Hugo-Schneider Str. 87
o511o7
Hasagwerke Leipzig Mosse
X X
382728.4 149o65 127o82 16o78
Fa. Hasag, Leipzig O5 1934
Leipzig 23 1 IVa 3
8 o o 4
03 06 051 350 265
MB

RBK
Ind.
N1
o/o35o/o235 IVa Geheim!
Paul Budin wwf B 114
Hans Führer 113
Dr. Georg Mumme Wwf st. B 119
Gustav Hessen Dir. 257
Alfred Schaffer 124
Paul Budin 114
Alfred Schaffer 124
Herbert Feustel 175
Paul Budin
Schneider Hg Leipzig o/o35o/o235
Hugo Schneider
Maschinenfabrik
Leipzig O 5
Hugo-Schneider-Str. 87
Leipzig 1863
A.-G. HRB 169
Hasag
A 43 A 12 R 53
MB

Figure 1.1 Hasag-Leipzig 'factory-card' (*Reichsbeitriebskarte*).

Source: BA, R 3/2014.

5. Werk Thermos-Langewiesen
6. Glashütte Grossbreitenbach
7. Werk Eisenach
8. Werk Oberweissbach
9. Werk Taucha bei Leipzig
10. Rhönglashütte.

The company's expansion convinced the shareholders, convened on 21 December 1942, to double its capital from 6,300,000 marks to 12,600,000. Although net profit for 1942 (DM 693,000), does not seem impressive, it must be remembered that in keeping with the characteristically German thrift typical of the firm's fiscal policy, it had again increased the reserve fund intended for development and investment. Outwardly, Hasag maintained the appearance of an ordinary civilian concern, its goals defined in the company handbook as: 'to operate factories and enterprises in the field of metalworking and related economic fields. The company is entitled to introduce new economic fields that further its aims, to open branches, to enter partnerships with other businesses and to work jointly with other businesses. The company is entitled to invest in these businesses and to open branches both in the country and abroad.'

Its list of products appears equally innocent: 'tin, iron strips, wire, brass poles and copper and aluminum barrels and strips, goods from various raw materials, particularly lighting fixtures and equipment for heating and cooking with gas, kerosene, benzene, alcohol and electricity, metalware of all sorts, including enamel, insulating materials and tools and lighting for motor vehicles'. Hasag belonged to no less than 19 branch associations and industrialist federations, including the munitions industry organization (Fachgruppe Waffenindustrie). The company profile in the handbook contains a section on partnerships which makes modest mention of a corporation by the name of Hasag-Kraków Metalworks (Hasag Eisen und Metallwerke G.m.b.H.-Krakau). This company was founded in February 1943 with a capital of 20 million zloty, at the listed value of 9,950,505 marks[6] (see Figure 1.2.). If we compare this figure to the founder capital of Hasag-Leipzig (DM 12,600,000), we may get some idea of the size of Hasag's share of the war booty (*Kriegsbeute*) from the Generalgouvernement.

The secret of the new company's success lay in the fact that Hasag had managed to secure a monopoly in the munitions industry in the G.G. In January 1943, Budin concluded negotiations with Hans Frank's administration for the purchase, at the ludicrous price of 16.5 million zloty, of three factories: a foundry at Raków, an ammunitions plant at Skarżysko-Kamienna and a grenade factory at Kielce. Three additional plants under the commisarial management (Kommissarische Verwaltung) of Hasag were added at Częstochowa.[7] The millions the company invested in this transaction paid off handsomely when each of the six factories set up Jewish forced labour camps in 1942–43. The free labour of 15,000 inmates contributed considerably to the blossoming of the firm in the Generalgouvernement.

There can be no doubt that profits from the Hasag factories in Poland were channelled back to the company's coffers in Leipzig. At the trial of Hasag's German foremen in 1948, Gustav Hessen, an executive of the firm, testified that the shares of the new company in the Generalgouvernement were divided up between Paul Budin and the Hasag-Leipzig concern. Hessen denied the accusations of inhuman living conditions for the Jewish prisoners by claiming that back in Leipzig they knew nothing of what was going on in the camps in the Generalgouvernement.[8]

This claim is totally indefensible: thousands of threads, both overt and covert, tied the Hasag factories in occupied Poland to the head office in Leipzig. As early as 4 June 1940, Egon Dalski, the manager of the Hasag-Skarżysko plants, appears on the commercial register (*Handelsregister*) as an authorized agent (*Procurist*) of Hasag-Leipzig. His power of attorney is recorded as being revoked in November 1943.[9] What is not recorded are the reasons for his dismissal: the theft of Jewish property in the Skarżysko plant and the drunken orgies with his comrades. The list of 'procurists' also includes the names of Gustaw Kuhne, Paul Geldmacher and other officials in various managerial positions in the Hasag factories in Poland.[10] All of them were well aware of the conditions in the labour camps, where Hasag removed its mask of

Hugo Schneider Aktiengesellschaft (Hasag), Leipzig

Besitz- und Betriebsbeschreibung

1. Werk Leipzig-Paunsdorf.
Fabrikanlagen: Teils Hoch- und teils Shedbau, alles massive Gebäude; Gleisanschluß. Maschinelle Einrichtungen: Messingwalzwerk, Maschineneinrichtungen für Bleche und Stangen; Metallwarenfabrik mit Geschirr-Ziehpressen, Pressen aller Art, Revolverbänke, Automaten; galvanische Anstalt, Schleiferei usw. usw. Kraftanlagen: Der zum Betriebe benötigte Kraft- und Lichtstrom wird im wesentlichen bezogen und in eigenen Transformatorenanlagen auf die erforderlichen Spannungen transformiert. Daneben erfolgt eigene Krafterzeugung durch eine Kondensator-Dampfmaschine mit direkt gekuppeltem Generator. Als Reserve steht eine Auspuffdampfmaschine mit durch Riemenübertragung angetriebenem Gleichstromgenerator zur Verfügung.

2. Werk Berlin-Köpenick.
Fabrikanlagen: Teils Hoch-, teils Shedbau, massiv. Maschi-

nelle Einrichtung: Metallbearbeitungsmaschinen. Kraftanlagen: Bezogener elektrischer Strom.
3. Betriebsstätte Altenburg (Thür.).
4. Betriebsstätte Meuselwitz (Thür.).
5. Werk Thermos-Langewiesen.
6. Glashütte Großbreitenbach (Thür.).
7. Werk Eisenach.
Anlagen zur Schwachstromlampen-Fabrikation.
8. Werk Oberweißbach (Thür.).
Anlagen zur Schwachstromlampen-Fabrikation.
9. Werk Taucha bei Leipzig.
10. Rhönglashütte Dermbach.
11. Beamtenwohnhäuser Leipzig-Sellerhausen.
Grundbesitz: 2264 qm, bebaut 430 qm, viergeschossig.

Beteiligungen

Hasag Eisen- und Metallwerke G. m. b. H., Krakau.
Gegründet: Februar 1943. Kapital: Zl. 20 000 000.— Zweck: Eisenhütte und Metallwarenfabriken. Beteiligung: 100 %.

Die Gesellschaft gehört folgenden Fachgruppen und Verbänden an:
1. Fachgruppe Leichtmetallwaren und verwandte Industriezweige der Wirtschaftsgruppe Metallwaren;
2. Fachgruppe Blechwarenindustrie und Fachgruppe Waffenindustrie und verwandte Geräte der Wirtschaftsgruppe Eisen, Stahl und Blechwarenindustrie;
3. Fachgruppe Kraftfahrzeugbestandteile und Zubehör der Wirtschaftsgruppe Fahrzeugindustrie;
4. Fachgruppe Metallhalbzeug-Industrie der Wirtschaftsgruppe X Metallindustrie;
5. Fachgruppe Glas verarbeitende und veredelnde Industrie der Wirtschaftsgruppe Glasindustrie;
6. Fachabteilungen Glühlampen (12), Isolier- und Preßstoffe (7) und Elektrische Leuchten (18) der Wirtschaftsgruppe Elektroindustrie;

Buchwert der Beteiligungen: RM 9 950 505.—

Buchwert der Wertpapiere: RM 2 453 027.65.

7. Wirtschaftsgruppe Chemische Industrie;
8. Wirtschaftsgruppe Nichteisenmetallindustrie;
9. Gemeinschaft zur Förderung des Drahtgewerbes;
10. Verband deutscher Emaillierwerke;
11. Vertragsgemeinschaft für Isolierflaschen;
12. Wirtschaftsverband der Elektrischen Beleuchtungsindustrie;
13. Verband deutscher Schwachstrom-Lampen-Fabrikanten;
14. Kartell deutscher Messingwerke;
15. Wirtschaftliche Vereinigung deutscher Messingwerke;
16. Ausfuhrgemeinschaft für Erzeugnisse der Nichteisen-Metallhalbzeugindustrie;
17. Aluminium-Walzwerk-Verband;
18. Deutscher Kupferdraht-Verband;
19. Kupferblech-Verband.

Statistik

Heutiges Grundkapital:
nom. RM 12 600 000.— Stammaktien in 12 200 Stücken zu je RM 1000.— (Nr. 1—12 200),
4 000 Stücken zu je RM 100.— (Nr. zw. 1—12 000).

Großaktionär: Dresdner Bank, Berlin (ca. 51%).

Kapital-Veränderungen

lt. Hauptvers. vom	Stammaktien	Vorzugsaktien	Kurs in %	Bezugsrecht	Bemerkungen
Kapital vor 1914	5.0				
erhöht bis 1923					
um Mill. M	120.0	2.0			
auf Mill. M	125.0	2.0			Umstellung auf Reichsmark 12½ : 1
22. 12. 24	(— 115.0)	(— 1.93)			Umstellung auf Reichsmark 200 : 7
"					
Mill. RM	10.0	0.07			Einziehung von Vorratsaktien
17. 12. 25	(— 4.0)				
25. 10. 26	6.0	0.07			Einziehung der Vorzugsaktien zu 115%
		(— 0.07)			
4. 7. 32	6.0				Kapitalherabsetzung 10 : 7
	(— 1.8)				
13. 12. 40	4.2	—			Kapitalberichtigung gemäß DAV vom 12. 6. 41,
	+ 2.1				lt. A.-R.-Beschluß vom 30.11.42; + Div. für 1941
Mill. RM	6.3		110	1 : 1	+ Div. ab 1. 1. 1942
21. 12. 42	+ 6.3				
Mill. RM	12.6				

Kurse und Dividenden

Börsen-Notiz: In Berlin und Leipzig. Ord.-Nr. 71 020. Lieferbar sind nom. RM 6 000 000.— Stammaktien.

Kurse		1934	1935	1936	1937	1938	1939	1940	1941	1942	1943
höchster	%	79.5	110	141.75	170.5	211.5	194	250	351	350.25	keine 173[1]
niedrigster	%	54	75	106.75	138	162	153.2	178.75	247.75	346	Notiz 167.75
letzter	%	73.5	109.5	135	160	195.25	189.5	248	337	351.5	166.75

[1] Notiz ab 1. Februar 1943 auf das berichtigte Kapital.

5260

Figure 1.2 Page from the 1943 *Handbook of Public German Companies*, referring to Hasag-Leipzig.

Source: StAL, Handbuch der deutschen Aktiengesellschaften, 1943, B.5.

respectability and showed its true face of corruption, exploitation and cruelty.

The prosperous years of the Dresdner Bank

Who really pulled the strings at Hasag-Leipzig? Officially, it was controlled by its own management (*Vorstand*) and board of directors (*Aufsichtsrat*). From 1933 the management was composed of: Paul Budin, general manager and chairman; Eng. Hans Führer, vice chairman; Georg Mumme, deputy chairman; and Gustav Hessen, deputy chairman.

The list of members of the board of directors is particularly interesting:

1. Dr Ernst Schön von Wildenegg, member of the board of Allgemeine Deutsche Credit-Anstalt, Leipzig, chairman;[11]
2. Hugo Zinsser, member of the board of Dresdner Bank, Berlin, vice-chairman;
3. Felix Bassermann, member of the board of Allgemeine Deutsche Credit-Anstalt, Leipzig;
4. Adolf Hartmann, manager of the Dresdner Bank, Leipzig;
5. Carl Höhn, retired factory manager, Leipzig;
6. Dr Richard Koch of Koch & Kienzel, Berlin.

The make-up of the board of directors thus sheds some light on the major powers controlling the company. A more precise picture is afforded by the list of shareholders attending the general meeting on 11 October, at which 31 shareholders controlling 80 per cent of the share capital were represented. They can be divided into three groups (see Table 1.1):

1. The German credit institution in Leipzig (Allgemeine Deutsche Credit-Anstalt, Leipzig), represented at the meeting by Kurt Pretsch, who personally owned 14.8 per cent of the firm's stock capital, and on the board of directors by von Wildenegg and Bassermann.
2. The Dresdner Bank, represented at the meeting by Georg Kaiser, who personally owned 25.5 per cent of the stock capital, and on the board of directors by Zinsser and Hartmann.

3. The Leipzig branch of the Bank of Germany (Deutsche Bank, Filiale Leipzig), represented by Eduard Pendorf.

Table 1.1 Shareholders of Hasag-Leipzig

Shareholder	Agent	Share Capital	%
Direktor Curt Pretsch, Leipzig		1,866,500	14.8
Allgemeine Deutsche Credit-Anstalt, Leipzig	Curt Pretsch	900,500	7.1
Georg Hauck & Sohn, Frankfurt a/M	Curt Pretsch	25,000	0.2
Bayr. Hypothek. u. Wechsel Bank, Nuremberg	Curt Pretsch	800	
Bayr. Hypothek. u. Wechsel Bank, Munich	Curt Pretsch	1,800	
Sächsische Bank, Filiale Leipzig	Curt Pretsch	8,100	
Paul Schauseil & Co, Halle	Curt Pretsch	20,000	0.2
Paul Schauseil & Co, Eilenburg	Curt Pretsch	900	
Meyer & Co, Leipzig	Curt Pretsch	20,000	0.2
Reichs-Kredit-Gesellschaft A.G., Berlin	Curt Pretsch	22,000	0.2
Sächsische Bank in Dresden	Curt Pretsch	15,000	0.1
		2,660,700	22.9
Deutsche Bank, Filiale Leipzig	Eduard Pendorf	620,000	4.9
Mendelssohn & Co, Berlin	Eduard Pendorf	3,000	
Creditanstalt-Bankverein, Wien	Eduard Pendorf	60,000	0.5
Wernigeroder Bank, Wernigerode	Eduard Pendorf	2,000	
L. Wolfrum & Co, Aussig	Eduard Pendorf	2,100	
Niederlausitzer Bank A.G., Cottbus	Eduard Pendorf	3,000	
Meklenburger Depositen u. Wechsel Bank	Eduard Pendorf	8,300	0.1
		698,400	5.5
Commerzbank in Leipzig, Leipzig	Karl Geithe	271,100	2.1
Prokurist Georg Kaiser, Leipzig		3,208,600	25.5
Dresdner Bank in Leipzig, Leipzig	Georg Kaiser	2,194,500	17.4
Dresdner Bank in Leipzig, Leipzig	Georg Kaiser	727,900	5.8
Dresdner Bank in Leipzig, Leipzig	Georg Kaiser	1,700	
Dresdner Bank in Leipzig, Leipzig	Georg Kaiser	26,400	0.2
Dresdner Bank in Leipzig, Leipzig	Georg Kaiser	11,000	0.1
Bayrische Staatsbank, Munich	Georg Kaiser	12,000	0.1
Bayrische Vereinsbank, Munich	Georg Kaiser	1,000	
Ostbank A.G., Posen	Georg Kaiser	5,000	
Länderbank Wien A.G., Wien	Georg Kaiser	24,000	0.2
B. Metzler s. Sohn & Co, Frankfurt/M	Georg Kaiser	25,000	0.2
Karl Dannecker, Leipzig	Georg Kaiser	900	
		6,238,000	49.5
Shareholders not represented at meeting		2,511,800	20.0
Total		12,600,00	100.0

The obvious conclusion to be drawn from the table is that Hasag was controlled largely by the Dresdner Bank-Leipzig, which, together with the 'procurist' (holding power of attorney for whom?) Georg Kaiser, held 49.5 per cent of the company's stock capital.

A glance into the not-so-distant past of the Dresdner Bank uncovers a few pages in its annals that are rather less than estimable. With Hitler's rise to power, the bank was a party to the 'Aryanization' of the Berliner Bank, owned by the Blechröder and Arnhold brothers. The authorities also deposited precious metals stolen from Jews in the Dresdner Bank's vaults.[12] The bank was similarly involved in the takeover of the Konzern Rawack und Grünfels, Hansche-Werke, and compelled to share the spoils with the Flick concern. With the occupation of Prague in 1939, the Dresdner Bank gained control of Escompetebank, the second largest bank in Czechoslovakia. Neither did it refrain from appropriating the Austrian accounts of Czech Jews. Not surprisingly, by acting so quickly it soon came to be known as 'the Nazis' financial institution'.[13]

The occupation of Poland offered the Dresdner Bank a broad arena for its activities, and along with the Reichsbank and the Deutsche Bank, it became one of the financial institutions most active in the takeover of Jewish property and the Polish economy. Several Polish banks fell into its hands, and it established its own branch in Kraków and other cities under the name Kommerzialbank. Agents of the Dresdner Bank also sat on the board of directors of Berghütte, a huge concern combining the coal mines and iron industry of Silesia in southern Poland.[14] The Dresdner Bank gained widest renown, however, as the 'SS-Bank', a title it earned as the favoured institution of senior SS officers for the handling of their own accounts.[15]

Neither the SS-Bank's control of Hasag, nor the fact that Budin himself was a highly placed functionary of the SS are sufficient proof that the concern was run at the dictates of the SS. In point of fact Hasag remained a private enterprise whose policy was set in accord with the demands of a capitalist economy. Indeed, in the autumn of 1943, the Nazi authorities and the shareholders began to go their separate ways, with the members of the financial world preferring to ensure their own future. In his chronicles, the economist Ludwik Landau wrote on 9 October 1943 that in defiance of all logic, there had been an astonishing rise in the stock prices of German industries, indicating that the buyers were divesting themselves of government bonds. The officials of the Nazi regime were well aware of the banks' hold on the German economy. In October the economic minister issued a directive to public companies demanding that they reduce the size of their boards of directors by removing agents of the banks![16] The degree to which this directive was obeyed can be seen by comparing the list of members of the Hasag board in 1942 and in 1945: it appears in fact that two more bank managers had been appointed.[17]

Another interesting fact about the postwar history of the Dresdner Bank can be found in an article published on 26 January 1955 in the Polish paper *Trybuna Ludu*:

> Hugo Zinsser, a member of the board of directors of the Dresdner Bank, was also one of the owners of the armaments concern Hasag-Leipzig. After the war, his name appeared on a list of war criminals with whom he was arrested, but he was rescued by the Americans and now serves as the manager of the Rhein-Main Bank in West Germany.[18]

The article does not mention the crimes with which Zinsser was charged. None the less, in view of the connections to American capital, we can only wonder who Hasag's slave labourers were actually working for.

In this context, the final column of the *Verzeichnis* is curious. Under the heading 'Foreign Holdings' (*Fremder Besitz*), the share capital of all those present at the meeting is listed (save for several small sums). Is it possible that the names of the banks and managers actually concealed the identities of other people who preferred to remain anonymous in the Third Reich (or other countries) and continued to do so even after its defeat? Or was this simply a ploy to evade taxes?

Enterprise in the Shadow of Defeat

In the summer of 1944 German industry was forced to deal with a new situation: the delusion of victory had long since faded, and it was clear that the time had come to salvage whatever they could. Evidence of this attitude can be found in the secret meeting of leading companies convened in Strassburg on 10 August 1944. Discussion focused on determining policy for the postwar period, including financial transactions with neutral countries and how to secure *Kriegsbeute* (war booty).[19]

On 19 June 1944, in an attempt to stave off imminent defeat, Hitler signed the 'Order Regarding the Concentration of Munitions and War Production', which gave the armaments minister the authority to determine the most urgent projects and channel all resources to them.[20] In line with this policy, the munitions plants were presented with three demands: to transfer a portion of their workers to the *Wehrmacht*; to develop new weaponry; and to step up mass production. However, the drop in the import of raw materials and forced labourers from Eastern Europe, as well as the disruption of the transportation system resulting from the bombings, made it impossible to fulfill all three demands. In order to remain in the game and exploit national resources until the very last minute, the firms could no longer plan production systematically, but were compelled to rely on their own resourcefulness and *ad hoc* solutions to all problems, including the procurement of new workers.

It should be remembered that the number of civilian workers in Germany, some 36 million, remained stable throughout the years of the war. The largest numbers were recorded in 1943 both for the *Wehrmacht* (9.6 million) and for the labour market (36.5 million). Despite the recruitment of workers for agriculture, these numbers did not drop in 1944 because thousands of people were sent back to the Reich as the Germans withdrew from occupied areas, forced back by the advance of the Soviet Army. Although the flow of forced labourers dwindled, in the summer of 1944 they still constituted about one-fifth of the total workforce in Germany,[21] and the general atmosphere of 'catch as catch can' applied to manpower as well.

Neither were the SS authorities, led by the WVHA (SS economic and administrative main office) willing to forego the opportunities presented by the war. The 'slave trade' at Buchenwald may serve as an example. According to the

Polish researcher Z. Zonik, from the autumn of 1944 and until the liberation of the camp, there were irregularities in the lists of prisoners. Nevertheless, the record that does exist presents an intriguing picture: At the end of 1944, at least 86 *Aussenkommandos* were at work in a number of factories owned by private industrialists. In January 1945 these squads comprised a total of around 105,000 prisoners, both men and women. In March 1945 there were 107 *Aussenkommandos* and by the end of the war the number had grown to 138 (see Figure 1.3).[22]

How was it that until the very last moment the factory-owners were so eager for workers from among the concentration camp inmates, thus putting millions of legitimate – illegitimate – marks into the pockets of the SS authorities and officials? The explanation was provided by Oswald Pohl, the head of the WVHA: the wages transferred by the plants to the Reich treasury through the WVHA were in net figures, after the factory owners had withheld 40 per cent for prisoner upkeep. Considering the subhuman living conditions of the inmates, 40 per cent seems exorbitant to say the least, so that concentration camp labour was far and away the cheapest alternative for private industry.[23]

The new directives issued by the Armaments Ministry and the frenzied search for manpower forced Hasag to adapt very quickly to changing realities. Budin knew that current munitions efforts for the ground forces focused on the infantry, and realized that the mass production of new weaponry was the best guarantee of the support of the Armaments Minister, Speer. It is likely that it was Budin himself who presented the new project to him. Whether or not this was the case, the stratagem produced the desired results: by special order of Hitler, Speer granted Budin extraordinary authority to increase production of anti-tank shoulder-missiles (*Sondervollmacht über Hochlauf Panzerfaust*). The project was classified as of highest priority in the new programme of munitions production.[24]

For the project to be successful, it also needed the approval of Speer's oldest rival, Himmler, who was put in charge of the arming of the ground forces in July 1944, and indeed this approval was forthcoming. Himmler's new appointment had

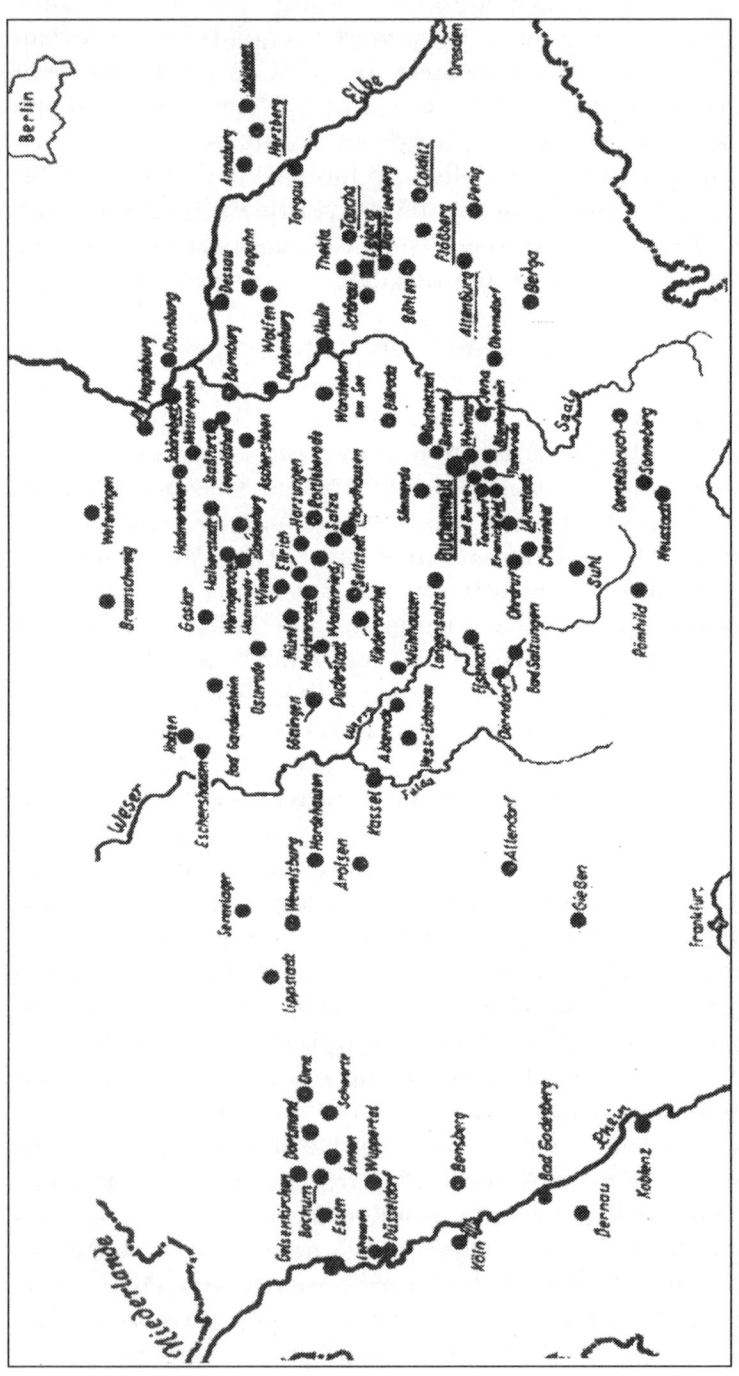

Figure 1.3 Map of the Buchenwald Camp *Aussenkommandos*.
Note: Hasag camps are underlined.
Source: Bucherwald: Mahnung und Verpflichtung (Frankfurt a/Main: Kongress Verlag, 1960)

other positive consequences for Hasag. In May, 1944 he decided to set up research laboratories in all the concentration camps. Here Jewish specialists would investigate issues of importance to the munitions industry. The idea was the brainchild of the SS High Commander of the General-gouvernement, HSSuPF Wilhelm Koppe, who had established a similar 'scientists commando' in the Płaszów camp. The report of its activities from 24 November 1944 lists, among other items, mathematical and ballistics investigations related to the new 'shoulder-missile project' of the Hasag concern.[25]

The project also required a large labour force, and to this end Hasag took four steps:

1. procuring forced labourers from European countries;
2. transferring Jews from the Hasag camps in the General-gouvernement to the firm's factories in the Reich;
3. procuring prisoners from concentration camps in Germany;
4. setting up new labour camps beside the Hasag plants in Germany.

Up until now, Budin had managed to adapt his labour force to suit production needs. Between 1941 and 1943, he transferred Polish workers from Hasag plants in the General-gouvernement to Germany, and managed to get groups of forced labourers from other countries, including Croatia.[26] In 1944 competition between the private sector and the WVHA, which employed camp inmates in its own factories, became sharper. As a result, in the spring of 1944 more foreign workers found themselves seized by the Gestapo and sent to concentration camps. Speer complained to Hitler that 30,000–40,000 employees were being arrested each month, and 'it's impossible to work like this!'[27]

Hasag was also hurt by the battle over labour. SS-Hauptsturmführer Albert Schwartz, in charge of work assignment in Buchenwald, testified that a transport of Poles from Łódź meant for Hasag was mistakenly directed to Buchenwald. Although the camp commanders knew these people were not prisoners, instead of being released they were, by order of the WVHA, reclassified as prisoners and designated an ordinary *Aussenkommando*.[28] Such incidents made it abundantly clear to Budin that he could not rely on a regular supply of forced labour.

As we have seen, Hasag was holding 15,000 Jews in the Generalgouvernement as an emergency reserve. However, years of experience in camp administration, and particularly the lessons he learned from the *Erntefest* in 1943, had taught Budin that the fate of the Jews was never certain.[29] It must be remembered that the destruction of the ghetto in Łódź began in June 1944, in the midst of the death march of Hungarian Jews to the ovens of Auschwitz. In addition, in view of the Russian advance, the Sipo (Sicherheitspolizei) and SD (Sicherheitsdienst) Commander in the Generalgouvernement, Bierkamp, issued an order in July of that year stating that if problems were encountered in the evacuation of labour camps, the Jewish prisoners were to be exterminated.[30] Meanwhile, the Russian offensive had been halted, the evacuation of the Jews appeared less urgent, and by intervention of General Maximilian Schindler, Armaments Inspector in the Generalgouvernement, the workers in the key munitions plants were assured immunity.[31]

The urgency of the new project appears to have left Hasag with only one option: the procurement of concentration camp prisoners. The company took advantage of its close ties with the Economics Office (appearing as number 9158 on the list of 'WVHA industrial organizations,' under 'special functions').[32] Budin did not hesitate to approach Oswald Pohl directly, without involving the other members of the Hasag board in the negotiations. He explained the imperative of the project and the need for thousands of prisoners for its implementation. In Pohl's opinion, 'Budin's demands were immense',[33] but negotiations were concluded successfully and assurances were given.

The infusion of thousands of prisoners into Hasag required the establishment of new camps. Budin had managed to set up 'company camps' (*Betriebslager*) in the Generalgouverne-ment which the WVHA could not touch, but this arrangement was not possible in Germany in 1944.[34] The only alternative was to house the prisoners in auxiliary Buchenwald camps (*Aussenlager*) as near as possible to the Hasag plants. Putting this plan into action required the collaboration of two individuals: SS-Standartenführer Gerhard Maurer, head of the work-assignment department (WVHA–AMT D II), and SS-Standartenführer Hermann Pister, commandant of Buchenwald. Pister also served as a manager of the German munitions plants (Deutsche Ausrüstungswerke-Buchenwald: DAW), an extremely profitable enterprise thanks to its connections with the military authorities. Hermann Pister was thus the most appropriate person for Budin to turn to.

Why a Camp for Women?

The reduction in the 'import' of foreign workers into Germany also affected the labour force in the military plants (*Wehrmacht-Betriebe*). According to official statistics of the Armaments Ministry, on 31 December 1944, 5,981,700 people were employed in 11,949 factories, with the figures in Table 1.2 demonstrating the changes that had taken place in the proportion of foreign workers.[35]

Table 1.2 Employment figures for the munitions industry

Data	No. of plants	No. of employees	Women Total	%	Foreign workers Total (incl. Ostarbeiter)	Foreign residents and Jews	POWs
20 June 1944	11,220	5,977,000	1,868,000	31.2	2,090,200	1,688,200	402,000
31 October 1944	12,198	6,224,100	2,152,000	34.5	2,276,400	2,014,004	262,000
31 December 1944	11,949	5,981,700	2,135,000	35.6	2,246,800	2,001,800	245,000

The manner in which the Jews are listed is of particular interest. Directives of the Armaments Ministry in regard to workforce statistics state that concentration and labour camp inmates of non-German descent, including Jews, are to appear together under the heading 'Others' (*Sonstige, Ausländer und Juden*).[36] It would appear that the Armaments Ministry did not wish to underscore the number of Jews for fear they might be removed from the plants.

The figures indicate a significant rise in the number of both plants and workers between June and October 1944. When both these figures drop towards the end of the year, however, there is a conspicuous increase in the percentage of women among factory personnel. This was not the result of the recruitment of additional German women, whose number barely changed throughout the war.[37] Rather, the workforce in the military plants was augmented by an influx of female prisoners, including Jews. The 'Personnel Report' of the *Wehrmacht-Betriebe* from 31 January 1945 reveals that of the 1,383,831 'others' (not including workers from the East – *Ostarbeiter*), 308,012, or 22 per cent, were women.[38] Considering the type of work involved, this is a very high proportion, warranting an investigation of Hasag's 'contribution' to this configuration.

It is well known that the large majority of concentration camps housed male inmates alone, e.g. (Buchenwald) or both men and women, e.g. (Auschwitz). The only exclusively women's camp was Ravensbrück. From mid-1942 it was decided that women from Ravensbrück could be transferred to the munitions industry on the condition, imposed by Himmler, that any firm wishing to do so first send a team of engineers and instructors to Ravensbrück to train the prisoners.[39] This directive indicates the lack of confidence in the women's technical ability, and it proved a failure. Nevertheless, with the growing demand for cheap labour (for a woman, considered an unskilled labourer, plants paid the WVHA only four marks, and in effect only two or three marks after deduction of upkeep), 34 'outside squads' of women were constituted by 1945. Of these, 23 were assigned to munitions factories.[40]

According to the data in the International Tracing Service (ITS), Arolsen, the large-scale procurement of women for the munitions industry began only in mid-August 1944. However, the core of the Hasag-Leipzig camp was already in place on 22 June 1944. On that day the camp was visited by agents of the authorities, who then went on to inspect the Hasag plants at Schlieben to check conditions for construction of an additional camp for 2,000 women prisoners who were to be sent from Ravensbrück. Hasag was represented in these discussions by Budin and the Schlieben plant manager, Merz, and Buchenwald by Hermann Pister, the head of the labour department Barnewald, and Dr Schiedlausky, the Waffen-SS garrison doctor.[41] It seems strange that the commandant of Ravensbrück, SS-Haupsturmführer Fritz Suhren, was absent from this meeting. An official explanation might be offered by the fact that although the *Aussenkommandos* of women were the administrative responsibility of their camp command, the technical implementation of all matters regarding work-assignments were handled by the Buchenwald labour procurement department.

The construction of a large camp for Women at Schlieben was obstructed by the dramatic events of July 1944 which were to change the course of the war. Europe was shaken by news of the failed attempt on Hitler's life, and in the middle of that month the Russians launched a new offensive. Germany declared 'total commitment to the war effort', and the munitions industry was again called on to speed up production and transfer a portion of their labour force to the *Wehrmacht*.

For Hasag, this was the signal to evacuate its camps in the *Generalgouvernement*. Of the ten 'company camps' dismantled in the Radom district, only the prisoners from Skarżysko-Kamienna and Kielce were transferred to other Hasag plants at Częstochowa and in Germany. Twelve hundred Jewish women were sent directly to Leipzig-Schönefeld, and 1,500 men ultimately ended up in Schlieben.[42] Once Budin received approval from the WVHA to set up another camp at Taucha, 900 men were transferred there from Płaszów in August 1944.[43]

The incoming transports from Poland prompted administrative changes. As we have seen, the *Aussenkommandos* of women from Ravensbrück served two 'masters', undoubtedly an unwieldy duplication of functions both for the commanders of Buchenwald and for Budin, who wanted 'his' people, that is, Hermann Pister and his subordinates, to handle these workers. Consequently, in a directive issued on 17 August 1944, Gerhard Maurer ordered that by the 31st of the month, the seven women's labour camps administered by Ravensbrück were to be transferred to the administrative authority of Buchenwald.[44] The list of camps is headed by three belonging to Hasag:

Table 1.3 Hasag camps under the aegis of Buchenwald

Location of Camp	No. of Prisoners on 15 August 1944
Leipzig-Schönefeld	2,951
Schlieben	998
Altenburg	1,000

The preferential treatment afforded Hasag is repeatedly apparent. On the list of 16 women's *Aussenkommandos* under Buchenwald from 25 November 1944, the five Hasag plants account together for about 50 per cent of the total number of prisoners (10,117 out of a total of 20,529).[45] By the end of 1944, Hasag had eight forced labour camps, their prisoner population on 31 January 1945 numbering 16,581, including 10,557 women (Jewish and otherwise) and 4,024 men (all Jews).[46] Hasag sustained its special status until the end of the war. In March 1945 Buchenwald administered 27 women's camps with a total of 26,000 prisoners. Hasag was the only concern to maintain five of these camps.

Table 1.4 List of Buchenwald Camp *Aussenkommandos* assigned to Hasag on 31 January 1945

Plant name	Products	Camp opened	No. of prisoners		
			Women Jews and others	Men (Jews)	Total
Leipzig-Schönefeld	Shoulder missile ammunition	1 September 1944 (w) 24 November 1944 (m)	5,067	221	5,288
Herzberg a/Elster	Explosives				2,000*
Schlieben	Shoulder missile	1 September 1944	242	2,339	2,581
Altenburg	Ammunition	1 September 1944	2,616	52	2,668
Taucha		7 September 1944 (w) 10 October 1944 (m)	1,256	426	1,682
Meuselwitz	Shoulder missile ammunition	6–9 October 1944	1,376	290	1,666
Colditz	Ammunition	29 November 1944			300
Flössberg		28 December 1944			396
Total			10,557	4,024	16,581

* As of 15 August 1944.

The list of Hasag camps (see above) reveals that in contrast to the relative precision with which the records of other camps were kept, there is a curious lack of data concerning the camp at Herzberg. In response to a question put to him on 31 July

1946, Oswald Pohl testified that he was not personally familiar with the camps run by the private sector. When his interrogator noted that seven camps were listed as belonging to Hasag, Pohl answered that 'there should be more'.[47] The fact is that the Herzberg camp does not always appear on lists of Buchenwald's *Aussenkommandos*. What was its dark secret?

After the war, confidential documents of the German Research Society (*Deutsche Forschungsgemeinschaft*) were discovered in the city of Wrocław in Poland concerning the activities of Nazi scientific institutions. Among them was a report from 24 June 1942 regarding the investigation of cases of poisoning by explosives at a pharmaceutical plant in Berlin. One of the members of the investigating team was Dr Fritz Jung, who presented a confidential overview of working conditions at the Hasag plant in Herzberg. In his report ('Bericht über gewerbliche Vergiftungen mit Dinitrobenzol'), Jung described the appalling conditions and high morbidity rate of those prisoners whose job it was to pack shells and bombs with explosives. Phenomena such as a drop of 30 per cent in haemoglobin, extreme anemia and digestive complaints were all too common. The report also refers to experiments carried out on the prisoners at various locations in order to study their sensitivity to explosives.[48] This document may contain a hint as to why such a low profile was kept for Herzberg, and we may safely assume that at least half of the 2,000 prisoners noted in 1944 were women.

Why did Hasag prefer women workers? Only the camps at Colditz and Flössberg were exclusively male; in all other locations there were in effect two separate camps and (with the sole exception of Schlieben) the women's facility was considerably larger. The WVHA would not have sent these women to Hasag against Budin's will. Known as 'an exemplary Nazi concern',[49] Hasag could undoubtedly have procured male workers had it so desired. Without question, the lower cost of a woman prisoner must have had a lot to do with it, but Budin would not have taken the risk of turning out large quantities of inferior ammunition were this a consequence of the employment of women. Rather, Budin's attitude to the employment of women appears decidedly modern, in contrast to Himmler's. The latter believed in the three traditional functions for women, 'children, church and kitchen' ('*Kinder, Kirche, Küche*'), and had demanded special instructors for them. Budin was the first industrialist in occupied Poland to assign women to operate machinery in every one of the Hasag plants, which produced a total of 17 different types of ammunition. Experience had taught him that women were no less technically proficient than men, and with the introduction of automation could adapt with extraordinary ease to any sort of work that did not demand exceptional physical strength.

Budin's success in procuring manpower (or womanpower) is indicated in a letter he wrote to Oswald Pohl (who forwarded it immediately to Himmler on 17 October 1944). It reads:

Within the framework of the special authority granted me by order of the Führer by the Armaments Minister Speer for purposes of the 'shoulder-missile project' of which the High SS Commander has also been informed, over the past weeks I have been compelled to apply nearly every day for assistance to SS-Standartenführer Gerhard Maurer, Oranienburg, and SS-Standartenführer Hermann Pister, Buchenwald, regarding the procurement of concentration camp prisoners.

Hasag is already working today with over 10,000 concentration camp prisoners and we are extremely pleased in terms of production and conduct. I regard it my duty to inform you of this, since without this assistance I would have not have been able, not even approximately, to achieve the results in the previous 'Infanterie' project and the present 'Panzerfaust' project that the facts evidence.[50]

This personnel policy paid off. In each of the Hasag plants, the machines operated at full capacity, with tens of thousands of cartons of shoulder-missiles loaded on to the trains rolling constantly eastward. In November 1944 alone, over one million shoulder-missiles were turned out. On receipt of the report from Hasag, Speer immediately informed Hitler of the success of the project, and on 30 November 1944 wrote personally to Budin (see Figure 1.4):

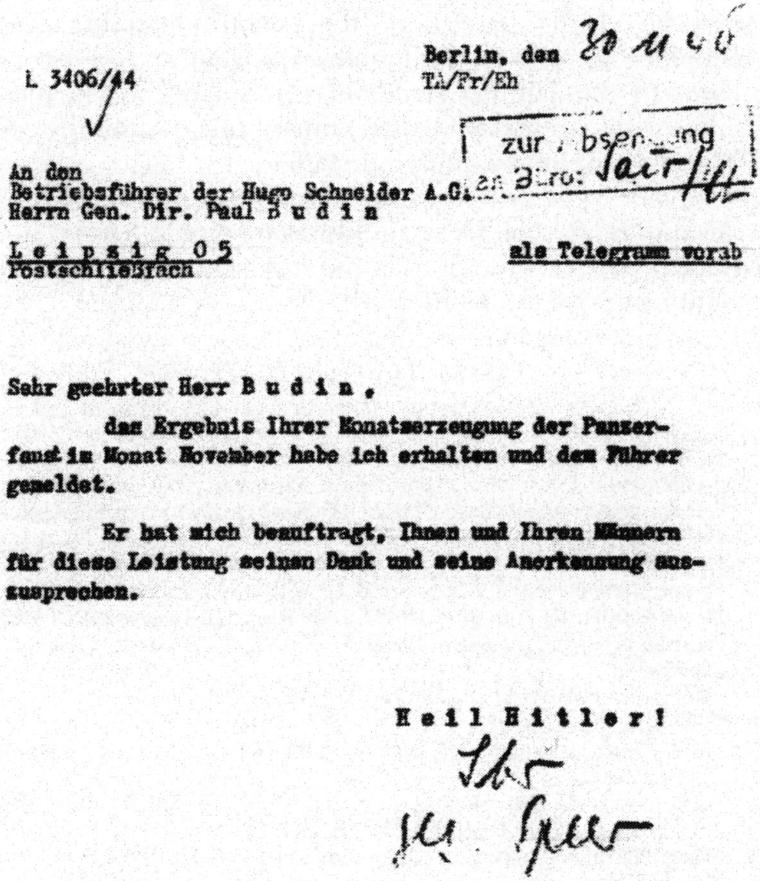

L 3406/44

Berlin, den *30 11 44*
T::/Fr/Eh

zur Absendung
am Büro: *Jair/44*

An den
Betriebsführer der Hugo Schneider A.G.
Herrn Gen. Dir. Paul B u d i n

L e i p z i g 0 5
Postschließfach

als Telegramm vorab

Sehr geehrter Herr B u d i n ,

    das Ergebnis Ihrer Monatserzeugung der Panzer-
faust im Monat November habe ich erhalten und dem Führer
gemeldet.

    Er hat mich beauftragt, Ihnen und Ihren Männern
für diese Leistung seinen Dank und seine Anerkennung aus-
zusprechen.

H e i l H i t l e r !

Ihr

M. Speer

Figure 1.4 Letter from Armaments Minister Speer to Paul Budin (30
November 1944), expressing Hitler's appreciation and gratitude for Hasag's
achievements.

Source: BA, R 3/1574/BI, 89.

Dear Mr Budin,

I received the figures of the monthly production of shoulder-missiles for the month of November and reported them to the Führer. The Führer has empowered me to express his appreciation and convey his gratitude for this achievement to you and your staff.[51]

According to the German historian Georg Janssen, the 'shoulder-missile project' was the last major munitions feat accomplished by the Third Reich.[52]

Notes

1. Ludwik Landau, *Kronika lat wojny i okupacji*, Vol. III, (Warsaw: Państwowe Wydawnictwo Naukowe, 1962), pp. 292–5.
2. 'Verzeichnis der in der ordentlichen Hauptversammlung der Hugo Schneider Aktiengesellschaft vom 11 Oktober 1943 erschienenen oder vertretenen Aktionären', Sächsisches Staatsarchiv Leipzig (StAL), AG Leipzig, HRB 169.
3. Karay, *Death Comes in Yellow*, pp. 2–5.
4. Hugo Schneider Aktiengesellschaft (Hasag), *Handbuch der deutschen Aktiengesellschaften* (1943), Band 5, pp. 5259–62 StAL. (Herefafter, *Handbuch*.)
5. 'Besitz und Betriebsbeschreibung', *Handbuch*, p. 5260.
6. 'Beteiligungen', *Handbuch*.
7. Hasag, *Encyclopedia of the Holocaust*, (Tel Aviv/New York: Macmillan 1990), p. 647.
8. Testimony of Gustav Hessen, Kamienna Trial, Sitzungen, Yad Vashem Archives, Jerusalem (YV), TR 10–7, p. 21.
9. Hasag, Handelsregister, Registerakten, StAL, 118 HRB-169.
10. Hasag an das Amtsgericht Leipzig, Leipzig, 18 February 1946, StAL, AG HRB 169. See: Karay, *Death Comes in Yellow*, pp. 39, 58, 96.
11. 'Hasag-Aufsichtsrat', *Handbuch*, p. 5259; the record of the Hasag bodies in the *Encyclopedia of the Holocaust* contains an error: the names Dr Ernst von Schön and von Wildenegg apparently refer to a single person, Ernst Schön von Wildenegg. See the testimony of Oswald Pohl from 31 July 1946, NI-388, p. 14.
12. Artur Eisenbach, *Hitlerowska polityka zagłady Żydów* (Warsaw: Książka i Wiedza, 1961), pp. 66, 399.
13. Franciszek Ryszka, *Państwo stanu wyjątkowego* (Wrocław: Ossolineum, 1964), pp. 395, 396.
14. Czesław Madajczyk, *Polityka III Rzeszy w okupowanej Polsce* (Warsaw: 1970), Part I, pp. 61, 522, 523.
15. Marian Podkowiński, 'Nie tylko Schacht', *Trybuna Ludu*, 26 January 1955.
16. Landau, *Kronika*, pp. 300, 346.
17. *Hasag an das Amtsgericht Leipzig.*
18. Podkowiński, 'Nie tylko Schacht'.

19. *Anatomie des Krieges*, Neue Dokumente (Berlin, 1969), p. 470, n. 1.
20. Anordnung zum Erlass des Führers über die Konzentration der Rüstung und Kriegsproduktion vom 19.6.1944 (RmfRüK), Bundesarchiv Koblenz (BA), R-3/3286.
21. Jürgen Kuczynski, *Die Geschichte der Lage der Arbeiter unter dem Kapitalismus* (Berlin: Tribune Verlag, 1964), pp. 282–4.
22. Wacław Czarnecki and Zygmunt Zonik, *Walczący obóz Buchenwald*, (Warsaw: Książka I Wiedza, 1969), pp. 148, 490-8.
23. Nur. doc. NI-382. cf. Czarnecki and Zonik, *Walczący obóz Buchenwald*, p. 155.
24. Georg Janssen, *Das Ministerium Speer: Deutschlands Rüstung im Krieg* (Berlin: Verlag Ullstein, 1968), p. 290.
25. Joseph Billig, *Les Camps de concentration dans l'économie du Reich hitlerien* (Paris: Presses Universitaires, 1973), p. 273.
26. Letter from P. Beisegal to Paul Budin from 19 September 1941, *Anatomie des Krieges*, p. 354. See Karay, *Death Comes in Yellow*, p. 29.
27. Albert Speer, *Der Sklavenstaat* (Stuttgart: DVA, 1981), pp. 79–80.
28. Nur. doc. NO-2125.
29. Felicja Karay, 'The Conflict Among German Authorities Over the Jewish Forced Labour Camps in the Generalgouvernement', (Hebrew) Yalkut Moreshet, 52 (April 1992), p. 116.
30. Order of the Sipo and SD Commander in the Generalgouvernement, Bierkamp, from 20 July 1944, *Documenta occupationis teutonicae* (Poznań, 1958), Vol. VI, p. 519.
31. Rüstungsinspektion im Generalgouvernement, Krakau, 20 July 1944, YV, JM/4530, p. 2/764974.
32. Nur. doc. NO-498.
33. Nur. doc. NI-388.
34. With regard to 'company camps' see Karay, *Death Comes in Yellow*, pp. 30, 32.
35. Reichminister für Rüstung und Kriegsproduktion (RmfRüK), Berlin, 23 February 1945, 'Ergebnis der Beschäftigtenmeldung. Stichtag 31 Dezember 1944', BA, R 3/3009.
36. Reichminister für Rüstung und Kriegsproduktion (RmfRüK), 'Runderlass für die Arbeitseinsatz, 10 November 1944', BA, R 3/1817.
37. Dietrich Eichholz, *Geschichte der deutschen Kriegswirtschaft 1939–1945* (Berlin: Akademic Verlag, 1971), pp. 83–5.
38. 'Beschäftigtenmeldung-Betriebe 11, 949', BA, R 3/3009.
39. Ino Arndt, *Das Frauenkonzentrationslager Ravensbrück: Studien zur Geschichte der Konzentrationslager* (Stuttgart, 1970), pp. 117–18.
40. Wanda Kiedrzyńska, *Ravensbrück, kobiecy obóz koncentracyjny*, (Warsaw: Klub Ravensbrück, 1969), p. 134.
41. 'Aktennotiz', Weimar-Buchenwald, 22 June 1944, Czarnecki and Zonik, *Walczący obóz Buchenwald*, Abb. 75.
42. See Karay, *Death Comes in Yellow*, pp. 229, 231.
43. Jacob Stendig, *Płaszów*, (Hebrew) (Tel Aviv, 1970), p. 154.
44. 'Einsatz weiblicher Häftlinge in der Rüstungsindustrie', Oranienburg 17 August 1944, *Buchenwald: Mahnung und Verpflichtung*, p. 256.
45. Vaupel, *Das Aussenkommando*, p. 72.
46. *Buchenwald: Mahnung und Verpflichtung*, pp. 252–5, 292–306; Czarnecki and Zonik, *Walczący obóz Buchenwald*, pp. 490–98.
47. Nur. doc. NI-388.

48. T. Czuj, C. Kempisty, Z. Ojrzyński, 'Działalność hitlerowskich instytutów naukowych w świetle tajnych dokumentów *Deutsche Forschungsgemeinschaft, odnalezionych we Wrocławiu'*, *Biuletyn Głównej Komisji Badań Zbrodni Hitlerowskich* (*BGKBZH*), XXVI (1975), p. 195.
49. *Buchenwald: Mahnung und Verpflichtung*, p. 75.
50. Nur. doc. NI-315.
51. RM. Speer to Gen. Dir. Budin, Berlin, 20 November 1944, BA, R 3 / 1574, Bl. 89.
52. Janssen, *Das Ministerium Speer*, p. 290.

2   The Camp

How the camp came into being

The first of the chain of Hasag camps to be set up was Leipzig-Schönefeld. Its history begins at some distance away, in the camp of Majdanek in occupied Poland, and is linked from the outset to its Commandant, Untersturmführer Wolfgang Plaul.

In the summer of 1943 Plaul visited Majdanek several times to supervise the transport of male prisoners to the camp at Buchenwald.[1] The purpose of his visits changed in the spring of 1944. To judge by the results, he was now charged with the task of selecting the group of female prisoners that were to become the 'founding mothers' of the Leipzig-Hasag camp. In April 1944 the Majdanek office began preparing a list of women destined for the new transport. The list included the whole of a large group of Polish political prisoners who had been sent to Majdanek in January 1943 from Pawiak, the infamous Warsaw prison, as well as a number of Polish women who had been at Majdanek for a long time, some of them functionaries in the camp's internal administration. On 19 April 1944 a 'special transport' of 566 Polish women and 10 female prisoners of other nationalities started on its way to Ravensbrück.[2]

Why were Poles chosen? According to Albert Schwartz, who was undoubtedly very familiar with the facts, 'when it came to workers, the category of prisoners or their nationality was of no importance, only their professional skills'.[3] It should be recalled that it was the commanders of Ravensbrück who had the most experience with female prisoners, since all the functionaries there were women from Germany, Poland and Czechoslovakia who had arrived on the earliest transports to the camp. According to the testimony of other women prisoners, many of them performed their duties so 'efficiently' that they earned the profound hatred of the rest of the inmates.[4] It is likely, then, that Majdanek's choice of Polish women was made on the basis of information received from Ravensbrück, as well as on Wolfgang Plaul's own observations. The transport reached Ravensbrück on 21 April 1944. The 'newcomers' were immediately placed in confinement for seven weeks. Contrary to custom, they were allowed to keep their striped prison uniforms from Majdanek, already an indication that this was not an ordinary transport. The women were subjected to countless medical tests, including a demeaning gynaecological examination. They were not sent out on work of any kind, and were closely guarded.[5]

The fateful day arrived on 9 June 1944. The rumour quickly spread through the camp that a 'special' group destined for Leipzig to work in the munitions plants was to be selected. Several debilitated women from the Majdanek transport were weeded out in the ensuing 'selection'. Eventually, 800 female prisoners were found suitable, the vast majority of them Poles from Majdanek who, according to one of them, appeared in considerably better shape than those who had spent some time in Ravensbrück.[6] The 'chosen ones' also included a number of Ukrainians and Yugoslavs, as well as a group of Russian prisoners of war.

This latter group was involved in an unusual incident. When they heard that they would have to work in munitions factories in Leipzig, the Russians declared that, even under threat of death, they would not agree to make bullets to be used against their brothers at the front. In order to break their resistance, the Ravensbrück commanders lined them up and made them stand for two full days with no food or water. But the Russian women did not break, and the camp authorities were forced to give in. Some 40 prisoners of war were assigned to various work details within the camp, including the kitchen. The story of their courage reverberated throughout the camp, and earned them universal admiration.[7]

On that same day, 9 June 1944, the transport arrived at Leipzig-Schönefeld, where the prisoners were received by Wolfgang Plaul, already a familiar face to some of the women from Majdanek. They were confined to isolated barracks at some distance from the Hasag factories. Conditions were surprisingly good: it was clean, there was plenty of bread, excellent soup and a variety of additions to the menu. Incredible! After the horrors of Ravensbrück, for many of the women, these luxuries made the place seem like a 'resort' (*kurort*)![8]

In July 1944 the first transport was joined by a few dozen new women from Ravensbrück, most of them Polish.[9] But they were still not enough to satisfy Hasag's production needs. Consequently, in June 1944 Budin had already looked into the possibility of procuring Hungarian Jews. That month, the Jews of Hungary were being sent directly to the ovens of Auschwitz, so that Ravensbrück remained the only reserve of female workers.

As Elisabeth Will, who was brought to the camp in January 1944, writes in her memoirs:

On 22 July 1944 a large transport left Ravensbrück for Hasag-Leipzig. In the selection preceding the transport, women prisoners from various countries were singled out: France, Poland, Czechoslovakia, the Ukraine, Russia, Greece, Holland, Germany, Hungary. There were also gypsies. The lucky ones were given new clothes, including underwear, a grey dress, a striped jacket, woollen socks and shoes. This changed the whole mood: I felt wonderful, all at once the atmosphere was different, our departure turned into a real victory parade... After Ravensbrück the world seemed very fine... Their arrival at Leipzig was greeted by an air raid siren and the prisoners looked on with pleasure at the panic of the Germans racing for the shelters.

There is a discrepancy in Elisabeth Will's testimony concerning the date and size of the transport. She writes that 2,000 women set out, and 1,000 gypsies disappeared along the way for some unknown reason. When the prisoners arrived at Leipzig, they found around 2,000 women there.[10] The previous statistics cited indicate that there were close to 900 women at Leipzig. If this international transport indeed arrived in late July, where had the other one thousand or so women come from? Apparently, they were the thousand 'gypsies' who disappeared along the way and were sent on ahead to the camp. (Elisabeth Will may also have included some of the Greek or Russian women under the heading of 'gypsies'.)

Another French prisoner, Lise Ricol-London, also describes this transport and the selection at Ravensbrück in her memoirs.[11] She claims the transport reached Leipzig on 21 July 1944 and its members were registered on the 'prisoner list' (*'Aufstellung'*) on 22 August 1944, starting from no. 1,274 and ending with no. 4,223 (the new numbers assigned to the women at Buchenwald). The list contains the names of the first 800 prisoners brought to the camp on 6 June, but it is unclear whether or not it also includes the names of the 70 women added in July. Thus, since there is a total of 2,950 names on the *Aufstellung*, the transport must have consisted of between 2,080 and 2,150 prisoners.[12]

The list does not contain the names of the 1,200 Jewish prisoners who arrived in Leipzig directly from the camp at Skarżysko, without ever being registered at Ravensbrück. However, the figure of 2,940–2,950 women transferred from Ravensbrück to Leipzig by the end of August 1944 coincides with the number in the camp register (2,951) mentioned in Maurer's directive of 17 August 1944.[13]

These were still not the last of the women prisoners procured by Hasag. In August, there was a reshuffling in the labour procurement division at Ravensbrück, bringing in SS-Oberscharführer Hans Pflaum, who has gone down in the annals of the camp as the 'cow-merchant' (*'marchand de vaches'*). Pflaum was particularly infamous for brutality towards the female prisoners, (he beat them mercilessly).[14] Part of his job was to select the inmates for the various munitions plant transports, and in this capacity he sent an additional 240 women of different nationalities to Leipzig. They entered the camp in three groups: the first (12) on 28 August 1944; the second (200) on 30 August 1944; and the third (28) on 5 September 1944.[15]

With the suppression of the Warsaw uprising in August 1944, tens of thousands of Poles were deported from the city, among them thousands of women who were sent to Ravensbrück. It was these women who made up the majority of another transport of 500 prisoners who arrived at the camp on 9 September.[16] Three of the prisoners in this transport, along with 12 others, appear on a separate list from 22 November 1944 indicating that they were sent from Auschwitz.[17]

From August 1944 there was a change in the disposition of Hungarian Jews, with some of them being sent to work at munitions plants. At last, Hasag was able to share in the 'spoils'. On 3 December 1944 a final transport of 500 women was added to the camp population. The main core of this group was 278 Jewish Hungarians, joined by small numbers of Jewish prisoners of German, French, Croatian, Slovenian, Dutch and several other nationalities.[18]

Table 2.1 Transports to Hasag-Leipzig Camp

Date of Arrival	Date of Registration	No. of women	Nationality	Sent from	Registration Nos	Note
9.6.44	22.8.44	800	Polish and other	Ravensbrück	In 'Aufstellung'	12
July 1944		73(?)	As above	Ravensbrück	1,201–1,272(?)	9, 12
21.7.44	22.8.44	2,140	Mixed	Ravensbrück	1,273–4,223 (incl 800 in 'Aufstellung')	10–12
4.8.44	5.8.44	1,200	Jewish	Skarżysko	1–1,200	21
29–30.8.44	9.10.44	212	Mixed	Ravensbrück	4,224–4,435	15
5.9.44	9.10.44	28	French	Ravensbrück	4,436–4,463	15
15.9.44	26.9.44	500	Polish and other	Ravensbrück	4,470–4,970	16
	22.11.44	12		Auschwitz	4,967–4,982	17
3.12.44	3.1.45	500	Mixed, (including 278 Hungarian Jews)	Ravensbrück	5,000–5,500	18
Total		5,465				

On 27 August 1944 the administrative procedure of transferring the Leipzig camp to the authority of Buchenwald was complete.[19] As noted above, the prisoners were now assigned new identification numbers. According to the memo regarding 'Distribution of Numbers to *Aussenkommandos* of Women' issued by Buchenwald's political department on 25 November 1944, the numbers from 1 to 10,000 were reserved for Hasag-Leipzig.[20] Had the numbers been assigned chronologically, the first 800 women who arrived in the camp in June should have been given the first ones, but this is not what happened. The registration of the female prisoners and

assignment of identification numbers began only after the arrival of the 1,200 Jewish women from Skarżysko, who were registered by the political department of Buchenwald and not Ravensbrück. This is one of the reasons why they received the first numbers: 1–1,200.[21] It is reasonable to assume that this allocation also stemmed from the camp authorities' desire to keep the Jewish women separate in order to facilitate supervision. Indeed, the numbers assigned to the 278 Hungarian Jews are similarly not in consecutive order, and appear together at the top of list of prisoners.

Despite fluctuations in the composition of the camp population, available sources indicate that it is unlikely that the total number of prisoners ever exceeded 5,500. The changes that occurred resulted not only from transports arriving, but also from those leaving the camp, among them:

1. Transports to Auschwitz of women weeded out in selections (the debilitated, ill, pregnant women and children), the majority of them Jewish.
2. The return of small groups or individual prisoners to Ravensbrück for administrative or other reasons.
3. The transfer of prisoners from one Hasag plant to another in accordance with production needs, changes in personnel, etc. In August 1944, for example, 80 women were sent to Schlieben, and in February 1945, a hundred went to Taucha.[22] Interestingly, while the exchange of prisoners among other Hasag camps was quite common, 'outgoing transports' from Leipzig became increasingly rare as early as the autumn of 1944.

With a population of 5,067 female prisoners on 31 January 1945, Hasag-Leipzig was the largest of all the women's auxiliary camps (*Aussenkommando*) administered by Buchenwald.

The commandant and his staff

Following accepted procedure, the staff of the Leipzig camp included a commandant and a team of female SS overseers (SS-*Aufseherinnen*). The first issue that warrants investigation are the special skills of Wolfgang Plaul that earned him the post of camp commandant and kept him from being sent to serve his country on the Eastern front, as might have been expected with a healthy young German man. There is no doubt that he already had a long, rich career behind him. Born in 1909, he joined the Nazi Party in 1931. Between 1935 and 1937 he was assigned to the concentration camps of Sachsenburg and Sachsenhausen, and in 1939 was at Wewelsburg. During this time, he also served in a firing squad. The years 1941–42 found him in Buchenwald, where he was the commandant of the preventive detention camp (*Schutzhaftlagerkommandant*). After a stint in the auxiliary camp Laura during 1943–44, he was appointed to the post of commandant of Hasag-Leipzig.[23]

According to Eugen Kogon, Plaul left his mark most notably on Buchenwald, where he was known as a hangman. In the well-documented fight for control between the political and criminal prisoners, he sided with the latter group, stripping the known communists of their authority and even planning their extermination. As befitting a man who bore Mozart's name, he showed himself to be a 'music-lover' by ordering the prisoners to sing as they pulled heavily laden carts. Rumour had it that it was he who gave these inmates their famous appellation 'the singing horses' (*Singende Pferde*). He also commanded the Jews to sing the demeaning 'Jews' song' (*Judenlied*) at every opportunity, one indication that his sobriquet 'the Jew-hater' was well-earned.[24]

It was probably by virtue of this 'glorious' past that Plaul was appointed commandant of the Hasag-Leipzig women's camp; a job that included responsibility for his staff. By order of Gerhard Maurer on 17 August 1944, a detachment of exterior guards and several SS overseers for the camp interior were to join the transport of prisoners from Ravensbrück. In view of the scarcity of manpower, it was difficult to recruit people for either function. The problem of the perimeter guards was solved by calling up SS men who were over-age or unfit for duty. The problem of finding enough women to oversee the camp was more difficult.

The terms of the agreement reached between Hasag and Buchenwald required Budin to send German (*Reichsdeutsche*) employees to be trained at Ravensbrück. Their number was to equal the number of SS overseers he was assigned. Budin naturally preferred to use the German Work Service (*Arbeitsdienst*) women in the Hasag plants to supervise the camp, but to do that he needed approval from the regional labour administration.[25] Such an arrangement would be in line with the accepted practice, by which German women were recruited into the ranks of the SS. This generally took place in one of three ways:

1. recruitment of factory personnel through the auspices of the local labour exchange with the approval of the regional labour director (*Arbeitsgau*);
2. conscription implemented by means of orders to local mayors to find appropriate candidates in their towns and transfer them to the authority of the SS;
3. recruitment of volunteers.

The women inducted into the SS did not have the right to object to or appeal against their conscription orders, and were required to undergo training at Ravensbrück. Presumably, those found unsuitable for the job during the course of this instruction were sent home.[26] Those who volunteered did so because they could expect higher wages and better conditions than they had enjoyed in their previous place of work. Compensation was determined according to age, seniority and family status. Thus, for example, an unmarried newly recruited SS overseer aged twenty-one or twenty-two earned 125 marks, while her married colleague earned 135. Uniforms and shoes were issued free of charge. The women themselves were responsible for other expenses, including taxes and the German Labour Front Levy (*Deutsche Arbeitsfront* – DAF), as detailed below:

Table 2.2 Monthly budget of a single SS overseer (expenses)

	Marks
Food	37.20
Accommodation (single room)	15.00
Taxes	7.50
DAF	2.40
Health insurance	10.00
Underwear and entertainment	43.00
Total	115.10

It is clear from these figures that the SS overseers did not live a life of luxury. The appeal of service in a concentration camp thus lay in the possibility of adding to their income by the theft of prisoner property. In 1942–43, some 3,000 German women completed their training at Ravensbrück. At the end of the six-week course, graduates were assigned posts in a camp for women or in the women's division of a concentration camp for both sexes.[27]

What sort of 'training' did these recruits receive? In 1966 one of them, Ulla Jürss, was tried and sentenced to life imprisonment for crimes against humanity. West German television (NDR) defined her 'studies' as 'training in deriding and exterminating human beings' (*'Schulung in Menschenverachtung und Zerstörung'*). The men and women on the course were described in the broadcast as epitomizing the German petty bourgeoisie: 'From this reign of absolute discipline, the average individual emerged as a murderer.'[28]

The memoirs of former Ravensbrück prisoners stress the fact that all the SS overseers, both married and single, were promiscuous with their colleagues, and tales were told in the camp of wild drunken orgies. In her attempt to find a psychological explanation for this behaviour, the former inmate Germaine Tillion suggests a connection between barbarity and debauchery, particularly among the women. Those overseers who permitted the lustful advances of SS men before the very eyes of the prisoners were the same women whose personal and original forms of brutality went far beyond the normal bounds of cruelty. Germaine noticed that, unlike the male SS officers who were not particularly handsome, most of the women were quite attractive. Not all of them were members of the Nazi Party, and a review of the data regarding some 200 of them reveals that they came from all sectors of German society.[29] Buchenwald records from 23 September 1944 list the female SS overseers in the various auxiliary camps, as given in Table 2.3:[30]

Table 2.3 Female overseers in auxiliary camps

Camp	No. of overseers
A.T.G. Leipzig	20
Hasag, Altenburg	19
Hasag, Leipzig	41
Hasag, Schlieben	20
Krupp, Essen	54
Verw. Chemie, Allendorf	6
Verw. Chemie, Hess. Lichtenau	26
Gerätebau, Werk Mühlhausen	15
Junkers, Makkleeberg	10
Kabelleitungswerk, Neustadt/Kbg	8
Rheinmetall Borsig A.G.	26
I.G. Farben, Wolfen	5
Lippst. Eisen und Metallwerke	8
Heeres Muna, Torgau	10
Total	268

The record shows that a total of 268 overseers were assigned to 14 outside squads, 80 of them in Hasag camps. Hasag-Leipzig is the second largest after Krupp in terms of staff members. A similar list from 31 January 1945 puts the number of SS guards at Hasag-Leipzig at 81, and the number of female overseers at 50.[31]

The members of the staff of overseers were not constant, with changes occurring both for objective (illness, etc.) and disciplinary reasons. One list for *Aussenkommando* Hasag-Leipzig compiled at Buchenwald (undated) contains only 47 names.[32] Another list of 94 SS women overseers attached to a letter of the National Committee of the Politically Persecuted in Bavaria from 23 September 1947 includes, in addition to those names already known, three more women noted as serving at Leipzig.[33] Nine additional names appear on various documents of the Buchenwald administration dealing with matters of personal equipment[34] (see Figure 2.1). These figures indicate that a total of 59 SS overseers were assigned to the camp at Leipzig at various times.

Following regular procedure, a head overseer (*SS-Oberaufseherin*) was also posted to Hasag-Leipzig. Officially, she was directly responsible to the camp commandant and it was her job to supervise the rank-and-file overseers and ensure that they, together with the prisoners, reported for

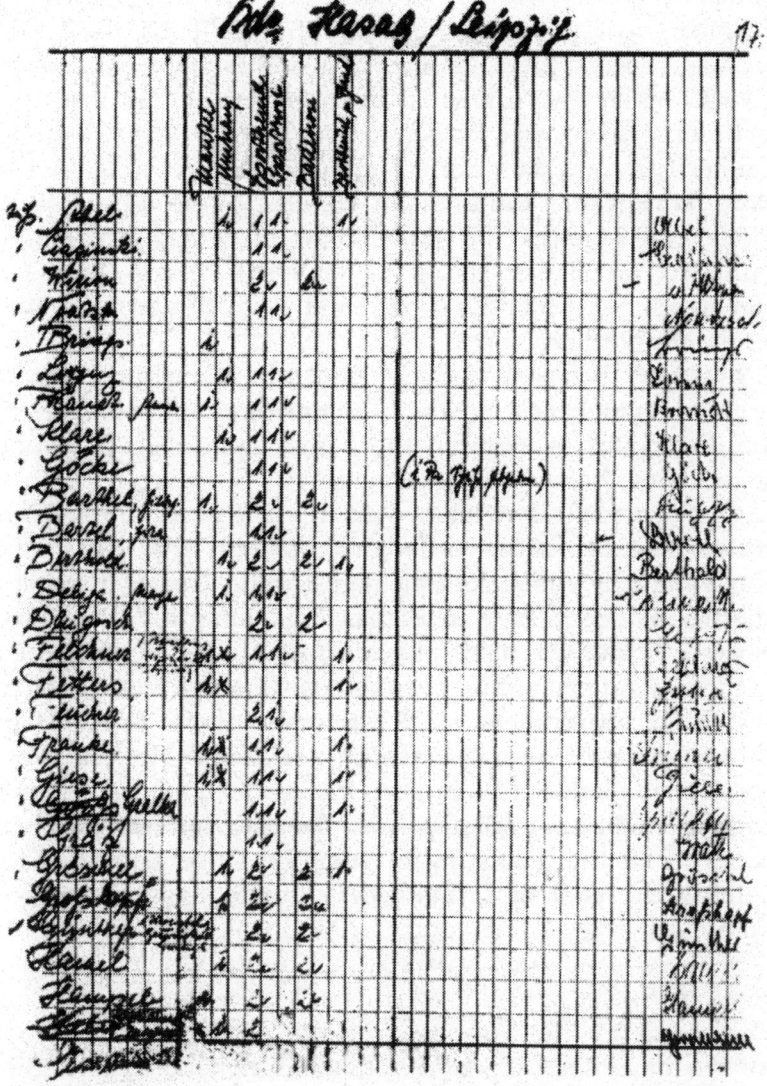

Figure 2.1 Page from the list of SS overseers assigned to Hasag-Leipzig Camp (clothing allotment).

Source: ThHSA, NS, 4 Bu, Vlg, 99, p. 171.

work in the plant, precisely on time. She herself was in charge of activities only within the camp itself, her duties including keeping a roster of those inmates who were ill. On the basis of existing sources, there is some confusion as to the name of this '*Oberka*', as she was known by the prisoners. In response to the testimony of several Polish women before the Polish War Crimes commission, an investigation was begun against the overseer Elfriede Kaltofen on charges of brutality toward the Leipzig inmates. She claimed that the *Oberaufseherin* in the camp was an SS overseer by the name of Saletsky, with Käthe Heber as her second-in-command. Arrest warrants were issued for both women.[35]

In Danuta Brzosko-Mędryk's book, the name of the '*Oberka*' is given as Heber-Sarnowsky.[36] Interestingly enough, despite the discrepancies between the names appearing in various testimonies, the same figure emerges: a tall, young, curvaceous and very attractive woman with the face of an angel, blond curls – and brutality worthy of a butcher. The two sources above may have mistaken the name of the '*Oberka*' for that of another overseer, Elise Saretzka, who came to Leipzig from Auschwitz and was also notorious for her extreme cruelty.

Official data is more reliable. According to a letter from the WVHA-D Department of 28 September 1944, Käthe Heber held the post of head overseer at that time.[37] Her name also appears in a letter of 28 January 1945 concerning the return of equipment,[38] but is missing from the list from March of that year.[39] From the beginning of 1945, Else Noatzsch, listed as holding the post of *Erstaufseherin*, seems to have replaced Käthe Heber.[40]

Reward and punishment Hasag-style

As we have seen, Speer's commendation of Paul Budin's achievements indicates that the manager of Hasag produced outstanding production figures even in the chaotic conditions already prevailing in the German economy in the summer of 1944. What was the secret of his success? Were the conditions in his camps so good that they motivated the 'Hasag slaves' to ever greater efforts, or was the opposite true – were the punishments such that they resulted in increased production?

In so far as Leipzig, by virtue of its size, exemplifies other camps as well, two major factors can be seen to have affected living conditions. On the one hand, the policy implemented in all concentration camps invariably dictated poorer conditions for women prisoners. At Auschwitz they were assigned to a much smaller area, lacking in the basic sanitary facilities, and were allotted smaller food rations. Shaving their heads and dressing them in the striped inmate uniforms divested them of both human and feminine semblance. To this was added further discrimination against the Jewish women. In the words of Rudolf Hess, the commandant of Auschwitz: 'The Jewish women died much faster than the men, despite the fact, as I have learned from experience, that *women are generally hardier and more resilient than men, both mentally and physically*'.[41] Hess attributed this to the inmates' mental state, ignoring the fact that the high death-rate was the result of the deplorable conditions in the camp.

On the other hand, Hasag's policy was also determined by the company's experience of running forced labour camps in the Generalgouvernement for Jewish inmates of both sexes. Here they learned that under harsh but identical conditions, the women fared better, suffering less from starvation, maintaining personal hygiene and remaining healthier. This greater endurance derived from several advantages: their heads were not shaved, nor were their clothes taken away from them; and they enjoyed relative 'freedom' within the camp, enabling them to establish 'trade' among themselves and to conduct a certain social life, including cultural activities.

Taking into account both approaches, Hasag, interested in obtaining the maximum output from 'its' women, adopted a 'zig-zag' policy with regard to the internal running of the camp. In contrast to the conditions in the concentration camps, the prisoners of Leipzig were housed not in huts, but in a large former factory building on Bautzener Strasse. The sign on the gate read '*Schutzhaftlager*' (preventive detention camp). The building, several storeys high, along with the area designated for officers, were surrounded by two high-voltage barbed wire fences and SS watch-towers. A number of additional wooden structures, separately fenced and known as Drugie Pole ('the Other Field') by the prisoners, also belonged to the camp, and were used to house some of the Poles and Hungarian Jews.[42]

The building, boasting several balconies, was surrounded by grass. The kitchen, a huge dining-hall, and the administration offices (*Schreibstube*) were on the ground floor. The cellar held the food stores, shelters, two large washrooms (*Waschräume*) with hot water in the faucets and showers, and relatively normal toilets (although they lacked doors). A small infirmary (*Revier*) was located on the first floor. Long corridors ran the length of each floor, leading into the dormitories or 'blocks', big high-ceilinged halls with efficient central heating. The blocks were divided by partitions that did not reach the ceiling. Each block slept several hundred women on pallets built four levels high. The prisoners were issued mattresses and blankets. A number of tables and benches occupied the centre of the block.

Figure 2.2 Coupon for the Hasag-Leipzig Camp canteen.

Source: Private collection.

There was also a canteen in the camp, where the inmates could make purchases in exchange for coupons to the value of one or two marks awarded for exemplary work in the plant (see Figure 2.2). These bore the inscription: 'SS-Standort-Kantine, Buchenwald, Aussenkommando, Wertmarke RM-2' (SS base canteen, Buchenwald outside squad, monetary coupon 1 DM).[43] They were handed out by the plant foremen or the *blokowa* (*Blockälteste:* block supervisor) in the camp. The canteen offered a sort of salad consisting of vegetables and snails in mayonnaise, or a portion of jam. If, as was generally the case, these were unavailable, the women could console themselves by buying a comb, a small mirror, a toothbrush, sometimes a bar of soap and, on very rare occasions, a pair of rubber shoes or fabric shoes with wooden soles. There were also sanitary pads (of no value to most of the women since the majority had ceased to menstruate) and even beaded necklaces,[44] although it was perfectly clear that should they dare to deck themselves in such adornments they would be beaten within an inch of their lives by the first SS overseer they encountered.

The policy of reward and punishment was particularly apparent in regard to personal appearance. On principle, the women's heads were not shaved and no numbers were tattooed on their arms. There is no doubt that, as Danuta Brzosko-Mędryk states, this accommodation 'prevented mental paralysis'. However, as in all concentration camps, the clothes brought from Ravensbrück were identical for everyone: undershirts, underpants, socks, a striped or grey dress and a jacket. Periodically, the dresses underwent disinfecting and the underwear was replaced. There was a head check every month, and anyone found to have lice had their head shaved. The 'lucky' ones got shoes, but most (and the Jews in particular) had to make do with wooden clogs. According to one testimony, brassieres were forbidden, but the inmates got round this by sewing them themselves. The injunction against belts was dodged by weaving rope bindings.[45]

As in all camps, the greatest problem was food. As far as we can tell from available testimony, each transport arriving in the camp enjoyed a 'honeymoon' period courtesy of Hasag. Their daily fare was the regular diet for munitions workers:

excellent soup, plentiful high-quality bread and a variety of supplements. As soon as the SS took over responsibility for supplies, however, conditions deteriorated. The bread ration was reduced, the quality of the soup declined, and the supplements – such as a slice of salami, a spoonful of jam, or a dollop of margarine, became so small they were barely able to hide the taste of the bitter 'coffee'. Hasag appears to have learned from experience that hygiene was more important to women than diet, and thus provided reasonable sanitary conditions in compensation for the meagre food rations.

Strangely enough, alongside the policy of food-deprivation, there was considerable concern for health services in the camp. In principle, matters of health were the province of the Buchenwald administration. According to the *Aussenkommando* records of 31 January 1945 compiled by the Waffen SS garrison doctor (*Der Standortarzt der Waffen-SS*), medical personnel in the 'Hasag-Leipzig camp' consisted of:[46]

On behalf of the SS health corps...Dressler
No. of doctors (prisoners)...4
No. of nurses (prisoners)...13

This was the largest medical staff of any of Buchenwald's auxiliary camps, the reason being, above all, a fear of epidemics which represented a two-fold risk. First, it was no longer a simple matter for Hasag to procure new transports of slave labourers, and second – and most importantly – the prisoners here worked in factories within a large city and side by side with Germans. Thus, in contrast to the 'infirmaries' in concentration camps and other forced labour camps that came to be known as 'corridors to death,' on the whole the Leipzig *Revier* offered the prisoners genuine health-care. The unit was virtually independent, with internal medicine, surgical and dental departments, all equipped with the basic instruments. A shack outside the main building housed a ward for infectious diseases. More complex operations, particularly if they were associated with work accidents, were performed in the hospital within the factory compound. Hasag provided the *Revier* with certain drugs and medical supplies. As a rule, the average number of patients at any one time did not exceed

200 – a result of conditions in the camp with its relatively low level of overcrowding and the provision of mattresses, blankets and heating. However, there were an alarming number of bedbugs and fleas. The battle against lice was more effective, since the plentiful hot water and soap ration made it possible to maintain personal hygiene. As Irene Pełka-Seńko describes it: 'It was typical of our camp – (humane) health services while at the same time they starved us like they did in the concentration camps.'[47] Indeed, as we have seen, in the winter months of 1944–45, hunger became the prisoners' most serious problem.

Another torment was the regime of assemblies (*Appell*) and punishments. There were two types of assemblies. The first were 'routine' roll-calls conducted each morning and evening, at which time the various supervisors counted the prisoners and reported the figures to the SS overseers. The second were punitive, collective punishment for all sorts of offences. In the wake of the most serious, such as the escape of a prisoner, the others would be made to stand or kneel for hours on end. An untidy block was also cause for a general disciplinary muster or *Strafappell*. Individual punishments were more inventive: head-shaving, three days of solitary confinement in a bunker with no food, being made to stand in the courtyard for several hours. The most severe penalty – 25 blows – was meted out at Buchenwald. Such an incident is described by one of the former inmates of that camp:

Once, in 1944, four women from the Hasag-Leipzig commando came to the camp [Buchenwald]. Three of them had committed some sort of offence and they were punished at the detention house by Oberscharführer Hermann Hofschultke with 25 blows. After he had administered the punishment, Hofschultke reported to his superior that he had carried out orders, adding: 'One of them, instead of 25, I gave her 40 blows, as hard as I could, but she was made of iron and didn't make a sound!' A little while later we heard that one of the women who had been punished had died of a heart attack. The SS men there laughed at Hofschultke for boasting before, saying: 'You beat a corpse and wasted your strength with your 40 blows!'[48]

As in all the Nazi camps, Hasag-Leipzig could implement their carrot-and-stick policy with the help of a team of functionaries: the *Lagerverwaltung*, the internal camp administration.

'Mistresses or slaves'?

Following Ravensbrück practice, the primary prisoner functionaries for each *Aussenkommando* were appointed before they left for the auxiliary camp. They were to serve as the core of the internal administration in the new camp. The former Majdanek inmates knew from experience just how great an influence the internal administration had on camp life. Therefore, before leaving Ravensbrück, they chose the major functionaries themselves, and their suggestions were approved in part by the commandant Wolfgang Plaul.[49] Danuta Brzosko-Mędryk's book *Matylda*, along with the extensive testimonies of Irena Pełka-Seńko and Maryla Perlberg-Reich, are the main sources for the various posts in the internal administration of the Hasag-Leipzig camp.

The central post of 'camp doyenne' (*Lagerälteste*) was held by Joanna Szumańska, a vain imposing woman with a crown of blond braids, the daughter of a geography professor at Lwów University and a former student and pianist. Before the war, she had socialized with Jews. According to her version of events, she had seen arrested for her part in a smuggling ring getting Jews into Hungary. According to another version, under interrogation in prison, she informed on the other members of the group. In Lwów she had been friendly with a Pole, Halina Kielar, and with Hanka Skowrońska, a Jewish woman with Aryan papers whose real name was Maryla Perlberg (today Reich). The three of them were sent to Majdanek, where they met and formed ties with the political prisoners from Pawiak.[50]

At Majdanek, Joanna served as the second *Lagerälteste* in the women's camp. According to Matylda Woliniewska, she was chosen for the job by her Majdanek friends because she had had the courage to resist the authorities' orders, had shown exceptional integrity and loyalty, and had not benefited from any of the privileges enjoyed by the functionaries in other camps. At the same time, she responded harshly to any undesirable behaviour on the part of the prisoners.[51] In contrast to this 'character reference', however, Danuta Brzosko-Mędryk claims that Joanna was selected for the 'camp police' (*Lagerpolizei*) at Majdanek by the SS overseer. When she asked to be excused from the post, she was beaten. None the less, when a transport of Jewish women from the Warsaw ghetto arrived, Joanna tried, unsuccessfully, to 'impose some order' on their blocks, and as a result often became angry and beat them.[52] In fact, she was notorious among the Jewish inmates at Majdanek for her brutality.[53]

It seems likely that Joanna Szumańska's appointment to the post of camp doyenne at Leipzig was promoted by the commandant Wolfgang Plaul, who knew her from Majdanek. In the new camp, she kept a low profile: she always wore the striped dress (the 'prominentes' in Ravensbrück sometimes wore civilian clothes), and the only privileges she enjoyed was a small two-room apartment.[54]

Joanna's second-in-command in charge of the camp police (*Lagerschutz* or *Lagerpolizei*) was Zinaida Bragińska, known as Zina. The more junior positions were generally held in rotation by different prisoners. These included:

- **Camp guard** (*Lagerschutz*): The function of 'policewoman' included helping to organize the roll-calls and count the prisoners, organizing work groups, inspecting the blocks, toilets, etc.
- **Administration offices** (*Schreibstube*): These were manned by Teresa Todtleben,[55] Halina Madurowicz, Alina Paradowska and others. The offices registered prisoners and prepared records of their status: healthy, ill, escapees, transfers to other camps, transports arriving and leaving, individual files, etc. All these figures were passed on to the offices at Buchenwald.[56]
- **Food stores**: the workers organised the distribution of bread and other food to the prisoners.
- **Supplies**: Jadwiga Lipska and others were responsible for these. According to the testimony of Jadwiga, her function was restricted to conveying instructions to the food stores as to the commodities to be supplied to the camp kitchen,

'and the amount of paper work involved was considerably greater than the amount of food'.[57]

- **Blocks**: A *Blockälteste* (or *'blokowa'*) was in charge of each block: a post usually held by a Polish inmate. Because of the language problems in the multinational camp, the *blokowa* would appoint an assistant (*sztubowa*, *Stubendienst*) who shared a common language with the prisoners in the block, and she would be in charge of order and cleanliness, food distribution, etc. Thus, for example, the French block had a head *sztubowa* (a Frenchwoman), who was entitled to choose an assistant and several 'group leaders' (*grupowa*) to dole out food. The Polish *blokowa* made do with using its connections with the camp offices and internal police.[58]
- **Kitchen**: There was one kitchen for all the inmates. In contrast to the other functions, only one Polish woman is mentioned as having worked here: Krystyna Winnicka.[59] Most of the women in the kitchen were Russian prisoners of war, remembered for their part in the 'rebellion' at Ravensbrück.[60] Ukrainians were assigned to help them. The prisoners of war were also assigned jobs in maintenance, disinfecting and gardening.
- **Canteen**: Coupons (*'bons'*) could be exchanged for a variety of items in the canteen.[61]

The infirmary, or *Revier*, was a separate unit with a large staff. As early as August, 1944, two prisoner doctors and one nurse were sent from Auschwitz.[62] According to Irena Pełka, with few exceptions, only Poles were employed here. Members of the staff included:

1. **Doctors**:
   - Internists: Dr Maria Iwanowna, a Russian and Dr Helena Wasiliewna, a Ukrainian (their family names are unknown).
   - Surgeons: Maria Pilichowska, also known as 'Dr' although she was actually a paramedic who worked with the professional nurse Sawicka.
   - Dentist – Dr Antonina Nieszczyńska.
2. *Revier* **secretary**: Krystyna Mostowska.
3. **Infectious diseases ward**: This was staffed by the

biologist Irena Todtleben and Barbara Narbutowicz.

4. **Nursing staff**: Only the professional nurses worked here permanently, with the auxiliary staff positions rotating among various prisoners, among those mentioned as serving as head nurse are: Halina Sliwińska, Elżbieta Pańczyszyn, Jadwiga Wolska, Elica Pulko (Slovenian), Jadwiga Kamieńska, Hanka Skowrońska, Helena Bieńkowska and Nina Fiodorczuk.

5. **Practical nurse**: Irena Pełka, with the assistance of four other women in the post of *sztubowa*, was in charge of distributing food to the patients, who received the same rations as the other prisoners. On very rare occasions, the *Revier* enjoyed supplements from the SS kitchen, such as a pitcher of milk or porridge.[63]

The problem of relations between the Polish functionaries and the prisoners of other nationalities is reported throughout the history of the camp. It must be mentioned, however, that there are two opposing views of the nature of internal administrations in general. Gilbert Dreyfus, a former prisoner of Mauthausen, maintains in his memoirs that the *Lagerverwaltung* was 'an almost incredible system that demonstrates the truly demonic genius of evil: the executioners were recruited from among the prisoners. The Nazis hoped that we would slaughter each other, and, in fact, their plan succeeded beyond all expectations.'[64] It was not by chance that Elizabeth Will chose the title 'Mistresses and slaves' (*Maitresses et esclaves*) for the chapter on the internal administration of Ravensbrück. In the women's camp as well, implementation of this system leads to a pessimistic conclusion, since the same objectives and conditions brought about the same sort of 'privileged status' exploited by the authorities, the same perversions and twisted passions, and the same crimes.[65]

A contradictory view is presented by Matylda Woliniewska, a Polish public official and social worker allied with the Socialist Party in Poland before the war. Under Nazi occupation, she joined an Underground organization, and was incarcerated in the Pawiak prison in Warsaw together with other political prisoners. From there she was transferred to Majdanek and then to Leipzig. At Majdanek she organized self-help in a number of areas, including among the Jewish women, and ran diverse cultural activities, all of which earned the admiration of her fellow inmates.[66] Her personality and enterprise are described at length in Danuta Brzosko-Mędryk's *Matylda*.

According to Matylda Woliniewska, the political prisoners sought to choose their own candidates for the various posts and regarded them as public servants. They bore a heavy moral responsibility in that they had to provide support and aid to the other prisoners in all aspects of camp life, to uphold justice, to mediate between the inmates and the camp authorities, and, as far as they could, to ameliorate the hardships imposed on prisoners.[67]

How these two contradictory approaches operated in reality, and which of them had a greater impact on the daily life in the Leipzig camp, will become clear as we continue to trace its history.

Notes

1. Danuta Brzosko-Mędryk, *Niebo bez ptaków*, (Warsaw: Min. Obrony Narodowej, 1968), p. 229.
2. Sondertransport – Überstellung von Lublin (nach Ravensbrück), 21 April 1944, Archiwum Państwowego Muzeum na Majdanku.
3. Testimony of Albert Schwartz, Nur. doc. No-2125.
4. Olga Wormser-Migot and Henri Michel, (eds) *La Tragédie de la déportation 1940–45, Temoignages de survivants*, (Paris: 1955), pp. 211–12.
5. Danuta Brzosko-Mędryk, *Matylda*, (Warsaw: Min. Obrony Narodowcj, 1970), pp. 41–4.
6. Testimony of Zofia Kołecka-Fugiel, YV, 0-33/4838.
7. 'The Debate Over the Behaviour of the Polish Women Functionaries in the Leipzig-Hasag Camp', letter from Matylda Woliniewska, April 1996, YV, 0-33/4237 (hereafter: 'The Debate').
8. Testimony of Jadwiga Wolska-Landowska, YV, 0-33/4238.
9. Testimony of Barbara Wójtowicz-Natanson, YV,0-33/4241.
10. Christian Bernadac, *Kommandos de femmes Ravensbrück* (Paris: M. Lafon, 1973), pp. 201–2.
11. Lise Ricol London, *La mégère de la rue Daguerre: Souvenirs de Résistance* (Paris: Editions du Seuil, 1995), pp. 327–8.
12. KL-BU, 22 August 1944, 'Aufstellung der weiblichen Häftlinge des Aussenkommandos Hasag-Leipzig von Konz. Lager Ravensbrück', Archiwum Głównej Komisji Badania Zbrodni przeciwko Narodowi Polskiemu, (AGK), Warszawa, KL Buchenwald, sygn. 55, pp. 1–60.
13. *Buchenwald: Mahnung und Verflictung*, p. 256.
14. Trial of Hans Pflaum at Rastadt, AGK, Zespół KL Ravensbrück, sygn. 55, pp. 7, 24.

15. KL Buchenwald, 9 October 1944, Weibliche Zugänge nach Aussenkommando Hasag-Leipzig, AGK, KL Buchenwald, sygn. 55, pp. 75–83.
16. Weimar–Buchenwald, 'Neuzugänge vom 26 Sept. 1944', AGK, KL Buchenwald, sygn. 55, pp. 66–74.
17. 'Frauenaussenkommando Hasag Leipzig-Schönefeld', Dr Irmgard Seidel, Gedenkstätte-Buchenwald, private collection.
18. Weimar–Buchenwald, 'Neuzugänge vom 3 Januar 1945', see note 16, pp. 75–83.
19. This date appears in a letter of 22 December 1944 from the directress of Ravensbrück regarding the transfer of the prisoner Danuta Brzosko to the administration office of the Buchenwald camp: See Brzosko-Mędryk, *Matylda*.
20. KL Buchenward, 25 November 1944, Nummerverteilung bei den weiblichen Aussenkommandos: Vaupel, *Das Aussenkommando*, p. 72.
21. Transport of 1,200 Jewish women from the Skarżysko–Kamienna camp, YV, JM/3963,3964.
22. Testimony of Zofia Fugiel, YV 033/4838.
23. Lebenslauf des Kommandoführers Wolfgang Plaul, Gedenkstätte Weimar–Buchenwald, Museum.
24. Eugen Kogon, *Der SS-Staat*, (Munich: Kinder Verlag, 1974), pp. 60, 96, 98, 288, 313.
25. '*Aktennotiz*'. Weimar–Buchenwald, 22 June 1944, Czarnecki and Zonik, *Wąlczący obóz Buchenwald*.
26. Vaupel, *Das Aussenkommando*, p. 76.
27. Germaine Tillion, *Ravensbrück*, (Paris: Editions du Seuil, 1973), pp. 92–3.
28. 'KZ–Bewacherin stellte Antrag auf Rehabilitierung', *Ravensbrück Blätter*, 82 (April 1995), p. 8.
29. Tillion, *Ravensbrück*, p. 88.
30. Weimar–Buchenwald, 23 September 1944, 'Aufstellung', Thüringisches Hauptstaatsarchiv Weimar (ThHSA), NS 4 Bu, Vlg. 99, p. 114.
31. KL Buchenwald, Frauen-Aussenkommandos, 31 Januar 1945, *Buchenwald: Mahnung und Verpflichtung*, p. 255.
32. KDO Hasag-Leipzig, ThHSA, NS 4 Bu, Vlg. 99, pp. 171–2.
33. Landesausschuss der pol. Verfolgten in Bayern, München, 23 September 1947, YV, M-21/234.
34. ThHSA, NS 4 Bu, Vlg. 99, pp. 97, 98, 113, 370.
35. Akta dochodzenia p-ko dozorcom obozu Hasag-Leipzig Charlotte Lehmann, Saletzky i Kathe Heber, YV, JM/3799, sygn. 294, k. 1-12.
36. Brzosko–Mędryk, *Matylda*, p. 61.
37. Nur. doc. NO-2109 (the name appears as Heberer in this document).
38. Arbeitslager Leipzig (Hasag), 28 January 1945, An die Verwaltung des KL Bu, ThHSA, NS 4 Bu, Vlg. 99, p. 98.
39. KDO Hasag-Leipzig, ThHSA, NS 4 Bu, Vlg. 99, pp. 171–2.
40. Letter from Dr Irmgard Seidel of 2 August 1995 (see note 17).
41. *Wspomnienia Rudolfa Hössa*, Jan Sehn (ed.), (Warsaw: Wydawnictwo Prawnicze, 1960), p. 133.
42. Brzosko–Mędryk, *Matylda*, p. 48.
43. Ibid.: see photographs.
44. Rut Kornblum-Rosenberger, *Neder* [Vow] (Tel Aviv: Moreshet-Sifriat Poalim, 1986), pp. 76–7; testimony of Bela Grossmitz, YV, M-1/E/1612/1495.

45. Testimony of Genia Grünberg-Reiser, YV, 0-33/3485.
46. See note 31, ibid.
47. Testimony of Irena Pełka-Seńko, YV, 0-33/4242.
48. *Buchenwald: Mahnung und Verpflichtung*, p. 121.
49. Brzosko–Mędryk, *Matylda*, p. 46.
50. Testimony of Maryla Perlberg-Reich (known as Hanka Skowrońska in the camp), YV, 0-33/3316.
51. Oświadczenie Matyldy Woliniewskiej o Joannie Szumańskiej, Lagerälteste w obozie Leipzig Schönefeld, YV, 0-33/4237.
52. Brzosko–Mędryk, *Niebo bez ptaków*, pp. 86, 172, 255.
53. Testimony of Janina Latowicz, YV, 0-3/1384.
54. Testimony of Maryla Reich.
55. Personal letter of Teresa Todtleben-Pool from 8 March 1994, private collection.
56. Oral testimony of Danuta Brzosko-Mędryk.
57. Testimony of Jadwiga Lipska-Węgrzecka, YV, 0-33/4240.
58. Ricol–London, *La mégère de la rue Daguerre*, pp. 330–31.
59. Krystyna Winnicka was the underground name of Barbara Wojtowicz-Natanson. Testimony of Barbara Wójtowicz–Natanson.
60. Woliniewska, 'The Debate'.
61. Oral testimony of Danuta Brzosko-Mędryk.
62. Danuta Czech, 'Kalendarium der Ereignisse im Konzentrationslager Auschwitz–Birkenau', *Hefte von Auschwitz*, 8 (1964), p. 64 (hereafter 'Kalendarium').
63. Testimonies of Irena Pełka-Seńko and Maryla Reich.
64. Wormser-Mijot and Michel (eds), *La Tragédie de la déportation*, p. 211.
65. Ibid., pp. 212–13.
66. Stanisława Demidowicz, 'Związek pięciu stworzeń,' *Dla Ciebie Polsko*, (Olsztyn: ZBOWID, 1988), p. 49.
67. Matylda Woliniewska, Collection of Documents, YV, 0-33 4237.

3   The Slaves

The long road to Paradise

Malka sat on the edge of her pallet, staring in amazement: was this real, or could she be dreaming? Here she sat is this huge room, all clean and scrubbed, her underwear and shirt freshly laundered, in one hand a thick slab of bread (and what fine bread it was!) spread with jam, and in the other a plate of salad... She tried to gather her thoughts... It was just yesterday that she had arrived in Leipzig.

A few days ago they had left the camp at Skarżysko, 1,200 women and 1,500 men, heading for an unknown destination... How far away it seemed now, that yellow hell! Where were the filthy barracks infested with lice and fleas? Malka looked around her: neat pallets, the last rays of the evening sun gleaming through the windows, everything sparkling clean. There, at Skarżysko, on very rare occasions she could wrangle herself a meagre can of hot water, for a price, in order to wash her yellow body. A chill ran through her when she remembered the bathhouse at Skarżysko, the floor covered in mud and faeces and a freezing wind blowing through the broken windows. Sometimes there wasn't even cold water... And here, hot showers!!! Unbelievable! Hot water! They even got soap... [1]

The journey to Leipzig took three days and three nights. At least 60–70 women were crammed into each truck. At the very last minute they threw in a few loaves of bread and water cans. There was no room to sit down. Outside the sun was blazing and inside it was unbearably stifling and oppressive. The buckets allotted to each car filled quickly and stank to high heaven. There was all-out war near each opening as people fought for a tiny breath of fresh air. Some of the older women couldn't take it, and fainted. When the train stopped

57

and they were given a little water, the women, mad with the heat and thirst, fell on the buckets, spilling their contents. It was pure hell inside the cars: the inmates screamed, prayed, wept, cursed. Some became totally indifferent: for such they were being taken to their death, to Auschwitz...

When no more prisoners could be crammed in, the ones remaining were loaded onto open, unroofed cars. A few of the women took this as a good sign: everyone knew that closed cars meant a journey to death. They even got a little bread along the way, which must mean they were being taken to a work camp.[2] But here as well, they were crowded in so tightly that even with everyone standing up there was no room to move. There were women who bit or hit their neighbours just to sit down.

> After standing up for 24 hours, I nearly fainted and fell over on my neighbour, and they yelled at me to get off. I grabbed a pot and threatened to break the head of anyone who tried to move me. I finally got them to let me squeeze in. There was a constant racket and shouting in the car. To keep us quiet, the Germans hurled stones at us, and even piss pots! Lola and a few other prisoners were badly hurt.[3]

The train sped westward. After the first day it was obvious that they had crossed the Polish border. Another day went by and the train stopped at Leipzig-Schönefeld. The men's cars were immediately uncoupled and went on towards Buchenwald. 'We were barely able to climb down from the cars, exhausted, filthy, thirsty.' The women were greeted by a large detachment of SS officers and overseers. The prisoners were lined up five across and marched out. They crossed through an industrial zone. The few Germans they passed in the street stared at them wide-eyed. They'd never seen anything like it before! Women with yellow, green, red, purple hair, yellow faces... How could they know that this was their 'legacy' from the Skarżysko plants where they had been set to work producing mines. The dust from the explosives, TNT and picric acid, had painted them all in bizarre colours.

The column reached the camp gate. Commandant Plaul was waiting for them, and scrutinized the prisoners closely, row by row.[4] What a transport! Twelve hundred Jewish women for the Hasag plants – pure gold! The new prisoners could hardly believe their eyes: a camp in a building with grass around it? But this was only the first of the surprises in store for them. Group by group they were directed to the cellar, where they found the local prisoners, Polish and Russian women. The orders were given: 'Get undressed! Hand over all your property, including valuables! Every last thing! Line up in front of the showers!'

Panic immediately ran through the ranks. Showers??? By now the Jews knew very well what was behind the doors to the showers in Auschwitz. The *'ka-elniks'*[5] who had been sent to Skarżysko from Majdanek started screaming hysterically: 'They're gas chambers!' There was a huge commotion, women yelling and crying, moving out of line. The Polish supervisors, not realizing at first what it was all about, rained blows on the inmates to try to restore some order, explaining they were genuine showers. Even Commandant Plaul himself appeared, causing the naked women to recoil in panic. Finally, the first group went inside and fearfully turned on the faucets... water! Real hot Water! What joy! Only if you have not felt the touch of a hot shower for years can you understand how ecstatic they were.

Next they were lined up to be checked for lice. If any were found, all the hair on the affected woman's body was shaved. Then they were given thick cotton underwear, and were ready to enter the camp. The Jewish prisoners were allotted four blocks, numbers 17, 18, 19 and 20, the largest of which held 600 women and the rest 200 each. Although the four storeys of two-woman pallets were a familiar sight, here each had a mattress and blanket! In the centre of the room were tables and benches, and what was that on the walls? Central heating radiators? And everything was so clean it was incredible! 'This is a palace, not a concentration camp!'[6] At last, it was time for the most important moment of all – food! Wide-eyed and hungry, the new prisoners gazed at the rations: half a loaf of delicious bread, a spoonful of salad, jam and even sweet coffee! What was going on? It was impossible; something must be wrong here... they couldn't be plying them with these delicacies just to kill them afterwards?

Malka awoke from her daydreaming: maybe, just maybe, they would let them live. And maybe she could save the pictures of her parents and sisters that she had managed to hang onto thus far. They had been told to hand over everything. Down there in the cellar, before she went into the shower, she had asked one of the Polish supervisors to hold them for her. The Polish woman shouted at her, saying she had no intention of jeopardizing herself for some Jew. But Malka didn't let up, pleading with her tearfully: we were both deported from Poland by a common enemy, we both dream of going back home. But your homeland and loving parents are waiting for you, and I've lost everything. All I have left are these pictures... The guard wiped her eyes, snatched the envelope of photographs from Malka's hand and shoved her back into line. Malka wasn't the only lucky one. In a similar manner Blanka Künreich was also able to save her family photos.[7]

The Jewish prisoners stayed in their blocks for several days, awaiting the dresses that had yet to arrive from Ravensbrück. Although they were forbidden to leave the room, many of the women found a way to check out the whole building during those first days. They met some of the other inmates, got a look at the other blocks, and brought back news: there were several thousand woman there from all over Europe; they would again be working in a factory; they already knew all about it! What a camp! There was even a canteen! The older women were less enthusiastic. Felicja Bannet-Schäftler, an educated woman nearing forty, viewed the situation rather more sceptically. She saw the pallets of the *blokowa* and the *sztubowa* near the window, separated from the others by sheets and blankets, the province of the 'ladies of the camp'. She saw the crowding, the bedbugs in the mattresses. She heard the sobbing of the women who had again been separated from their loved ones, their husbands, brothers, sons.[8] What fate awaited them back there in Buchenwald?

On registration day, tables holding boxes of camp files were set up in the block. All of the *Schreibstube* workers were recruited for the task. There was a long line in front of each one. Every now and then the '*Oberka*' would come in and strike out at prisoners indiscriminately. There was a two-part

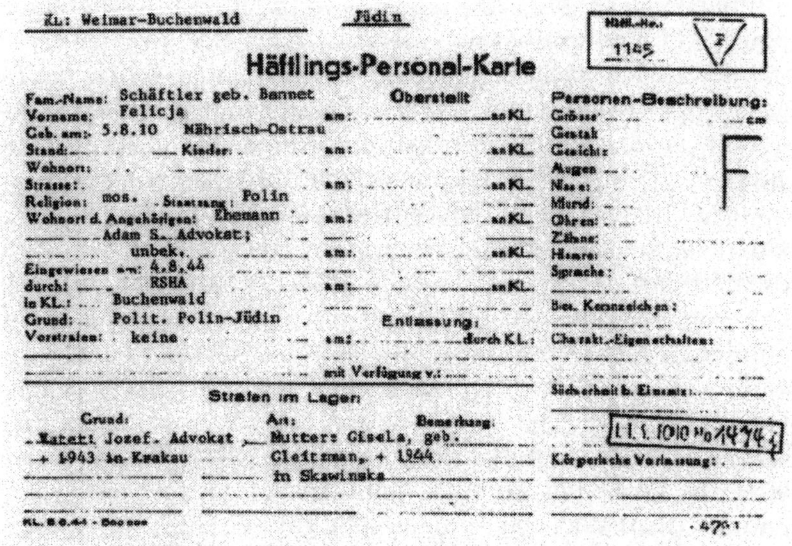
KL: Weimar-Buchenwald Jüdin
Häftlings-Personal-Karte
Häftl.-Nr. 1145
Fam.-Name: Schäftler geb. Bannet
Vorname: Felicja
Geb. am: 5.8.10 Mährisch-Ostrau
Stand: Kinder:
Wohnort:
Strasse:
Religion: mos. Staatsang.: Polin
Wohnort d. Angehörigen: Ehemann Adam S. Advokat; unbek.
Eingewiesen am: 4.8.44
durch: RSHA
in KL.: Buchenwald
Grund: Polit. Polin-Jüdin
Vorstrafen: keine
Überstellt am: an KL.
Entlassung: am: durch KL.: mit Verfügung v.:
Personen-Beschreibung: Grösse: cm Gestalt Gesicht: Augen Nase: Mund: Ohren: Zähne: Haare: Sprache:
Bes. Kennzeichen:
Charakt.-Eigenschaften:
Sicherheit b. Einsatz:
Körperliche Veranlagung:
Strafen im Lager:
Grund: Art: Bemerkung:
Vater: Josef. Advokat + 1943 in Krakau; Mutter: Gisela, geb. Gleitzman, + 1944 in Skawinska
F
KL. 8.6.44

Figure 3.1 Felicja Bannet-Schäftler's personal prisoner card.

Source: YV, BU (B) 51.

personal card (*Häftlings-Personal-Karte*) for each woman. The upper half held her number, name, date of birth, family status, religion, prewar address, parents' names and father's occupation. Date of arrival in the camp was noted as 4 August 1944, and under 'supplied by' appeared RSHA (Reich Main Security Office). 'Reason for arrest' read '*Polit. Polin Jüdin*' (political, Polish Jew).[9] The bottom half of the card listed the prisoner's occupation and the articles of clothing that the inmate had turned over on arrival in the camp. This item was left empty for the women from Skarżysko. According to Sara Shalem, the prisoners were asked to sign a document stating that they had been arrested for immoral behaviour.[10]

As they stood in line, it was whispered that for purposes of registration, it was best not to be too young or over thirty-five. Similarly, they would do well not to boast of a university education, and to declare a 'practical' occupation. Taking this advice, some of the younger girls added a couple of years to their age. On the other hand, Felicja Bannet-Schäftler declared herself to be a 34-year-old hat-maker. She was assigned number 1,145 of the 1,200 allocated to the Jewish women (see Figure 3.1). The number was sewn on to the sleeve of her dress and on to her jacket. Notably, non-Jewish prisoners were given not only a number, but also a red triangle with the letter of their nationality: P for Polish, F for French, and so on. The badge of the Russian prisoners of war bore the letters SU.[11]

Within a few days, concentration camp uniforms were issued to the newcomers: one single blue and grey striped dress known as a *'pasiak'*. The *blokowas* informed them, that they were responsible for this dress and were expected to launder it in their free time, since they would not be getting another. In addition, they were each given a striped jacket, socks, wooden clogs, and a bowl, spoon and cup. Such luxuries! There had been no bowls at Skarżysko; they had had to eat out of empty tin cans. Could it be that the Jews were going to be treated like human beings at Leipzig?

Impatiently, they awaited their first day of work. They were bored just sitting in the block. Here and there, a familiar melody could be heard, but it already had new words:[12]

> Hasag is our father,
> The best father there is!
> He promises us
> Long years of happiness!
> In Leipzig – a paradise on earth!
> There's bread and butter, and salad green,
> Luxury homes are where we live,
> Four storeys high – and the pallets are clean,
> From Hasag we get toilets and showers right here,
> And they give us the clothes of prisoners to wear!

The words had not changed very much; they were still Germans after all, and you could never tell:

> The commandant's for
> Law and order, no more!
> That we calm our nerves
> Before we become
> A can of preserves...

And the chain drags on

Today they would be going to work for the first time. Reveille was at 4 a.m. Outside it was still dark and cold. Quickly, they had to put their pallets in order, bolt down a slice of bread, if they had any left from the day before, and gulp the coffee that was handed out in haste. Hundreds of women from all the blocks poured out, the supervisors shouting and hurrying the stragglers.[13] The first SS overseers arrived. There was 'Sowa' ('Owl' in Polish) with her crinkly hair and ugly face who spoke excellent Polish as she shoved them and struck them to straighten the lines. Beside her was 'Holenderka' ('the Dutch woman'), an attractive blonde infamous throughout the camp for her cruelty. She not only hit them with her whip; she used her fists too.[14] In fact, this first encounter with the SS overseers is mentioned in numerous testimonies. The newcomers who had not passed through Ravensbrück had never before seen women in SS uniform. Since they never introduced themselves, they were known only by the nicknames they were given, and in view of the lack of any precise description, it is impossible to identify them.[15]

When the prisoners were lined up, the officials appeared: Joanna the *Lagerälteste*, the '*Oberka*', and the commandant. Each *blokowa* took her place at the entrance to her block and made her report: how many in the work detail, how many ill and remaining in camp. Commandant Plaul delivered a speech, as he did whenever a new transport arrived. Thus, for example, in summer 1944, he received the French women with the warning: 'If you don't work, you don't eat. Your primary duty is – obedience.'[16] He chose different words for the Jews:

I am in charge of this prisoner camp. You are prisoners of war under the inspection of the Red Cross, and you have rights. Should anyone abuse them, you are invited to complain to me and the offender will be punished ... You will work in the Hasag-Werke Leipzig-Schönefeld munitions and ammunition factory. You will be paid in coupons redeemable at the camp canteen where you can purchase whatever you need. I am hoping for your cooperation. I now wish you pleasant work and am expecting you to help in the war effort of my fatherland, Germany.[17]

His words convinced the Jewish prisoners that this was not just another German ruse; rather, they did indeed constitute vital manpower for Hasag. After all, they were trained experienced workers! By now it was 5.30 a.m. Roll-call was complete and the women marched toward the gate in rows of five. They were arranged according to their place of work, each group identified as a 'commando'. They headed for the factory. Armed SS guards marched on both sides of the column, joined by the overseers. They were not permitted to talk or to turn their heads: *Halt die Klappe!* (Shut your mouth!). Thousands of women marched in time, the thousands of pairs of wooden clogs raising clouds of dust. 'Left! Left!' Anyone who didn't keep up got herself a shove. The guards didn't strike them (they were passing through populated streets). 'Left! Left!' The guard dogs ran between the rows, ready to sink their jaws into anyone who stepped out of line. Every now and then there was a disturbance, with women panicking and screaming. Setting the dogs on them was one of the favorite diversions of the overseer known as 'Drynda' ('rickety wagon' in Polish). In a chillingly vivid description, Danuta Brzosko-Mędryk tells of the enormous dog that attacked her, and how she escaped with her life at the very last second.[18]

The Hasag plant was about two kilometres from the camp. They could see it in the distance, a row of large, mostly red-brick buildings. Each housed several big factory floors surrounded by a number of smaller rooms. The work commandos split up and were swallowed up one by one. Inside, Germans were already rushing about. The work day started at precisely six o'clock. There were only a few German foremen on site, and the small number of German men at work were either elderly or crippled. During that period, even people born in 1895–1897 were being conscripted into the *Wehrmacht*, and Armaments Minister Speer was still waiting for Himmler to accede to his request to demob skilled labourers with essential occupations and send them back to the munitions plants.[19] There were more German women, either factory workers or assigned to supervise the prisoners.

All the non-German men in the plant were slave labourers who fell into one of two categories. The first category comprised prisoners housed in several fenced-in barracks near the Hasag-

Leipzig camp. Most of them worked in the 'polygon' outside under extremely harsh conditions. According to Danuta Brzosko-Mędryk, this was a small commando of Frenchmen, Italians and other nationalities. They were in very poor physical shape and were constantly rotated.[20] This may have been the group referred to as the male outside squad numbering only 150 on 21 November 1944 (no Jews are mentioned who were listed as a separate *Aussenkommando*).[21] The second category comprised the 'free' forced labourers, mostly Polish, although there were also some Italians, Yugoslavs and Czechs. They were ostensibly allowed freedom of movement and could leave the camps in which they were housed, but had to report for work daily and were under constant supervision. Hasag had set up a large camp for Polish workers as early as the first year of the war.[22] Paul Budin displayed such 'concern' for his Poles, that in March 1944 he tried to arrange to bring the Kraków Philharmonic Orchestra to Leipzig to play for them! He was forced to abandon this plan because of the objections of the governor of the Generalgouvernement, Hans Frank, who did not wish for the musicians to see Leipzig in ruins and make this fact generally known.[23]

The prisoners from the Leipzig camp became the main body of Hasag's factory personnel. The Jewish women who arrived in August 1944, were greeted by the head foreman, Friedrich, who handed out their work assignments. They were told that they were involved in the production of *S-Zü*, an enigmatic name interpreted by the women as short for *Zünder*, referring to detonators of various sorts. With the German instructors offering no further information, the women eventually became aware only in general terms that their 'products' were connected with the manufacture of shoulder-missiles, shells of different sizes, and airplane parts. Friedrich may have been told in advance of their previous experience, as some of them found themselves assigned to machines similar to those they had operated at Hasag-Skarżysko. As a rule, because of the full automation in the plant, the prisoners worked on a single component and had no idea what sort of weaponry it belonged to.

On the whole, working conditions were bearable (there were modern sanitary facilities), but there were considerable

Figure 3.2 Paul Budin, General Manager of Hasag.

Source: NMG, Buchenwald.

differences between the various departments. Contradictory to the claims made in certain testimonies, the Jewish workers were not assigned to the more difficult jobs, and in most departments, the personnel was multinational. This was even true in the most arduous of all, the machine department, manned by both a day and a night shift.[24] Felicja Bannet-

Schäftler was posted here, and describes the work in her journal:

> The glass ceiling lets in the heat of the sun. Dozens of electrical machines, large and small, emit even more heat into the air, which is suffused with the stench of sweat, rancid oil and low-grade grease. We are stupefied by the noise of motors, the screech of saws and drills, the shouts of foremen and overseers, cursing in every language under the sun, and the killing pace of the work. Sweat pours into your eyes, your hands repeat the same gestures mechanically. The quota, for the moment, is five crates. There are over 450 nuts in every crate. Each has to be fixed into the machine and drilled with six bits of different shapes and sizes. The electric machine does the drilling automatically, but the bits, fitted onto a sort of miniature tower that looks something like the gun turret on a warship, have to be changed with a manual crank. One, two, three, four, five, six with your right hand, then use your left hand to take out the finished nut and stick in another one. Six operations with your right hand, two with your left hand, for a total of $5 \times 450 \times 8 = 18,000$ movements in the 12-hour work day, 1,500 an hour. It was like Chaplin's movie.[25]

A group of prisoners was assigned to the drilling machines that heated up so much that the workers had to pour soapy water over their hands and the metal parts that drilled the holes. Even worse were the machines that dripped hot oil. To this day, Halina Zuckerman remembers the burns on her hands and face caused by splattering oil.[26] The work was hard, laborious and exhausting. Twelve hours that crawled by like an eternity in the monotonous, unrelenting whirl of activity.

> Every day I work
> Twelve hours in production.
> Can you see? Among the machines
> The hours slither like a snake?
> They shriek in the gloom of morning,
> And flow by one by one,
> Ponderous, dark and long,
> Twelve they are – the working hours.

Every day the same number for all of us.
We screw, twist, and twist again,
Bang and saw and stamp.
They go by sticky
From our sweat and blood,
From the effort we put in and our yearning for God.
Twelve heavily laden hours
The unchanging quota
Twelve for each and every one – the daily quota.[27]

Jews, Poles and Frenchwomen worked in the Hasag
Nordwerk plant, where there was no ventilation in the
summer since the window had to be kept closed because of
the blackout regulations. The heat, stifling air and sweat
became intolerable. Over time, the lack of air caused many of
the women to suffer from anemia. Danuta Brzosko-Mędryk,
who worked here for a while, describes a typical incident.
Because of the unbearable heat, the prisoners tried to take a
drink from the faucet whenever they could, until they were
forbidden to do so and then found it wrapped in rags. One
day there was a visit from a review committee of *Wehrmacht*
officers who were shown around by Commandant Plaul and
the foremen. When the entourage reached Danuta, one of the
officers asked her how the work was. Knowing she spoke
German, the other prisoners pushed her forward. She
complained of the heat, the lack of sleep and the shut-off
faucet. The next day they found it working again.[28] The Jewish
women also found another way to get some relief from the
heat. Although forbidden to do so, they removed their
undershirts and pants and worked only in their dresses.

The heat was even more oppressive because of the rubber
aprons they were forced to wear in order to protect their dresses
– government property! They were also issued hair-nets so that
their hair would not get caught in the machines. 'This concern,'
states Felicja Bannet-Schäftler, 'verged on the grotesque. On the
one hand, the SS were killing us, and on the other the plant was
giving out hairnets! But there was a certain logic in this: a corpse
at the machine meant a halt in production, the need to repair the
machine, a waste of raw materials! What seemed grotesque was
actually careful calculation!'[29]

68

The Polish prisoner Zofia Kołecka describes work in the machine department. At the far end of the huge hall near the door there were steel poles four metres long. Periodically, she would have to cart one of these extremely heavy poles to the machine, stick it in the allotted holes, and turn on the machine, which made bullets. The bullets had to be scrutinized constantly with the appropriate devices. The work went on for 12 hours, and there was also a night shift.[30] The night shift was the hardest to bear. In addition to a 'lunch-break' when soup was handed out, there was also another ten-minute break during which the women fell into a deep sleep. The night shift suffered severely from lack of sleep, since it was virtually impossible to get more than four or five hours rest during the day in the camp because of the noise, the food distribution, the need to report for assembly, etc. It is not surprising that the worst work accidents occurred at night, as in the case of the woman whose hair got caught in a machine.[31] Sara Bojer lost a finger in the factory, and was lucky enough to be sent for immediate treatment. Tema Baner was less fortunate when her arm got caught in the machine.[32]

Some jobs were much easier. *Hala F* was considered a particularly good department. It occupied a large hall where French, Polish, Jewish and German women worked, sometimes joined by male foreign labourers. Manufacturing shell components, they worked only a day shift here.[33] Blanka Künreich toiled at one of the benches checking 'cups' (apparently shell-casings), tossing the flawed ones into a basket and arranging those she passed on a tray which she handed over to Maria Schächter, who stamped them with a manually operated device.[34] Romualda Stramik, a 17-year-old Polish girl who had already been through Majdanek and Ravensbrück, was also very lucky. She sat comfortably and stamped casings with their factory numbers: type, year and lot number.[35]

Large doors led from the main hall to other rooms where small teams were at work.

In one of them, eight to ten girls sat on two sides of a work bench with two Germans at the head doing the same thing we did. Shell components with small holes, called

Bodenschraube, rolled along the bench like on an assembly line. Using tweezers, we stuck small detonators, called *Zündhütchen*, into the holes, so in camp slang it was called the *Zündhütchen* department.[36]

SS overseers patrolled all the departments keeping their eyes on the prisoners. Speaking with the Germans or the male workers was forbidden, and any woman caught doing so was risking a few slaps across the face or three days in the bunker. Even the German men were afraid of the overseers. 'Miotła' ('broom' in Polish), a tall, thin, ugly woman who viciously slapped the women she felt were taking too long in the toilet, was particularly notorious.[37]

Fortunately for the prisoners, they were also guarded by overseers of a different sort. There was 'Gitla', who treated them well and once even took the trouble to ask why they called her by that name. The women found it hard to supply a suitable answer, and finally explained they had chosen the nickname because of her resemblance to the film actress of the same name.[38] Gaunt little 'Myszka' ('little mouse' in Polish) is also remembered favourably for not hitting or provoking the prisoners. Some of them managed to get close enough for her to confide her personal history to them. Her father had refused to join the SS, and she had been forced to volunteer in his stead in order to atone for his shameful behaviour and ensure that the authorities did not take their revenge on him. Her kindness somewhat alleviated the pain of the blows from 'Holenderka', who had the habit of bursting into the 'laboratory' in order to make her presence felt.[39]

The group assigned to the laboratory included, among others, the noted poets Henryka and Ilona Karmel, whose poetry had already earned them a name in Skarżysko,[40] Mata Hollender, known as a 'lobbyist' for her knowledge of German, and Ester Nessel and her mother, Mrs Kurtz, who was pregnant when she arrived in Leipzig. What sort of work did they do there? This is Henryka Karmel's reply:

> You ask what's my job?
> What is it I do?
> Well, ladies and gentlemen, the bullets I review.
> A nice occupation, it helps time go by:

If the bullets kill they're good,
'Shmelz' if they don't make you die.
So remember, because this is fine advice indeed:
Whatever kills is good,
All the rest – we don't need ...[41]

Fifteen women, including Ruth Kornblum and Ziuta Rotenberg, worked in another room performing optical tests of the installation of warheads on anti-aircraft missiles. It was relatively easy, albeit monotonous, work, causing Ruth to ask to be transferred to the department where the fuses of anti-aircraft shells were galvanized. Working with tubs full of poisonous substances was more difficult, but at least it was more interesting.[42]

These prisoners' descriptions are supported by the cold facts. In terms of the number of work days and working hours, Hasag-Leipzig led the other companies manned by Buchenwald inmates (see Table 3.1).

We won't help kill our brothers?

The number of work days that the Hasag slave labourers contributed to the war effort of the Third Reich raises the question of whether the prisoners might have tried to sabotage production. At that time, with the defeat of Germany appearing increasingly imminent, the idea of escape was very tempting. Despite the fact that for a foreigner unfamiliar with the language, or with his or her surroundings, the odds of a successful escape attempt were virtually nil, there were those who took the risk. As the Russian front drew closer, more and more Polish workers, who had relative freedom of movement, took off. In response, on 7 May 1944, the general manager of Hasag, Paul Budin, posted the following warning (see Figure 3.3):[44]

NOTICE

In recent weeks, Polish men and women – mostly women – have absconded. I would again draw your attention to the fact that we will deal harshly with any attempt to escape,

Table 3.1 Working hours and average number of Buchenwald
Frauenaussenkommandos per day in industrial plants (February 1945)[43]

Company	No. of hours	No. of work days	Average no. of prisoners per day
Allg. Solvay-Werke Bernburg	12,455	1,310	55
ATG, Leipzig	102,892	9,767	407
Bayer. Motorenwerke, Abterode	39,371	3,523	147
Dort.-Hörder Hüttenver. Dortmund	121,620	11,940	497
Fabrik Allendorf GmbH	249,285	24,299	1,012
GmbH Fabrik Hessisch-Lichtenau	187,562	17,863	944
Gehrt, Penig	139,452	17,166	715
Gerätebau GmbH, Mühlhausen	97,337	13,102	546
Hasag, Altenburg	539,752	48,277	2,011
Hasag, Leipzig	**1,009,306**	**92,997**	**3,875**
Hasag, Meuselwitz	270,774	24,994	1,041
Hasag, Schlieben	61,510	6,151	256
Hasag, Taucha	306,401	28,124	1,171
Heerbrandt, Raguhn	38,059	3,487	145
Heeres-Muna, Torgau	65,780	5,980	249
IG Farben, Wolfen	64,878	5,898	245
Junkers, Aschersleben	133,482	11,880	495
Junkers, Markkleeberg	375,276	34,116	1,421
Kabel-u. Leitungswerke, Neustadt	84,398	7,521	313
Krupp, Essen	107,625	12,395	516
Lippstädter Eisen u. Metallwerke	200,596	19,403	808
Polte, Duderstadt	226,121	19,732	822
Polte, Magdeburg	525,492	47,772	1,990
Rheinmetall Borsig, Sömmerda	291,426	27,371	1,140
Wasag, Elsnig	31,000	2,824	118
Westf. Metall-Industrie, Lippstadt	78,141	7,331	305
Total	5,359,981	505,223	21,051

and all escapees will be caught sooner or later. They can
expect severe punishment, since, at this time in particular,
we expressly regard abandoning work in our plant as
serious sabotage.

In accord with the orders I have received from the
supreme authorities, I hereby issue this grave warning. All
Polish men and women should be aware that the present
difficult stage of the war does not make it possible to satisfy
the will of the individual – and this is true both for Germans
and for Poles – and that every worker in our plant, whether
German or foreign, and starting with myself, is charged
with the duty of working his shift to the very end, until the
battle with Bolshevism is decided!

OGŁOSZENIE!

W ostatnich tygodniach ścięła pełny .... i kobiety, w czym przeważa liczba kobiet.

Ponownie zwracam uwagę, że każdy wypadek .... będzie surowo ścigany i że my wcześniej czy później złapego .... ich srogo kara, gdyż właśnie teraz opuszczenie procy w naszej fabryce nie może być nazywane inaczej, jak ciężkim sabotażem.

W ramach udzielonego mi od władz wyższych rozkazu, przestrzegam z naciskiem. Każdy z Polaków i Polek musi o tym wiedzieć, że obecna ciężka faza wojenna nie pozwala uwzględnić życzeń osób pojedynczych – tyczy to tak samo Niemców jak i Polaków – i że dla ku. dego członka naszej załogi. obojętnie czy to Niemiec, czy pracownik zagraniczny, a zał. ... jąc ode mnie, jest tylko jeden jedyny obowiązek, mianowicie

praca do ostateczności na wyznaczonym stanowisku w tej najcięższej walce z bolszewizmem.

Kto inaczej myśli, musiałby to później gorzko odpokutować, bo bolszewizm nie oszczędziłby i jego, tylko by go strc . .ał.

My musimy nadal przy twardej pracy stać w jednym szeregu. Wysiłek pracy Polaków w HASAGU jest zawsze przezemnie uznany, przy czym mnie często boli, że życzenia osobiste, choć usprawiedliwiona, nie mogą być przezemnie uwzględnione, tak samo jak ja swoje życzenia odsunąć i z nich zrezygnować muszę.

P. BUDIN

Lei,p7.g. dnie 7 m.o.. 1944

BEKANNTMACHUNG!

P. BUDIN

Figure 3.3 Notice from Paul Budin to Hasag employees, 7 May 1944.

Source: Brzosko-Mędryk, Matylda.

Anyone believing differently will bear the responsibility, because Bolshevism will not show him mercy, but rather, will tread him under.

We must continue to stand together in our strenuous labour. I have always praised the efforts of the Poles employed at Hasag, and I am often troubled that I can not accede to their personal wishes, even when justified, just as I am compelled to deny and put aside my own wishes.

Leipzig, 7 May 1944

P. Budin

The fact that 'free' forced labourers were escaping undoubtedly lay behind Budin's eagerness to procure prisoners for his workforce. When the Leipzig camp was set up, it soon became obvious that the prisoners were so closely guarded on their way to the plant that escape was not feasible. The few incidents vaguely referred to in the testimonies all relate to Russians. According to Maria Schächter, this was made possible by the help of factory workers. Since she knew a little Ukrainian, Maria made friends with two girls who worked in the kitchen and sometimes gave her soup. One of them managed to escape and, in reprisal, the golden braids of which the other, Sonya, was so proud, were chopped off.[45] Ester Nessel adds that on another occasion they learned that several Russian women had escaped. 'This was in February, 1945, on a Sunday, when, as usual, I was washing my only dress like the other women. Suddenly the whole camp was called out for a *Strafappell*. We had to stand outside all day in our wet clothes in the freezing cold'.[46]

Another incident is related by Paula Gimes:

I managed to hold onto a good civilian jacket, and once a Russian woman asked me if I would trade it to her in exchange for bread. I knew she wanted to escape, so I agreed. Three Russians ran away then. One of them was caught and was punished with blows and being locked up in the bunker. In a punitive assembly, ten women were selected and their heads were shaved.[47]

This may be the same *Strafappell* referred to in the journal of the Polish woman Stanisława Demidowicz:

One day two girls from our block escaped. We were summoned to a disciplinary assembly and our block was made to stand apart from the others. The camp commandant came and ordered every other row to step forward and picked out each fifth girl. All the others were sent back to the blocks, and the victims were sent to the cellar where their heads were shaved. There were 17 from our block alone, all young girls, and some had such beautiful hair! You there, in the free world, cannot imagine how awful they looked. After all, here, a woman's hair is her only grace.[48]

Of all the incidents reported, none ended in a death sentence and no mention is made of transport to Auschwitz or Ravensbrück. None the less, the reign of terror effectively achieved its aim: there were no more escape attempts. The only option remaining for striking at the military power of Germany was to sabotage production. However, in late 1944 the dilemma faced by every forced labourer became even keener: saboteurs could expect the death penalty, as set down in the order issued by Gerhard Maurer on 11 April 1944.[49] Why should they stick their necks out? Would a few damaged shells or missiles decide the outcome of the war? On the other hand, they were being used against their brothers and friends who were fighting for their freedom at the front! Did the reign of terror imposed on the slave labourers release them from the guilt of collaborating with the enemy? What did the prisoners themselves think? The following poem by Gela Meiersdorf gives us some idea:

The factory is quiet,
Not much work
Anywhere...
But that is not possible,
We can not rest here!
And so – new production
Must roll out again!
Again the crates pile up,

Boxes, tools and boards rounded up,
And the highly complex work is taken up:
What? Are the spark plugs being undone
And their reassembly now begun!
I too have a part in this contest now,
I'll finish my quota quick – and how!
I'll measure and count the cogwheels too,
I'll check and I'll polish every screw,
So they're smooth, not a bit of sawdust left,
And flexible enough for any check,
They should not miss their mark, Oh Heaven forbid!

And then I awake and open my eyes:
This is not just any industrial enterprise!
This is meant to murder, destroy, annihilate...
A shudder of terror runs through my bones,
Dizzy with fear, my head bows low,
Visions of hell now fill my eyes:
The people of Europe – in blood they lie!
And I whisper the words: abomination and calumny...
History will judge!
Just wait and see...[50]

'Our work was tragic, because without knowing it, we were helping the Germans to kill our brothers and friends.'[51] Did many of the prisoners suffer this sense of guilt? To judge by the testimonies available to me, the answer is no. We have no knowledge of any act of heroism such as that organized by the Russian prisoners of war at Ravensbrück who refused to work even when faced with the threat of death.[52] For all the other nationalities, including the Jewish women, there appears to have been a clear division: a few risked getting into trouble; the rest went about their work. The worsening of conditions in the winter of 1944–45, together with the fear of punishment, further demoralized the prisoners. To this were added alarming rumours that 'we would never leave here alive, that they would make mincemeat [*siekanka*] of us and blow up the whole camp. It is said that the Germans in the factory are spreading these rumours on purpose to depress us even more and console themselves for the defeats at the front.'[53]

Nevertheless, there were indeed incidents of sabotage. The group of political prisoners from Majdanek who worked in the Hasag-Nordwerk plant devised a unique custom to encourage sabotage: the announcement of the number of rejected components (*Ausschuss*) as a 'gift' to any woman celebrating her birthday! When Matylda Woliniewska was found to be the main instigator of this practice, there were women who succeeded in smuggling 'presents' for her collection through the security check at the gate: damaged bullets and shell-casings. She hid them in her bed, and when they got to be too many, she knew how to get rid of them. Even some foreign workers collaborated with her.[54]

The French women, proud of their status as political prisoners, also took the issue of sabotage very seriously. As Suzanne Chaumet-Leboindre relates in her memoirs: 'I operated a very complicated milling machine with a young Russian girl. It was hard to work together because we didn't understand each other... We had to process 1,500 shell casings per 12-hour shift, standing up. We were supposed to use three inspection devices all the time to check that the casings were okay... We only did it when the German foreman was around. I never learned to stop the machine when it wasn't working properly, and sometimes I broke it myself... The supervisors complained that the French women were lousy workers.'[55] Lise Ricol, who arrived in the camp with a large group of underground activists, reports that wherever they worked they committed sabotage 'as much as possible'.[56]

The Jewish women also performed acts of sabotage, despite the far greater danger of punishment (they risked transport to Auschwitz, not merely confinement to the bunker or having their heads shaved). None the less, it may be said that their attitude to sabotage was no different from that of the others: most heard nothing and knew nothing; a few acted. Typically, those women who report acts of sabotage are the same ones who initiated the practice at Hasag-Skarżysko, among them Felicja Bannet-Schäftler:

I have a Dutch supervisor, a young blond boy as mean as an ape, goes out of his way to prove his exaggerated loyalty, does the dirty work of the tyrant for the foreman... If my hand shakes as it performs one of the thousands of daily motions, the touchy machine responds instantly by stopping, a split second is enough, the drill gets caught and bang! It's broken. The vigilant Dutchman comes running, stops the machine and fits in a new drill bit. Bang, bang! – In one shift three bits broke. The routine notion of systematic sabotage instilled at Skarżysko jumps at the chance. The next day I break a few more drill bits on purpose. The Dutchman gets angry, shrieks *'pass auf'* [watch out]. After five days he's had enough. He's getting suspicious. Threatens to tell the SS overseer. I have to be careful.[57]

Another form of sabotage involved reducing the quota. Malka Granatsztajn, who worked alongside her sister, found an original way to do this:

I had to carry a certain number of heavy crates each day and I wanted to help my sister who was very weak. I didn't meet my quota and I convinced other girls to do the same thing. Once the supervisor came up to me and warned me that they were already talking about me and it might cost me my life... When the German foreman asked me who I was carrying the crates for, I said that I was helping my sister who was ill and I couldn't fulfill my quota. The foreman was a musician, and apparently an anti-Nazi. He helped me carry the crates and eventually transferred us both to an easier job.[58]

The foreman Friedrich, the one best known by the Jewish women, is remembered as an 'informer' who reported poor work to the SS overseers, resulting in three days in the bunker without food for the offender.[59] There seems to have been a reason for his behaviour:

'Little Friedrich' (*der kleine Friedrich*) goes wild. He races from one station to the next, cursing and threatening. He comes back with whole crates of nuts rejected by the inspection devices and we have to do them again. We smile contentedly, understanding without the need for words.

Along with our lack of skill and our poor physical condition, undoubtedly about 50 per cent are cases of sabotage. But with all the meters and the damned inspection devices, it's going to be a lot harder for us here than at Skarżysko.[60]

Attempts at sabotage sometimes improved relations with the foreign workers. Luna Fuss-Kaufman remembers:

There wasn't a specific quota for the lathe I worked on, but the machines worked day and night without a stop. I actually understood exactly how the lathe worked (nobody knew that, of course) and I knew how to position the blades so that they would break. Naturally, this caused a waste of metal and a halt in production. Every time it happened, I'd run, in despair, to the German engineer who ran the whole floor to tell him that the machine had broken down again. A Polish technician worked with me supervising the operation of the machine. He was a nice young man who would sometimes bring me bread, a little butter, or something else to eat. He knew very well what I was doing to the lathe, but he never said a word to anyone about me, even when the Germans complained that he wasn't watching the machine closely enough. I was never punished in any way, and if I'd been caught, it would have been much worse.[61]

But relations were not always so good, as Frania Brand-Siegman recalls:

I worked in F Hall with a Frenchwoman who was always asking me how much the other Jewish women and I had done. What business was it of hers? Personally, I never did a single piece more than the quota demanded. She did more, so I told her she made herself out to be a great patriot in words, but not in deeds... Sabotage was completely out of the question, it was impossible because they watched us so closely.[62]

At the same time, Frania admits that at her previous assignment working with Friedrich at a lathe that dripped hot oil, she sometimes dared to reduce the quota of three and a half crates. When Friedrich finally took down her identification number, she became frightened that she would be taken out and shot 'because there were cases like that'. Her remarks are not supported by any other testimony, and she herself was then transferred to a much easier job.

To the extent that it is at all possible to sum up the sabotage activities of the Leipzig prisoners, it can be stated they shared certain features. In terms of organization, there was no connection between the various acts of sabotage. They were performed either on the initiative of the individual prisoner for reasons of conscience, or in small groups of one nationality with a common political background or previous experience of underground activities. Neither is there evidence of any connection between the local initiatives and the Underground in Buchenwald.

Despite all credit to the prisoners for their courage and enterprise, the overall impression of what was accomplished by sabotage is not encouraging. All in all, it took place on a very small scale, and had no effect whatsoever on war production in general. Romualda, who also tries to play up her part in sabotage efforts, sums up its true significance: 'This activity was still very important for raising the morale of the prisoners, who didn't want to give up their struggle against the enemy by any available means even under camp conditions.'[63] In other words, sabotage was a spiritual balm for the tortured souls of the prisoners forced to labour against their menfolk.

Notes

1. Testimony of Malka (Mala) Zuckerbrot-Hottner, YV, 0-33/1655.
2. Testimony of Bracha Bar Ilan, YV, 0-33/4839.
3. Testimony of Barbara Reibscheid, YV, 0-16/1911; cf. Bina Herstein, YV, 0-33/1796; Jeta Jolinger, YV, 0-33/3419.
4. Testimony of Roza Zelwer, YV, 0-3/1074.
5. The prisoners from Majdanek were known in Skarżysko as 'ka-elniks' because of the letters KL (*Konzentrationslager*) painted on their clothes.
6. Kornblum–Rosenberger, *Neder*, pp. 70–71.
7. Testimony of Blanka Künreich-Ickowicz, YV, 0-33/3421.
8. Journal of Felicja Bannet-Schäftler, YV, 0-33/4096.
9. KL Weimar-Buchenwald, Häftlings-Personal-Karte, Nr. 1145, YV, BU-(B)51.
10. Testimony of Sara Iwańska-Shalem, YV, 0-33/3332.

11. Bannet-Schäftler, *'Journal'*, p. 12.
12. This is a new version of a song sung at Skarżysko; see Karay, *Death Comes in Yellow*, p. 209. See also: testimony of Rena Taubenblatt-Fradkin, YV, 0-16/249. It appears in the testimony of Ester Netzer (known as Ester Nessel in the camp), YV, 0-33/650.
13. Testimony of Hanka Kornfeld, YV, 0-16/502.
14. Kornblum-Rosenberger, *Neder*, p. 71; oral testimony of Sara Rosental-Stern.
15. See Chapter 2, notes 30, 38.
16. Ricol-London, *La mégère de la rue Daguerre*, p. 329.
17. Kornblum-Rosenberger, *Neder*, p. 72.
18. Brzosko–Mędryk, *Matylda*, p. 62.
19. Fernschreiben an den Reichsführer SS, 8 September 1944, BA, R 3/1615, p. 103.
20. Brzosko–Mędryk, *Matylda*, pp. 48–9.
21. KL Buchenwald, 31 Januar 1945, Jüdische *Aussenkommandos*, *Buchenwald: Mahnung und Verpflichtung*, p. 252.
22. Eva Seeber, *Robotnicy przymusowi w faszystowskiej gospodarce wojennej*, (Warsaw: Książka i Wiedza, 1972), p. 270.
23. Arbeitssitzung am 3 March 1944, Hans Frank, Tagebuch, YV, JM/21, Nr. 11, p. 34.
24. Testimony of Hanka Szklanka-Wolańska, YV, 0-3/1174.
25. Bannet-Schäftler, *'Journal'*, pp. 13-14.
26. Testimony of Halina Zuckerman-Razowski, YV, 0-33/3287.
27. The author of this poem is unknown. It appears in the testimony of Malka Hottner (see note 1).
28. Brzosko–Mędryk, *Matylda*, p. 53.
29. Bannet-Schäftler, *'Journal'*, p. 17.
30. Testimony of Zofia Fugiel.
31. *Les Françaises à Ravensbrück*, (Paris: Sallimard, 1965), pp. 138–9.
32. Testimonies of Sara Wolf-Bojer, YV, 0-33/3287; Tema Baner, YV, M-1/E/325/228.
33. Testimony of Malka Budyn-Katz, YV, 0-33/3272.
34. Testimony of Blanka Ickowicz.
35. Romualda Stramik, 'Los zakładniczki', in Maria Teodorowicz (ed.), *Nadzieją była wolność*. (Olsztyn: TON, 1991), p. 73.
36. Testimony of Felicja Schächter-Karay, YV, 0-33/1812.
37. Testimony of Lilian Lichtensztejn-Goldberg, YV, 0-33/4837.
38. Testimony of Rina Cypres, YV, 0-33/1857.
39. Testimony of Ester Netzer.
40. Felicja Karay, 'The Social and Cultural Life of the Prisoners in the Jewish Forced Labour Camp at Skarżysko-Kamienna', *Holocaust and Genocide Studies*, 8:1 (Spring 1994), pp. 18–19.
41. Henryka and Ilona Karmel, poems, YV, 0-33/1852.
42. Kornblum-Rosenberger, *Neder*, pp. 73, 77.
43. Erika Buchmann, *Die Frauen von Ravensbrück*, (Berlin, Kongresa Verlag, 1960), pp. 60–61.
44. Brzosko–Mędryk, *Matylda*.
45. Testimony of Maria Schächter-Lewinger, YV, 0-33/1802.
46. Testimony of Ester Netzer.
47. Testimony of Paula Gimes, YV, 0-3/1080.
48. Stanisława Demidowicz, 'List z Buchenwaldu', *Gazeta Olsztyńska*, (26 December 1993), p. 10.

49. Nur. doc. NO-1556.
50. Collected poems of Gela Meiersdorf, YV, 0-3/869. (hereafter Meiersdorf 'Poems').
51. Testimony of Rina Taubenblatt-Fradkin, YV, 0-16/249.
52. Testimonies of Maryla Reich and Irena Seńko.
53. Demidowicz, 'List z Buchenwaldu', p. 10.
54. Matylda Woliniewska, *'Przeciw przemocy'*, YV, 0-33/4237.
55. Bernadac, *Kommandos de femmes Ravensbrück*, p. 203.
56. Ricol-London, *La Mégère de la rue Daguerre*, p. 205.
57. Bannet-Schäftler, *'Journal'*, p. 15.
58. Testimony of Malka Granatsztajn, YV, 0-3/3323; cf. Felicja Karay, 'Women in the Forced Labor Camps', in, D. Ofer and L.Weitzman (eds), *Women in the Holocaust* (New Haven, CT: Yale University Press, 1998), pp. 293–4.
59. Testimony of Ester Belzowska, YV, M-1/E/1628/1516.
60. Bannet-Schäftler, *'Journal'*, p. 16.
61. Testimony of Luna Fuss-Kaufman, YV, 0-33/1819.
62. Testimony of Frania Brand-Siegman, YV, 0-3/2979.
63. Stramik, 'Los zakładniczki'.

4   Changing Times

The road to the factory

It is Autumn, 1944. The women are marching off to work again. In columns of five they pass through the gate, one commando after the other. The overseers shout out orders, they straighten the lines, the wooden clogs clatter, and the columns march in perfect order past the camp guards. Outside it is still dark: the night mists have not yet lifted. The grey procession moves through the deserted streets of Leipzig. It is raining. The figures advance slowly, their clogs slipping in the wet mud on the ground. The SS guards form a tight cordon around the women, lest one of them should try to make a run for it into a dark alley. Each of the prisoners on the far right and left of every tenth row carries a large lantern. They have to hold it steady so it doesn't sway as they walk. If it does, they feel the whip on their backs. Their flimsy dresses are soaked by the rain, freezing them to the bone. Every now and then a harsh bark breaks the silence: '*Schneller! Links! Links!*' They march on: Russians, Jews, Poles, Greeks, Czechoslovakians, gypsies, French.

Like a giant caterpillar, the column of women moves along the street. The light of the lanterns casts a red glow over their striped dresses and illuminates the heavy bodies of the watchdogs prancing beside the guards. Ahead, outside the circle of light, the street lies in total darkness, and the stumps of the trees brought down by a stray bomb look like twisted shadows. There is silence everywhere, save for the clatter of the wooden clogs and the occasional growl of one of the dogs culminating in a sharp bark.[1]

Dawn breaks. The first pedestrians appear in the streets. They stare silently at the strange creatures in their striped dresses. Some gape in wonder, others in pity, and there are also those who whistle and call out 'Dirty Jews!' or curse the Russians.[2] But on the whole they just look on with indifference. They are already accustomed to these processions, the march of the numbers:

> Numbers, numbers,
> One, two, ten, twenty
> Unnamed suffering,
> Their bodies
> Wrapped in rags –
> Sharp pain.
> A marching prison...
> The shimmering light of lanterns, rifles.
> The rain falls, drop by drop.
> Rain?
> Perhaps – tears?...[3]
>
> (Henryka Karmel)

The rain stops. The first rays of sunlight break through the clouds. There are more people in the street now. 'They're well-dressed, they're free, living a normal life, not behind bars like us, they don't suffer humiliations, the unimaginable cruelty that is our lot in this vale of tears!'[4] The street noises sound close and familiar, and at the same time, distant and alien. As if those people, out there, in freedom, were moving like puppets behind some invisible wall... What's going through those Germans' minds? Are they afraid that the war will end? But bombs are falling on Leipzig night and day! 'And what will they say when it's over? That they didn't know anything, that they never heard of slave labourers, of camp inmates... knew nothing about it? We were marched through the whole city! Everyone could see us!'[5]

The march of the mannequins. Fives, hundreds, thousands. Another mile to the factory. They are not allowed to turn their heads, but Henia steals a glance. Over there is the young couple they sometimes pass on the way. Maybe they go to work together? The man has a limp; the woman holds him by the hand. Henia sighs, remembering her husband... Where is he now? Is he still alive?

Every day I see them, not talking, aglow
Gazing at each other with so much love.
And my heart breathes a sigh, will someone, some day,
Hold my hand in the very same way?
And I think: such a dress, the blue, so fair
The dress that woman has to wear...[6]

(Henryka Karmel)

Tall fruit trees grow on both sides of the street. They are so beautiful. Yellow pears, red apples... Helena looks down – maybe another miracle will happen? A couple of days ago two pears fell on the ground right in front of her! She picked them up carefully, barely getting away with it without being struck. Of course she gave the other women in her row a bite too.[7] What a feast! They were so sweet, those two wonderful, juicy pears...

At night, a storm and gusty winds
Shook the pears off the trees onto the ground
Where they rolled up to the pavement...
In the morning, a long sad line
Of prisoners
And a soldier beside them...
Surreptitiously she bent and picked them up,
And the soldier, an old kind-hearted grandfatherly sort,
Pretended not to see the girls
But was so very ashamed
That those pears could give them such joy...[8]

(Henryka Karmel)

They have already reached the last crossing before the factory. Why does the walk seem so long today? Is it the rain, or exhaustion? They march on. 'I remember a tall German standing at this point along the way every single day... It's odd... He would stare at us as if he were looking for someone... He was waiting for us there when we left work too.'[9]

As we return from work in a long grey line
Through the noisy streets in the broiling sunshine

I see you standing there, a mystery,
On a corner of German street, alien and hostile
And I know it is we you are awaiting, yes you are...
Your tall figure I can see from afar,
I feel the penetrating look in your eyes
Asking us to say something, tell you why,
Gleaming restlessly, a question they speak,
Something they want to say, or perhaps to seek?...
Or is that you burn in shame... I can't divine
At the women marching in a long grey line,
And are trying to say the blame is not with you...
Or are you waiting for your lover to appear out of the
    blue,
The one who made you happy, the light that made your
    life glow,
And suddenly went out in the land where the Visla
    flows...
I cannot tell... but it gave me pleasure to know,
That at the end of the day, somewhere from afar,
I would see your tall figure, and there you are,
Standing there, so upright, a mystery,
On an alien, hostile street in Germany...[10]

(Henryka Karmel)

Apples for the 'whores'

Another routine day in the factory had begun. But Ester could not understand why suddenly today her *Meister*, Brüchard, was ordering her into a side room to clean the instruments. When she went in, Brüchard quickly closed the door and took a huge slice of cake out of the pocket of his smock: 'It's for you, eat!' Surprised, Ester tried to hide it in her pocket so she could share it with her mother, but Brüchard would not allow it and ordered her to finish it quickly, 'because if anyone sees you, they'll arrest me'. Having no other choice, Ester swallowed down the whole piece of cake. She knew she was not the only one who Brüchard sometimes rewarded with a tasty 'treat'. He helped almost all the women in 'his' group, where Mata Hollender served as an interpreter for the women who did not speak German. The *Meister* had frequently brought medicines for women who needed them, and was particularly solicitous toward Hanka Kurtz, who was pregnant.[11]

Was Brüchard's behaviour unusual for a German in the plant? The testimony of numerous Jewish and Polish women indicate that the Germans were initially hostile and antagonistic because the SS portrayed the prisoners as criminals, thieves and whores.[12] At first the women were unaware of this last soubriquet, until they learned of it by chance. It must be recalled that unlike the Hasag factories in Poland, there was no 'middle level' of Polish overseers or prisoner *kapos* in Leipzig. Thus, despite the injunctions and threat of punishment, there was direct contact between the inmates and the local staff. Paradoxically, the label of 'whore' prompted the blossoming of a complex tissue of relations with the German bosses.

A large number of testimonies describe the initial shock: 'One day when I got to work,' relates Luna Fuss, 'the German foreman asked me why I had been arrested because I looked too young to be a whore. He was amazed to hear that I had been arrested because I was Jewish.' Similarly, Henia Buchman tells of being asked: 'How come young girls like you are already prostitutes?'[13] Just how ludicrous the Nazi propaganda was is demonstrated by an incident involving Haneczka that sent shock waves throughout the factory. Haneczka (her family name is unknown), only 12 years old, had succeeded in passing herself off as older than her real age. It was not so easy, however, to pull the wool over the sharp eyes of her elderly German forewoman, who on one occasion lashed out at her saying it was inconceivable that such a sweet quiet young girl could have sunk so low. At first the child did not understand what she was talking about, but when she understood what she was being accused of, she burst into tears, which did not, however, convince the angry forewoman of her innocence.[14]

The answer to the riddle of the source of the misinformation can be found in the testimony of Rena Taubenblatt. A short item in a local paper (secretly given to her by her foreman, Peter Fursch, in the automation hall) reported that Leipzig had long been '*judenrein*' until the recent arrival of a group of Jewish women arrested for prostitution whom the authorities were attempting to rehabilitate as 'productive elements'. Rena managed to make it clear to Fursch that she herself was no *Dirne* (prostitute), but rather came from an honest, decent bourgeois home. She even told him of how her father had died and what had happened to her in the ghettos and camps. Hearing her story, Fursch confessed that he was ashamed to be German, and promised to help.[15]

Without a doubt, the Germans soon realized that many of the prisoners displayed the fine education and behaviour typical of a good *Kinderstube* (upbringing). The 'whore affair' was the subject of a ditty that went around all the departments:

> I, a whore no. 906, I write poems!
> You don't believe me?
> Well it's true.
> Trust me,
> My father never stole,
> And I am no whore,
> Or in a nicer phrase: a lady of the night,
> I am a fine upstanding woman, and always was,
> But to use the popular term,
> Just not quite the right race . . . [16]
>
> (Henryka Karmel)

Even given the discrepancies among the various testimonies, it seems quite clear that in time the Germans' attitude to the prisoners improved. Fursch's assistant, an elderly German man nicknamed *'Dziadek'* ('grandpa' in Polish) was particularly popular. His real name was probably Altmann. According to Rena Cypres, it was he who asked her if she was happy that the Russians might make it to Leipzig. 'Whatever happens, I told him, I'm not happy, because they'll accuse me of collaborating with the Germans.' She, too, had a 'guardian angel' in the form of a German electrician named Josef who would sometimes bring her bread and occasionally apples![17] Even the foreman Friedrich, who struck fear into all the women, treated them humanely from time to time and contrary to their apprehensions, would transfer the prisoners who had trouble operating the more complicated machinery to easier jobs. On the whole, the foremen came to the women's aid in cases of accident or illness, although they had to be circumspect about it.[18]

We cannot, however, conclude that this was the general pattern. There were also foremen like Hermann Krüger in the *S-Zü* department who played it both ways: although he offered no help to the prisoners, he declared that he was not a member of the Nazi party, had never heard of the Final Solution, and had no idea of the crimes for which the women had been arrested. He did, however, argue with the SS overseers, protesting against their striking the prisoners and also against the stingy soup rations.[19] Other Germans, such as Keller, in charge of checking bullets, feigned indifference,[20] while still others, such as Richard from the automation department, displayed outright hostility.[21]

The German women who worked in the plant as labourers or forewomen were generally quite ordinary people, Hasag employees or typical members of the bourgeoisie. It was only natural that working with women from all over Europe, and particularly with Jews, aroused their curiosity and made it impossible for them to obey the prohibition against consorting with the prisoners. The first time the SS overseers were out of sight, questions and answers were exchanged, and thus a broad fabric of human relations slowly evolved.

Fela Schächter recalls that in the *Zündhütchen* department,

> there were two German women, one young and the other older. The sandwiches they brought to work with them were quite paltry, and I don't remember them ever sharing them with me. They themselves were afraid of the overseer 'Miotła', but when she moved away from the door, we would sometimes chat. That's how they found out we weren't prostitutes, but decent educated girls. I remember how amazed I was when I realized that the woman I was talking to didn't even know that Columbus discovered America! Once the older woman complained that we might bring lice into the plant. That made me mad, and I had the audacity to say that the German soldiers at the front also had lice.[22]

Speaking of lice, an enticing young blonde German woman

who was very popular with the men worked alongside Blanka Künreich. Rumour had it that she had several children, each by a different father. On one occasion when the head foreman of Hala F showed up for a routine inspection, she demanded that the prisoners be disinfected because she had found lice in her home. The foreman, who seemed a pleasant, quiet sort, replied that he had never noticed lice on the prisoners, and suggested she check the man she had been sleeping with lately. This genial foreman, however, was not Blanka's 'guardian'. When examining the shell parts, she would throw the wrappings into a waste basket that was emptied periodically by an elderly German worker. One day he brought the basket back and hinted that she should take a look inside. To her astonishment, she found an apple and a tomato![23]

> What's this?
> A tomato, red
> In secret laid
> Smiling at me, a friend?
> No, it's not a tomato red
> It's from a heart that is rent
> Broken, in pity it bled . . . [24]
> (Henryka Karmel)

According to Ester Szymkiewicz, who worked with German women in the bomb detonator (*Bombenanzünder*) department, there were many who wanted to help the prisoners but were afraid of informers. Nevertheless, they shared their bread with the inmates and brought them underwear and stockings from home.[25] Helena Schächter has fond memories of her supervisor Gertrud, who sometimes gave her a sandwich or an apple. But things were not always so serene. It so happened that stately Eda Fenik was assigned a German supervisor who hated her with a passion. Since the German woman was short and hunchbacked, however, she had to stand on a chair whenever she wanted to show her displeasure by giving Eda a number of sharp slaps on her face, which were accompanied by hearty cursing.[26]

Malka Zuckerbrot, a religious woman, was unusually fortunate. The German woman who worked alongside her (probably the wife of the electrician Robb), told her in secret about her son who was fatally wounded on the Eastern Front. To Malka's great surprise, she discovered that the German was quite familiar with the intricacies of Jewish tradition, and knew exactly when each holiday fell. When Malka asked where this knowledge came from, the German revealed that she had hidden a family of Jewish acquaintances for quite some time until they were informed on and picked up by the Gestapo. Malka describes what happened on Yom Kippur:

> I fasted, like many of us did. During the break, 'my' German came over and stuck something in my hand. I stole a glance and there in my fist was a red apple wrapped in paper with the words: 'Remember, today is Yom Kippur, a fast day. Eat this apple tonight. I wish you and all your friends a good year and quick redemption...' I was shocked. In this cruel world around us there still beat a human heart, and it lit a spark of hope!

Ida Kelberg-Buszmicz, only 14 years old, also remembers the elderly German woman who occasionally stuck a slice of bread in her hand, and when no one could hear, would whisper: 'Soon, my child, hold on, soon the war will be over.'[27]

The prisoners sometimes chose to show their appreciation for the humane treatment they received from the Germans. The French women who worked with little Nina Tiberger made Christmas ornaments from coloured wrapping papers and Nina presented them to the foreman as a gift. He replied by wishing her and her friends that they be liberated in the coming year.[28] This was not the only instance of 'friendly relations'. Luna Fuss, who enjoyed the patronage of the overseer known as 'Laleczka' ('little doll' in Polish), made her a present of a doll she fashioned out of rags, even dressing it in a striped dress with a number on her chest.

Relations between the prisoners and their German bosses was not limited to the surreptitious offer of a slice of bread or an apple. Sometimes unexpected circumstances required the women to turn to the Germans directly for help. Such a case involved the German forewoman in Hala F, Frau Romer.[29] As a rule, she did not overly interfere in their work, always spoke to the prisoners softly and courteously – '*une grande dame*', and when she learned that one of the women was pregnant, she invariably made sure she received a double soup ration.[30] One day the rumour spread through Hala F that some of the workers were being transferred to a different plant. The news panicked diminutive Fela Schächter, who was in the camp together with her sisters. As fate would have it, in the corridor on her way to the toilet she ran into the forewoman sporting a new coat. Taking her courage into her hands, she greeted her, adding with a touch of *naiveté*: 'How nice you look, *Frau Meisterin*,' and then made the request that she not be separated from her sisters. They remained together, and to this day she does not know whether it had anything to do with her innocent compliment.

It was Yom Kippur, 1944. Many of the prisoners fasted, including a large number of those who were not observant. When Frau Romer noticed the unusual behaviour of those Jewish women who were not standing in line for soup at the noonday break, she asked Ziuta Hartman why. Ziuta explained that they were fasting to honour the memory of the dead, adding a few 'unnecessary' remarks regarding exactly which dead she was referring to. The *Meisterin* listened closely, and then suddenly blurted out: '*Mein Gott, mein Sohn war auch dort!*' (My God, my son was there too). 'When I realized what I had said,' writes Ziuta, 'I told the forewoman that if she reported our conversation to the SS overseer, we would both be taken out and killed.'[31]

Naturally, the Germans dared not talk to the prisoners, particularly the Jews, about their own troubles. None the less, at times, they would let fall a few words that indicated their distress and bitterness over their fate:

> *Herr Meister* must have forgotten
> That it was forbidden, and how,
> He gave us a very curious look,
> And stopped his work for now.
> And as we have said,
> Forbidden it was to be heard,
> Yet suddenly out of his mouth there came,
> An unstoppable stream of words.

That from the Eastern Front his son,
Had wounded returned from the fray
Arriving in time to bury his wife,
The other in hospital lay.
His leg they'd had to amputate,
Nothing could save him now,
And his despair was immensely great.
Another in Italy fought,
For months from him not a word did he hear,
And everyone knew that thousands of men
Were falling every day there.
Even the 16-year-old lad
Who'd just yesterday played in the sand,
They wouldn't let him stay at home,
Sent him too to some far-off land.
He spoke of how they'd said goodbye
Before their final touch...
But then he coughed and silent fell
He'd already said too much...[32]

(Henryka Karmel)

There were also some tragic cases. Ruth Kornblum, who had been transferred to a different workplace at her own request, enjoyed the beneficence of her new foreman, old Wilhelm. Although he declared himself a loyal supporter of 'the Führer', he did not approve of the anti-Jewish policy. Every day for lunch he brought a pot full of food from home which he shared with 'his girls'. Since they were working with toxic materials, he arranged for them to be issued rubber boots, and occasionally even a glass of milk. When Ruth and another prisoner told Wilhelm that their fathers had served in the German Army in the First World War, he became a real friend to them. Until the sad day in the spring of 1944 when the girls arrived at the plant and found Wilhelm hanging from a rope. He left them the pot of food with a note, reading: *I can no longer bear the shame of defeat. I realize we were all wrong. My wish for you is that you regain your freedom and every now and then remember old Wilhelm who loved you like daughters.*[33]

As in any other situation and every human society, there were better days and worse days in the factory. Despite the unchanging daily routine, the tension could be felt in the air. Was it that the Germans believed the end of the war was coming and they would be going down in defeat? Or was there an authentic change in their attitude to the prisoners in general, and the Jewish women in particular? Let us not forget that most of the Germans who earned the appreciation of the prisoners are described as elderly, that is, aged fifty to sixty, and had thus assimilated less of Hitler's theories. Undoubtedly, there were also those among them who were kindhearted by nature. Nevertheless, many testimonies contain no mention whatsoever of any assistance from the Germans. Felicja Bannet-Schäftler protests in her journal against fat supervisors who wolfed down a large breakfast without it ever occurring to them to sneak a slice of bread to a starving prisoner. Still, the fact that many former inmates make a point of recording the behaviour of 'good Germans' must be significant.

In this regard, it should be noted that the credibility of testimony of any kind depends on two factors: the witness must not be subject to any pressure and must not wish to receive any secondary benefit from his or her testimony. In these terms, there can be no doubt that the relatively large number of references to the humanitarian behaviour of Germans can not derive from considerations of self-interest. On the contrary, given the desire to honour the memory of the victims of the Holocaust and to record for posterity the torments suffered by the survivors, as well as potential demands for compensation of some kind, it would seem in the witnesses' interest to depict the Germans in the most negative light possible.

Sources reveal that in the other Hasag camps, the nice Germans, the 'ordinary people' employed by Hasag, some of whom were ex-communists, underwent a startling metamorphosis in 1942–43. With the anticipation of victory in battle and unlimited power over others, they soon turned into sadists who beat the prisoners and used every opportunity to increase their wealth at the expense of their victims. Any German who dared to help a Jewish prisoner was risking not only internment in a concentration camp, but also ostracism by his colleagues for his 'crimes'.[34]

What, then, brought about the change for the better at Leipzig? According to Lise London, there was a significant turnover of supervisors in the plant because of the demands of army recruitment, and those who remained treated the prisoners better than their predecessors, not reporting incidents of bad conduct or sabotage to the SS overseers.[35] Was their behaviour dictated only by fear of the approaching front or the awareness that they, like their compatriots, would bear responsibility for Germany's crimes? It does not seem likely, as Felicja Bannet-Schäftler claims, that the SS overseers at Leipzig 'did not have the guts to tell the civilian population the truth about us'.[36] In late 1944 the German population was well aware of the fate of the Jews and the meaning of the term 'concentration camp'. For this reason, the prisoners were generally skeptical and regarded any displays of humanitarianism with suspicion. 'The Germans at Leipzig were very afraid of the SS, afraid of each other, afraid of their own shadow. True, they treated us more decently than in Poland.' Luna Fuss adds: 'As the end of the war drew near, the Germans became more humane. My SS overseer revealed a kind heart, but how she behaved before, nobody knows.'[37]

The logical conclusion seems to be that the conduct of the German supervisors at Leipzig toward the prisoners in general, and the Jewish women in particular, was influenced primarily by objective factors: the imminent end to the war, the fear of defeat, and the urgent need to construct an 'alibi', both individually and collectively. Even some SS overseers were starting to worry about the future, and chose to temper their behaviour in the presence of the civilian population. Let us not forget that any surreptitious offer of a word of comfort or a slice of bread was made while Leipzig was being heavily bombed.

The shelling

Throughout 1944 Hasag had to contend with the damage caused by the bombs that fell on the Leipzig factories. Once the camp was set up, injecting new manpower into the plants, it was necessary to hasten the repair of the ruined facilities. Procedure demanded that the Hasag management notify the

Labour Headquarters Light Munitions, of the damage in order to be issued the proper construction permits. Budin, however, would usually begin repairs on his own authority, leaving the local Armaments Officer to obtain the necessary permits.[38] Thanks to this practice, production delays were avoided.

The atmosphere of feverish work pervaded the Hasag plants until late in September 1944, when the first changes began to be felt. Until that time, music was sometimes played over the loudspeakers installed on the factory floors, with news from the front broadcast at noon. Both ceased at the end of that September. 'First we were told that the radio was broken and then we were not told anything. We knew why! We were not supposed to learn of Germany's great "victories", with her soldiers on the retreat at Kiev, Lvov and Warsaw ... So we were glad when they stopped playing the radio.'[39]

The winter was exhausting for the prisoners, with the savage pressure in the factory getting even worse. Hasag tried to 'raise morale' in its own inimitable way. As we have said, 'wages' were paid in the form of coupons in exchange for which the women could purchase small items at the canteen. Not all the women were lucky enough to receive these, however, since the foremen considered them rewards for good work. But the prisoners regarded the coupons in a different light. Lacking sources for the attitude of the women of other nationalities, we can only relate to that of the Poles, French and Jews. In the case of the Poles, Matylda Woliniewska encouraged the organization of a group of 'Pawiak prisoners' who refused to accept coupons in protest against the forcing of political prisoners to produce munitions that were being used against their own nation. Matylda tried to convince women of other nationalities to join the 'boycott'.[40]

The French political prisoners also refused the coupons. 'That was our decision, even though we were starving!' states Lise London. 'The meaning of our refusal was utterly clear to the SS overseers, who made a lot of us pay heavily for it.' The supervisors did not understand what it was all about until Angele Romey explained their position.[41] The affair resounded throughout all the factory departments, and was commemorated in this poem:

For excellent work, you get a prize!
The German said
And the Frenchwoman replied:
Merci, but no thanks.
I work because you force me to
It's a matter of the heart, you understand, don't you?
Don't thank me, don't you see
That rewarding me
For creating death for my nation
Is shameful to me?[42]

(Henryka Karmel)

It should be noted, however, that the Polish prisoners (at least until the liberation of Poland by the Red Army) were receiving parcels from home.[43] Parcels also arrived occasionally for the French through the Red Cross. The Jewish women had no way of getting any outside aid, and were more debilitated. Thus the large majority (if not all) of them accepted the coupons, hoping to be able to purchase a pair of cloth shoes,[44] a precious item without which they could not expect to survive. In addition to the coupons, the supervisors gave out vouchers for an extra soup ration to those women who exceeded their quota. Some of the Jewish prisoners worked hard for this voucher, while others decided not to make the effort.[45]

Hunger in the camp grew progressively worse, with the march back and forth to the factory, in addition to the 12-hour working day, sharpening the women's appetite. In February 1945, the bread ration was reduced to one fifth of a loaf. Potatoes cooked in their skins had disappeared long ago. The soup ration doled out at the factory thus became the main meal of the starving prisoners, so that not surprisingly its appearance at noon became the highpoint of the day. As Paulina Buchenholz puts it: 'I was kept alive by sleep, a hot shower, and the soup. Life revolved around the soup, and I felt as if I lived for one goal alone: SOUP! I worked all day, went to sleep, and got up with one thought in my mind: today I'll get my soup!'[46] The 'sweet soup', containing groats and macaroni, aroused the greatest enthusiasm. Initially it was on the menu once a week: 'To this day I remember how it tasted. We were always thrilled when it came.'[47]

In the course of time, the taste of the sweet soup was forgotten as well. More and more often, the vats brought to the plant held turnip soup, which gave the prisoners severe diarrhoea. 'I remember one time,' notes Fela Schächter, 'when we were standing in line for soup at the lunch break, and as soon as we finished it we had to run to the toilets. Some of the German foremen standing around saw what was happening, and one of them joked: *"Die Suppe läuft über!"* (The soup is spilling over).'[48]

The sirens went off again in mid-January 1945. From that time on, shelling was stepped up, the bombardments now coming even in broad daylight. On some days as early as ten in the morning, and then again at noon, the women were ordered to stop the machines and go down to the shelters, which were roomy and well-equipped. *'Los, schneller!'* the overseers would shout angrily. The prisoners went downstairs in high spirits! Eda could not help herself from laughing out loud, which instantly 'earned' her a stinging slap across the face. Never mind! They enjoyed the 'hullabaloo' and the break from work.

Sometimes we sat in the shelter for two or three hours. The spirit of gaiety refreshed our tormented bodies... It was forbidden to speak out loud in the shelter. We were constantly watched by the overseers. Idiots, they must have been scared the bomb would hear us and fall on them. If it only could! But the all-clear sounded and we had to go back to the machines. And then – new orders: we had to meet our quota despite the interruptions in the workday.[49]

How did the prisoners find the strength to survive under these conditions? Sometimes encouragement came from unexpected quarters. On one occasion crates of Russian munitions, war booty, were delivered to Hala F to be cleaned and readied for shipment to the front. Inside, the women found messages in Yiddish: 'Jews, hold on, you will soon be delivered!'[50] Every now and then foreign workers would shout from a distance: 'Hitler is *kaput*! The war is almost over!' French prisoners of war who were working nearby passed news from the front to their compatriots, along with sewing materials and even books – no less important.[51] Now and then Czech and Polish workers found the opportunity to whisper 'Hang in there!' to one of the prisoners, and if they dared to risk it, sneaked cigarettes or bread to 'their' girls, or perhaps even helped them with some particularly strenuous task.[52]

Towa Zilberberg relates the following incident:

> Once I was working the night shift. The work was exhausting and I couldn't keep my eyes open… All of a sudden I found that a man who looked Jewish but who spoke an unfamiliar foreign language was standing beside me. I managed to make out that he was Italian… He stood there, and seeing how tired I was began to work side by side with me, doing some of my work. To this day I don't know who he was. Was he a prisoner like us?… Maybe a Jew?[53]

Although they worked together, no mention is made in any of the testimonies of romantic relations between the prisoners and the foreign workers. This goes to show how well the SS overseers performed their duties. It was easier for friendships to develop among the inmates working side by side. Bina Herstein, who worked in Hermann Krüger's department, became friendly with a Frenchwoman who translated the instructions for her. Eda Lewin recalls her French friend who volunteered for work at Hasag in order to be closer to her husband, who was a prisoner of war. She told Eda what was going on in the outside world and often brought her a bit of food. The women also took advantage of the presence of other nationalities to learn foreign languages. Claiming to be giving each other instructions regarding their work, they whispered back and forth, and thus learned French, English or Russian. German was not a particularly popular language of study, for obvious reasons. Danuta Brzosko managed to compose a Polish–English dictionary. Sara Shalem, Ester Nessel and others also tried to learn as they worked.

Another of the forbidden methods the women used to help pass the time during their many hours of tedious labour was to write poems or copy them out under the table and learn them off by heart. They tried to remember the poems they had been taught in school and wrote new ones on their own situation. It is no exaggeration to say that this 'hobby' occupied women of all nationalities. Among the Jewish prisoners, the most popular poems were those penned by Henryka and Ilona Karmel. Rena Taubenblatt recorded a large number of the Karmel sisters' creations in a notebook that was at the centre of a tragi-comic incident. A Polish woman named Marysia asked Rena to lend her the notebook because she wanted to copy the poems and smuggle them to the 'other side.' Marysia hid in the toilet with it to read the poems. To her great misfortune, she was caught by the foreman Richard, who took the notebook away from her. At Rena's request, two German-speaking Jewish supervisors intervened and assured the incensed foreman that the poems were entirely innocent. Richard ordered them to translate one of them for him, and by chance the book opened to Henryka's poem 'On English Capitalists':

> Seated comfortably in their leather armchairs in their
>   luxurious offices
> They discuss and record and debate,
> Divide and subtract, add and multiply.
> The greatest benefit at minimum loss calculate.
> That they are speaking of human beings, the world, and
>   nations
> That's nothing! It has no place in their calculations!
> Take it slowly, we'll make it in time, don't worry,
> We can't do it all at once, and there is no hurry.
> So what if the game goes on a bit more
> So what if there's anguish and horror and gore
> After all, gentlemen, that's the meaning of war!
> Nonsense!
> Dear Sirs!
> Can't you hear my words?
> That just isn't right, you're playing with life!
> But those gentlemen just count their money day and night.[54]
>
> (Henryka Karmel)

The foreman liked the poem so much that he gave the notebook back to Marysia who was, by the way, a very attractive young woman. The Karmel sisters' poems were

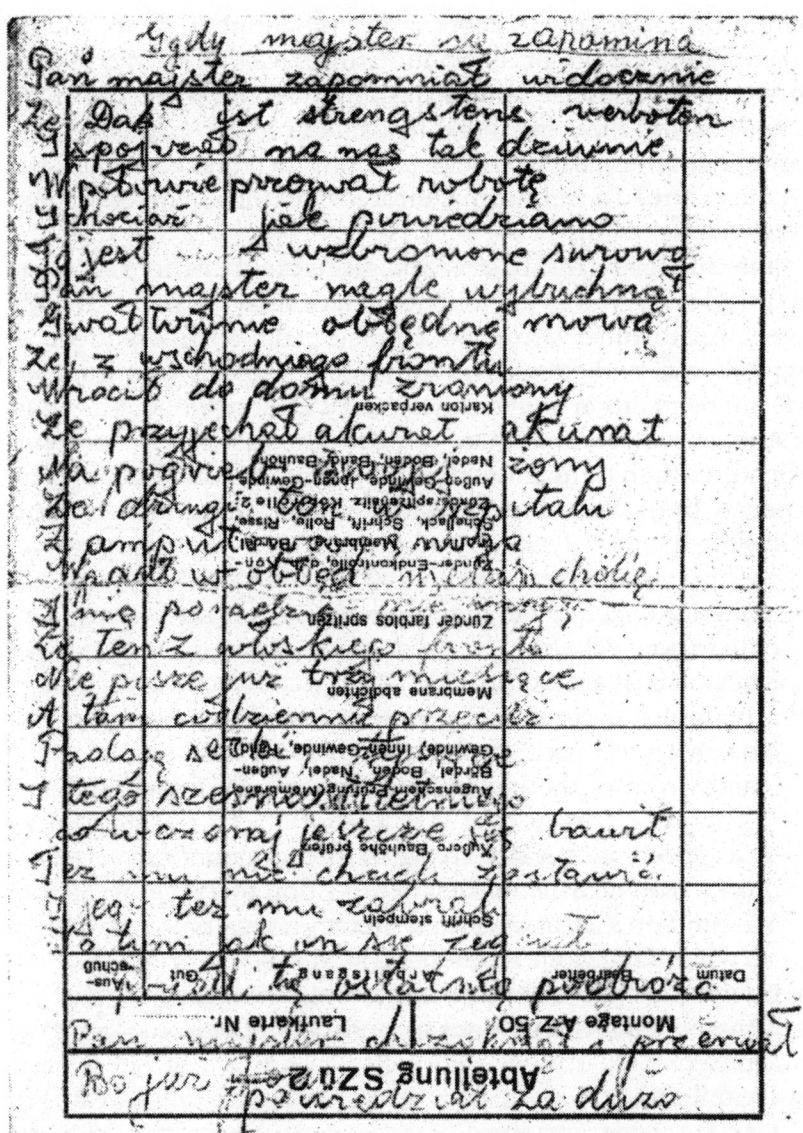

Figure 4.1 Poem by Henryka Karmel, written on a Department *S-Zü 2* work-card.

Source: Margulies-Timberg, YV, 0-48/47d-3.

copied by many of the prisoners, among them Malka Zuckerbrot, Fela Schächter and Ester Nessel. Ela Wachtel got hold of the official production figures forms in the *S-Zü* department to use for this purpose. For many years she took great care to preserve the forms on which she wrote out the poems, until they found their way to the archives of Yad Vashem (see Figure 4.1).[55]

Despite the hardship, there was a certain benefit to working in the factory: it was possible to make contact with the outside world. The Polish women had the best chances of doing so. As we have seen, there was an infirmary on the factory grounds where even rather complex surgery was performed. The head surgeon was a Pole, Dr Tomasz Goryński, who worked together with a doctor from the Buchenwald camp. The nurses from the Leipzig camp would bring the surgical patients to the infirmary and then remain in the operating theatre with the two doctors, with no German guards in attendance. They used the opportunity to pass letters from their compatriots, through the doctors, to friends and relatives incarcerated at Buchenwald.[56] There were also illicit relations with women prisoners from Ravensbrück. One of these, Helonowa, confirms that she received letters that were smuggled out of the Hasag-Leipzig camp by Polish inmates, and she passed them on.[57] It is likely that the Karmel poems also reached the 'outside' in a similar manner.

Zofia Kołecka describes the organization of illegal correspondence. Messages to family members were written on postcards marked with numbers. Mieczysław Kotwica, a Pole who worked in Zofia's department, was given a list of addresses with corresponding numbers. He would add the address and post them. Sadly, Zofia and two of her friends were caught at the camp gate with some 40 illegal postcards in their possession. The three of them were sentenced to six days in the bunker, where they suffered from cold, hunger and rats, and then were transferred to the camp at Taucha.[58]

There were also a few Germans in the plant who were willing to take the risk of conveying crumbs of information about the outside world to the prisoners. A young, one-eyed German electrician by the name of Robb, 'suspected' of being a communist, worked in Hala F. He regularly brought Maria

Schächter news of the situation at the front and in the rest of the world, whispering it to her furtively when he came to 'fix' her machine. Newspapers were even more precious. Every now and then, Meister Fursch would hide a paper in Rena Taubenblatt's clothes locker.[59] Smuggled into camp at great danger, it became a treasure, the news items arousing hope and faith and providing a source of strength for continued survival. Malka Zuckerbrot describes such an incident:

One day, late in 1944, 'my' German woman came onto the floor and whispered to me: 'Go to the toilet. I left you a paper there. They're going to establish a Jewish state in Palestine.' I hurried down to the toilets where a scrunched up copy of *Die Leipziger Zeitung* was tossed in a corner. I read it with tremendous excitement; after all, I had been cut off from the world for two years. And what an article! A Jewish army had been established in Palestine! The Jewish Brigade. There was also a photograph of Jewish soldiers in uniform. I stared at it for a long time: God in heaven, they were wearing a Star of David on their arm with such pride! I went back to work and sent some of my friends to the toilet to read it. It was a great day for us! Maybe, just maybe, we would make it. Maybe, despite everything, someone would rescue us.

Thus the days passed in work and rest, despair and hope, day following night, night following day... to work in the morning, back to camp at night, day after day after day...

Notes

1. Ilona Karmel, 'Al pat lechem' [On a Crust of Bread], *Al Ha-Mishmar*, (19 June 1961), p. 3.
2. Kornblum-Rosenberger, *Neder*, p. 73.
3. Henryka Karmel, 'My', *Spiew za drutami* (New York: Association of Friends of Our Tribune, 1947), p. 12.
4. Testimony of Felicja Silberstein-Shahar, YV, 0-33/3334.
5. Testimony of Eda Fenik, YV, 0-3/1272.
6. H. Karmel, 'Westchnienie', Ela Margulies-Timberg Collection, YV, 0-48/47d-3.
7. Testimony of Helena Schächter-Zorski, YV, 0-33/1797.
8. H. Karmel, 'Gruszki', *Spiew za drutami*, p. 19.
9. Testimony of Eda Lewin-Jewin, YV, 0-33/1838.

10. H. Karmel, 'Gdy wracamy', Margulies-Timberg Collection.
11. Testimony of Ester Netzer; Henryka Karmel-Wolfe, YV, 0-33/1852.
12. Testimony of Fela Blatt-Blum, YV, 0-33/1839.
13. Testimony of Henia Buchman-Strelski, *We Remember: Twenty-four Members of Kibbutz Megiddo Testify* (Hebrew), (Tel Aviv: Morehet-Sifriat Poalim, 1988), p. 70 (hereafter: *We Remember*).
14. Bannet-Schäftler, *'Journal'*, p. 26.
15. Testimony of Rina Fradkin, YV, 0-16/249.
16. H. Karmel, 'Migawki', Margulies-Timberg Collection.
17. Testimony of Rina Cypres, YV, 0-33/1857.
18. Testimony of Lea Muskatenblut, YV, 0-33/1801.
19. Testimony of Bina Herstein; Letter from Shoshana Adler, 3 May 1992, private collection.
20. Testimony of Jeta Jolinger, YV, 0-33/3419.
21. Testimony of Rina Fradkin.
22. Testimony of Felicja Karay.
23. Testimony of Blanka Ickowicz.
24. H. Karmel, 'Dar podrzucony,' *Śpiew za drutami*, p. 18.
25. Testimony of Ester Szymkiewicz, YV, M-1/E/1210/1276/
26. Testimonies of Helena Zorski and Eda Fenik.
27. Testimony of Ida Kelberg-Buszmicz, YV, 0-3/2798.
28. Nurit Harit (formerly Nina Thieberger), oral testimony.
29. We cannot be certain whether her name was Romer or Riemer; testimony of Miriam Eitan, YV, 0-33/2834.
30. Testimony of Frania Siegman.
31. Testimony of Ziuta Rotenberg-Hartman, YV, 0-33/1851.
32. H. Karmel, 'Gdy majster się zapomina', Margulies-Timberg Collection.
33. Kornblum-Rosenberger, *Neder*, p. 80.
34. See the incident involving Karl Herold, Karay, *Death Comes in Yellow*, pp. 96–97.
35. Ricol-London, *La mégère de la rue Daguerre*, p. 341.
36. Bannet-Schäftler, *'Journal'*, p. 26.
37. Testimonies of Ester Netzer and Luna Kaufman.
38. Hasag an den Reichsminister für Rüstung und Kriegsproduktion, Leipzig, 21 August 1944, BA, R 3/3232.
39. Bannet-Schäftler, *'Journal'*, p. 24.
40. Brzosko-Mędryk, *Matylda*, p. 55.
41. Ricol-London, *La mégère de la rue Daguerre*, p. 341.
42. Henryka Karmel; the poem appears in the testimony of Malka Hottner.
43. Brzosko-Mędryk, *Matylda*, pp. 50-51.
44. Testimony of Frania Siegman.
45. Testimonies of Eda Jewin and Luna Kaufman.
46. Memoirs from the war and concentration camps, by Paulina Buchenholz, YV, 0-33/E/142-2-1.
47. Testimony of Helena Feig-Kurzman, YV, 0-33/3280.
48. Testimony of Felicja Karay.
49. Testimony of Eda Jewin; Bannet-Schäftler, *Journal*, p. 31.
50. Testimony of Malka Hottner.
51. Ricol-London, *La mégère de la rue Daguerre*, p. 337.
52. Kornblum-Rosenberger, *Neder*, p. 79; testimony of Halina Razowski.
53. Towa Zilberberg, *Mama, Your Prayers Have Been Answered!* (Hebrew) (Tel Aviv: Bney Brak, 1994), p. 240.

54. Poems of Henryka and Ilona Karmel, Żydowski Instytut Historyczny (ŻIH), Warsaw, sygn. 246, nr. 108.
55. Margulies-Timberg Collection.
56. Testimony of Irena Seńko.
57. Urszula Wińska, Zwyciężyły wartości, Wspomnienia z Ravensbrück, (Gdańsk: Wyd. Morskie, 1985), p. 238.
58. Testimony of Zofia Fugiel.
59. Each of the prisoners had a small locker in which she kept her jacket and personal items during work; see the testimony of Rena Fradkin.

5 High-Level Politics at Hasag-Leipzig

Commandant Plaul's 'enlightened' regime

The tall figure of Commandant Wolfgang Plaul rarely appeared in the corridors of the Leipzig camp, and indeed he is seldom mentioned in the testimonies of the prisoners. Although they knew nothing of his previous record, experience had taught them to keep a safe distance from any SS officer. The Polish women called him '*Kogut*' (Polish for 'rooster') because of his protruding Adam's apple, and sometimes he was referred to by the nickname '*Głupi Jasio*' (Jasio the fool).[1] Did the name suit him? Or did Plaul perhaps succeed in operating the camp in the spirit of the times, that is, out of concern for his future, which no longer seemed so bright?

Descriptions of the Commandant's behaviour are quite varied, so that we can not give an unequivocal answer to this question. Danuta Brzosko, who spoke German, had worked as a charwoman in the SS officers' casino at Majdanek and knew Plaul well. She describes him as a hot-tempered man, famed for his violent flare-ups, who beat the women and liked to unleash his vengeance on them. Indeed, when she arrived at Leipzig, he assigned her to the hardest work in the plant because of her 'impudence'. At the same time, in the role of interpreter she did not hesitate to convey her fellow prisoners' requests to him, such as permission to receive parcels from home or to send letters out of the camp. In most cases, he granted these requests.[2]

Only few people had close contact with the Commandant, and, as stated above, his presence was felt mainly during inspections or spot checks at the camp gate. In the testimony of Jewish prisoners, he is depicted in a reasonably positive light, particularly in comparison to the 'demonic figure' of the Buchenwald Commandant (most likely a reference to Hermann Pister), who periodically made surprise appearances during inspections, using the opportunity to strike one prisoner or another.[3] Although rumour had it that in his previous positions Plaul had been a hangman and treated the prisoners with brutality, at Leipzig he managed to improve his image considerably. The general opinion of him was that he treated all the women equally, in accordance with his motto: *'Bei mir gibt's keine Rassenunterschiede; alle Häftlinge sind gleich'* (For me there are no race differences; all prisoners are equal).[4]

Figure 5.1 *Untersturmführer* Wolfgang Plaul, Commandant of Hasag-Leipzig.

Source: NMG, Buchenwald.

His unusual impartiality is also attested to by an incident related by Danuta Brzosko. It may be recalled that when the Polish uprising was put down in August 1944, hundreds of women from Warsaw were brought to the camp. Once when she was in the toilet and could not be seen, Danuta overhead a conversation between two of the 'new girls' in an adjacent cubicle. They were typical stall-holders from the famous 'Zieleniak' vegetable market in Warsaw. One was complaining bitterly to the other about the failure of their delegation to Commandant Plaul: 'We told him we didn't want to wear the red triangle, like those political prisoners... My friend, I had a horse and carriage, and what now? I have to clean shit here...' To Wolfgang Plaul's credit, it must be said that he did not grant their request, kicking and cursing the market-folk as he threw them out of his office.[5]

According to Rut Kornblum, the Commandant was also willing to listen to the prisoners' complaints. On one occasion, several Jewish women decided to complain to him of the abuse they received at the hands of the overseers 'Sowa' and 'Holenderka'. Plaul received them politely and promised to deal with the matter, although he never did. On the other hand, he did accede to the women's request for notebooks, pencils, and even paints, and this time followed it through. It is therefore not surprising that he is lauded as 'a good, kind commandant'.

At times his behaviour was decidedly odd. During one inspection he asked Malka Zuckerbrot her name. Trembling in fear, she told him. Plaul burst out in a roar of laughter, saying: '*Ach, so! Hast doch deine Ernährung von deinem Name*' (Is that so! Then you can live off your name!)[6] Malka did not know what to make of his response. On a more serious occasion she had a stroke of luck. In her mattress she had hidden family photographs she had managed to smuggle into the camp with the help of a Polish supervisor, and they were discovered by one of the SS overseers. When Malka was hauled in to be interrogated, Plaul asked her if she had relatives in Palestine, which army her father had served in during the First World War, and so on. Terrified, she was barely able to answer him. The Commandant concluded the interrogation with the dramatic declaration: 'The war is finished, but so are we!' – and let her go. Felicja Bannet-Schäftler, however, gives a less attractive picture of Plaul in her journal, depicting him as a fastidious man who did not wish to dirty his hands by striking the prisoners, but who nevertheless referred to them contemptuously as a '*Schweinepack*' (a pack of swine).

Who, then, did Plaul's 'dirty work'? Two groups were available for the job: the staff of SS overseers headed by the '*Oberka*', and the internal administration under Joanna Szumańska. The following incident illustrates the 'balance of power' between these two 'mistresses' of the camp. It happened in the spring of 1945, during roll-call. The women were pouring out, but not at a speed that suited Joanna, and she shoved one of the Russians. Her victim, a 'prisoner of war' who demanded to be treated accordingly, hit her back. Joanna immediately complained to the '*Oberka*' (who, on the basis of the description, appears to have been Käthe Heber). During the roll-call, Käthe slapped the Russian woman across the face repeatedly, drawing blood. The silent mass of prisoners were filled with rage, and there was a clear sense of mutiny in the air. (The Red Army was already on German land!) When the Russian was sent back to her place, the women beside her heard her whisper: 'Just wait!'[7]

The '*Oberka*' beat the inmates with her fists as well, becoming incensed if she found any contraband during inspection at the camp gate: items such as a piece of bread, an apple, or paper or rags pilfered from the factory. A new prisoner's first experience of her displeasure always came as a surprise, for it was hard to believe that such an attractive woman, with her brown eyes and golden curls, could behave with such brutality. Her favourite collective punishment was a general roll-call in which all the women were ordered to assume a kneeling position. Not surprisingly, she was hated with a passion, and not a single testimony has even one good word to say about her.

The overseers under the '*Oberka*' belonged to two work details: the escort detail which guarded the prisoners on the way to and in the factory; and the camp detail in charge of guard duties inside the camp. While in the factory, the overseers had to give some thought to the presence of civilians; 'at home', far from prying eyes, their power was unlimited. They spent most of their time in the camp conducting inspections: were the prisoners taking too long in the washroom, were they in the corridors without good reason, were the rooms properly cleaned and straightened, etc.

As 'graduates of Ravensbrück', they knew all too well how

to cause the prisoners the greatest distress. They conducted frequent searches of the pallets, turning over blankets and mattresses and disposing of anything that might ease the inmates' lot, if only a little: sewing materials, a knife, an extra pair of underpants or some rags that served as a towel. The most dangerous item that could be found were photographs (as in the case of Malka Zuckerbrot). Any forbidden articles of clothing or valuable mementos that had miraculously survived previous searches were immediately confiscated, (i.e. stolen).

Why were the overseers so eager to supplement their 'income'? Not only were they not paid well, as we have seen, but with their transfer to the jurisdiction of Buchenwald, supervision of them seems to have been significantly tightened. This impression is strengthened by the lengthy correspondence between the Buchenwald clothing storehouse and administration on the one hand, and *Aussenkommando* Hasag-Leipzig on the other. The letters sent between December 1944 and April 1945 contain repeated complaints of the overseers' wastefulness and irresponsibility: 'These overseers must be cautioned to take better care of the government property for which they are responsible. Their attitude and handling of the situation is sloppy and improper. The maintenance of law and order relies on the conscientiousness of individuals.'[8] (See Figure 5.2).

What occasioned these reprimands? Elsa had not returned a pair of gloves, Margaret was missing a blouse and Herta had lost a pair of socks! Most of their colleagues were guilty of similar crimes. Anyone reading this correspondence cannot fail to find it both incredible and ludicrous. Their world was falling apart around them, yet the Buchenwald commanders had nothing more to worry about than a pair of socks! Nor did they relent. The derelict overseers were forced to repay the value of any unreturned item into the Buchenwald coffers.[9] It is not surprising that these women are described by Danuta Brzosko as hungry for power and full of rage. The names of several of them appear on the lists of war criminals: Ursula Abeling, Margarete Deliga and Gretel Rössler.[10] It cannot be denied, however, that a number of overseers are mentioned favourably. Paula Gimes' testimony is a model of fairness,

```
            W a f f e n - ½
Konzentrationslager Buchenwald          (15)Weimar-Buchenwald,den 4.2.1945
      Verwaltung -
V3a-Az.: 15½a(w)-2.45./Sch5.

Betreff: Bekleidung der ½-Aufseherinnen
Bezug  : dort.Schr.v.28.1.1945
Anlagen: -½-

An das
W a f f e n - ½
Konzentrationslager Buchenwald
Arbeitskommando: Hasag-Leipzig
- Verwaltung -

(1o)L e i p z i g
Hugo Schneidersr.

In der Anlage werden Forderungsnachweise für die ½-Aufseherinnen:
    Edith  D e l i g a . . . . . . . . . Endbetrag RM  11,45
    Gerta  P ö s : h e . . . . . . . . .  -- " -   "    -,40
    Olga   A b e l . . . . . . . . . . . . . . .  -- " -  "   14,--
    Anna   B r a n d . . . . . . . . . .  -- " -   "   25,1o
    Else   D l u g o s c h . . . . . . .  -- " -   "   14,--
    Hedwig F l u c h e r . . . . . . . .  -- " -   "   25,3o
    Anneliese G i e s e . . . . . . . . .  --" -   "   65,4o
zum Einzug der Beträge und zur Einzahlung an die ½-Standortkasse Weimar-Bu-
chenwald,überreicht.
Den ½-Aufseherinnen ist allgemein zu eröffnen,daß sie künftig besser als b:
her das ihnen anvertraute Reichseigentum schützen und bewahren.Diese locke:
Auffassungen und Handhabungen sind ganz und gar nicht am Platze.Aus der So
faltigkeit der Einzelnen baut sich das Ganze zu einer guten Ordnung zusa.m.
```

Figure 5.2 Portion of a letter from Buchenwald headquarters to Hasag-Leipzig regarding SS overseers' missing items of clothing.

Source: ThHSA, Ns 4 BU, Vlg, 99, p. 47.

describing the merciless overseer formerly at Auschwitz, but not forgetting the 'girl with the dog' who she would send on ahead to warn the prisoners of her approach. With obvious emotion, Paula also remembers the *Aufseherin* who saved her life by getting her out of the infirmary just before a selection.[11]

The overseer most often mentioned in the testimonies was a short plump blonde woman by the name of Anneliese, perhaps the only one who can be positively identified.[12] She was in charge of the Jewish block, and proclaimed solemnly that she would treat them all well. She earned her popularity not only by keeping that promise, but also by virtue of the 'juicy' affairs she was involved in. With no men in the camp, there was not much to gossip about, until it was learned that Anneliese was a lesbian who periodically invited one or other of the inmates to a midnight tryst in the shelter. Public opinion was mixed. On the one hand, she was appreciated for her fair and reasonable treatment, but on the other, the prisoners were suspicious that she might be trying to get too close to them. As for her 'victim' of the moment, she clearly enjoyed a significant improvement in food and clothes. This aroused no public outrage, but rather disgust and regret over the demoralization of the woman. The authorities eventually became aware of the situation and Anneliese was transferred to another camp. Her last companion was sentenced to three days in the bunker.[13]

Depictions of the conduct of the SS overseers do not paint an overly sombre picture. On the contrary, the example set by the brutal '*Oberka*' does not seem to have dictated the behaviour of all her subordinates. They treated the prisoners more or less evenhandedly, and there do not appear to be complaints of greater cruelty to the members of one nationality or the other. To what extent this situation served the purposes of Commandant Plaul can only become clear by an examination of the status of the 'camp elder', Joanna Szumańska.

The confrontation with the Russian woman related above is evidence that Joanna did not routinely strike the inmates. It may be recalled that from the first mentions made of her, she is shown to have both good and bad points. The spiritual leader of the political prisoners from Poland, Matylda Woliniewska, actually gives her a 'character reference'.[14] None the less, it was an open secret in the camp that Joanna's friends from Majdanek enjoyed her unreserved support.[15]

What do the Jewish women have to say about her? Maryla Reich, who had passed for a Pole in Majdanek, relates that Joanna knew she was a Jew, protected her from harm and saved her life during the *Erntefest* (campaign of extermination) in 1943. Her guardianship continued in Leipzig, where Joanna's door was always open to Maryla, who invariably found a plate of bread and sausage waiting for her there on the table. Indeed, Maryla states in her testimony that she never heard of any acts of cruelty on Joanna's part in the Leipzig camp. Felicja Silberstein, 'just one of the Jews', adds: 'Joanna was good to me. She demanded strict obedience from us, because that was part of her job, it was what was required of her.'[16] It was rumoured in camp that Commandant Plaul had a romantic relationship with the '*Lagerälteste*' and that she used this 'to make life easier for us'.[17] Several Jewish members of the intelligentsia adopt a neutral position, admitting that while Joanna's behaviour could be erratic on the whole she treated them 'OK'.[18]

In contrast to her defenders, however, there is a large group of Jewish prisoners who unanimously accuse Joanna of hostile, demeaning and oppressive treatment.[19] In Felicja Bannet-Schäftler's journal we find that 'she was a servant of the totally inhumane Hitlerism who deserves to be hanged. It was only when talking with the Commandant that she struck a seductive feminine pose, staring at him adoringly as she awaited his orders'.[20] Animosity toward Joanna grew stronger when the 'ka-elniks' arrived from Skarżysko and told of her brutality at Majdanek, where she was known as 'Tygrys' (Polish for 'tigress') because she bared her teeth when she beat them.[21] At Leipzig she ordered night-time roll-calls even in the freezing cold, and anyone who did not keep in line was punished by having her soup and bread taken away the following day.[22] On Sundays she sent the Jewish women to clean in place of the Poles whose job this was. 'If there had been a crematorium there,' claims Dora Sroka, 'Joanna would have been the first stoker.'[23]

Following the war, Joanna Szumańska was arrested after being identified by several Jewish women. According to information received from Matylda Woliniewska, she was released two months later by the Polish War Crimes Commission due to lack of evidence. She later married the Jewish pianist Andrzej Szulc, with whom she tried to emigrate to Chile, but on the way, while in Paris, she was again recognized by a number of former prisoners and arrested. Frenchwomen, as well as Jews, testified against her, accusing her of brutality toward the Jewish women, greed and extravagance. Her husband sought witnesses for the defence who would testify that she was appointed by the camp commandant and behaved commendably. The details of the trial are unavailable, but it concluded with Joanna's release, after which she and her husband settled in the United States.

The serious accusations voiced against Joanna Szumańska are telling. Psychologists might claim that the fact that Joanna and the 'Oberka' showed no desire to correct the negative impression they made attests to their sadistic nature and lack of rationality, that is, a concern for the future. Or perhaps it was the anticipation of German defeat that drove the 'mistresses' to wield their power over the helpless slaves for as long as they could?

One thing is certain: Commandant Plaul was very pleased to have found the golden mean between two conflicting desires. On the one hand, he wished to keep a low profile in order to save his own skin when the sky fell in. This accounts for the infrequency of his appearances in the camp, his declarations of justice and equality, his permission for cultural activities, and so on. On the other hand, he wished to remain a harsh SS officer who inspired fear, the supreme authority. His expertise in the running of concentration camps was apparent in two crucial decisions he made: to give a free hand to the '*Oberka*' and her amazons, thereby exempting him from the need to become too closely involved in the internal affairs of the camp, and to place internal authority exclusively in the hands of the Poles. The annals of the camp reveal how these steps affected every aspect of the prisoners' lives, while at the same time furthering the goals of their masters.

And every nationality shall be separate...

The previous Sunday had been eventful. There had been an 'undesirable congregation' of prisoners in the courtyard in the evening, and as a result they were all ordered out for a punitive roll-call. What was it that had angered the authorities? Within a week, Ilona Karmel presented her friends with a new poem. (After all, she could not be expected to ignore an occurrence that had thrown shock waves throughout the whole camp!)

In the prison courtyard there's a crowd,
In the prison courtyard, the noise is loud:
'*Ich verstehe nicht*', '*Je ne comprends pas...*'
'*Nie ponimaju*', '*Qu'est-ce que c'est?*'
'God, I don't understand, it's so bad today...'
The women are Polish, French and Jew,
Czechoslovakian and Greek,
And Ukrainian too,

Each one alone, no family near,
Exhausted, saddened, all prisoners here.
    But suddenly, what's that? Can you hear?
    A song of lament, like life it aches,
    With a ringing power, through the noise it breaks
    And with its passion it pierces the soul,
    Firing the young blood of one and all!
O my brothers who are free, listen to the song!
Hear it bewail and weep and grieving break,
Choking, sobbing, as it struggles and shakes,
So deeply sad, but why – don't ask to hear,
It is sung by women who are prisoners here.
    Suddenly one from out of the crowd,
    Leapt into the circle like a storm from a cloud,
    She looked around, her hands she clapped,
    And started to dance like her mind had snapped!
    Spinning like a top! What a wondrous dance!
    And the pain and sorrow become things of the past,
    The women are happy and glowing in glee
    As if the fields of their homeland they can suddenly see
    As if they can breathe in the wonderful smell
    Of the earth of Russia they love so well...
The French and the Czechs all stand and stare
Alongside the Poles and the Jewish girls here,
And beyond the fence a German pair
Stop with their children to watch the dancing there,
Even the guard lays down his gun
To watch the dance that his heart has won.
    O listen to her sing, despite the hunger and need
    She may be a slave, but she still is free!
    They can dance, these proud Russians can do,
    It's for them that the tanks are breaking through,
    Making the evil go up in flame,
    The red flags are flying in their name!
    They stand there merry, laughing, gay
    Holding their heads up high today,
    With strength and hope and faith in their eyes,
    O Russia, Russia, Russia, mine...
Suddenly the dancer is shoved out of place,
And the cruel whip lands on her face,

Instantly her eyes go dark and dead
As they fall on the fence gazing straight ahead,
Yearning for space, for freedom and flowers,
As she stands in the roll-call that goes on for hours.
   Thus in a German prison, sombre and glum,
   The whip gets the better of the freedom song.[24]

                 (Ilona Karmel)

Ilona Karmel's poem may be considered a metaphor for the situation in the camp: a mix of many nationalities with no real common language, and suddenly, a spontaneous outburst of admiration for a prisoner who dared to thumb her nose at the oppressors, earning cheers of solidarity from all those present, an enthusiastic response that was brutallity put down by the German whip honouring the age-old principle of 'divide and conquer'.

The German authorities effected this policy in a number of ways:

They seek through threats, hard labour, starvation and oppression to destroy the humanity of this polyglot mass of people... while at the same time pitting nationality against nationality (which was the saddest thing of all for us) by internally preventing any show of cooperation or solidarity. They treat each nationality differently, deliberately ignoring any geopolitical unity or common citizenship... Hitler's entire national policy, based on division and the conditional support of minorities in order to destroy countries from within, is reflected here as in a distorting mirror.[25]

Thus they separated the Czechs from the Slovakians. Women who were previously citizens of the Soviet Union were now replaced by Russians, Ukrainians and Belarussians. The Walloons were kept separate from the Flemish, with no acknowledgement of Belgian citizenship. The women from Yugoslavia were divided up into Croatians, Serbs, etc. There were also small groups of prisoners from Greece, Holland, Italy, a few from Germany and even some from England. Each large national contingent was housed in a separate block. In principle, visiting between the blocks was forbidden.

The differences in the treatment of the various groups gave the lie to Commandant Plaul's solemn proclamations of 'equality among all prisoners'.[26] The disparities came to bear in a variety of areas, not all immediately apparent. Thus, for example, the Russians were the most closely guarded, and those who demanded to be recognized as prisoners of war were punished for the slightest infraction and assigned the most arduous work. As one of them testifies:

After refusing to work in the munitions factories while still in Ravensbrück, the Commandant of the Leipzig camp warned us that we would have to work in the camp, adding: 'I'll make sure the conditions are such that you will get down on your knees and beg me to send you to the plant.' And he kept his word. We would be woken up at two in the morning. We had to bring vats of hot coffee into the camp. Then they would make us run to the construction site. We built a prisoner camp and buildings for the guards. The work was extremely hard and the quotas so high that we couldn't meet them... They quickmarched us to work in the storerooms, the laundry... every single day they rained punishments down on our heads.[27]

Those who worked in the kitchen were somewhat more fortunate.

The Ukrainians were assigned to help the Russians in the kitchen, peeling vegetables and so on. In contrast to the harsh treatment of the Russians, the authorities tended to ignore breaches of discipline on the part of the Ukrainian women. As soon as a truck arrived with potatoes or turnips, the cry went up: 'Olga! Marussia!' Within seconds, the Ukrainians would swarm out from every doorway and leap onto the truck with monkey-like agility. By the time the guard in the watchtower realized what was going on, they had already disappeared with the spoils.[28]

The Czechs were the victims of cruel treatment: not only were they watched very closely but also subjected to frequent searches of their blocks by the SS overseers. Felicja Bannet-Schäftler claims this was justified, describing the Czechs as 'masters of conspiracy. They were polite, but suspicious of foreigners. For them, every nook and cranny was an underground cell of the resistance movement'.[29] The Slovakians had it somewhat easier, and the authorities were particularly tolerant of the Frenchwomen. As for the Jewish prisoners, Plaul's policy was conspicuously hypocritical. For example, they were, in principle, subject to the same conditions as all the other inmates, and indeed, when the transport from Skarżysko arrived, Plaul acceded to their request and appointed several of them to posts in the camp. However, the Polish 'prominents' protested vociferously, and as a result Plaul rescinded his decision and appointed Poles to these posts instead.[30] This behaviour contradicted accepted practice in multinational concentration camps, which dictated the naming of *kapos* from among the various nationalities in order to further divisiveness in the prisoner population. Why then did Plaul appoint only Poles to all the *Lagerverwaltung* functions?

Matylda Woliniewska seeks an objective explanation by stressing that the Polish women were the largest group and the first to be brought to the camp. Although they arrived together with Russian prisoners of war who had refused to work in the munitions plants and 'were supposed to perform the administrative functions in the camp, when it was discovered that they did not speak German, the remaining posts – save for the kitchen – were handed over to the Poles by force of circumstance'.[31]

This ingenuous explanation does not tally with the undisputed fact that Plaul had the authority to appoint functionaries of every nationality and from each transport, regardless of when they arrived in the camp. Furthermore, there were a number of Czechoslovakian, Hungarian and Jewish women who spoke fluent German. There can, therefore, be no doubt that the commandant decided to create a 'Polish regime' in order to promote his own goals. The situation was bound to increase divisiveness among the Poles themselves, as well as to make them the object of hatred on the part of prisoners of other nationalities.

This was not the only issue that divided the prisoner population in the Leipzig camp. The fact that it was a women-only camp raises the question of whether the same ideological, national and religious conflicts that characterized

Europe in general, and were brought into the camps by male prisoners, were also part of the consciousness of female inmates. The Frenchman Albert Rohmer, a prisoner at Buchenwald, describes relations among several of the national groups in that camp. He regarded the Russians in general as strong men who were good with their hands and knew how to adapt to circumstances. They displayed a genuine national solidarity, and despised the Poles in particular. As for the Germans, 'Stalin will slash their throats when he comes.' In point of fact, they appeared to be overgrown children, a bit wild, easily excited, kindhearted if you were able to get close to them, and grateful for any help. On the other hand, Rohmer was surprised by the hatred the Poles harboured equally for their neighbors both to the east and west and their unexpected hostility toward the French as well. He concludes that the Poles were not only arrogant, but also 'people consumed by hate'.[32]

It is interesting to compare these comments with those of a Polish prisoner in the Leipzig camp, Irena Pełka-Seńko:

> Everyone knew of the Polish–Soviet animosity, but it never overstepped the bounds dictated by prisoner solidarity against their captors. When it came down it to, we, the Polish women, did not have much reason to be overly fond of the Russian prisoners of war, after they had stabbed us in the back at the beginning of the war. Nevertheless – if I may digress on a personal note – it was a Russian prisoner of war who, in gratitude for the care given to a friend of hers who had the flu, came to our 'foreign Polish room' and brought me wild flowers she picked when she worked outside the camp. But the Russians also often and demonstrably sang a song that was very offensive to Polish ears: 'We shall remember the atman bitches, we shall remember the Polish *pans* (masters)...' They also complained that only Poles worked in the infirmary and wanted at least one Russian nurse. But although we agreed, they didn't let any of them accept this post, probably out of fear of 'treachery'.[33]

The Polish women accused the Russian prisoners of war of being excessively nationalistic, isolationist and haughty.

Relations between the Ukrainians and the Poles, whose countries had been hostile to one another for many years, were not much better. The Ukrainians felt extremely self-confident, even threatening the Poles: 'We'll show you as soon as our boys get here.'[34]

It cannot really be said that the Frenchwomen adopted a position of neutrality under these circumstances. Lise London and her friends, who had been active in the French communist Underground, looked up to the Russians and admired their courage and solidarity, although they lamented their insularity and mistrust of the other prisoners.[35] The Poles, on the other hand, were accused of being 'anti-Soviet, anti-Semitic and virtually collaborating with the German regime'. After the war, Lise London and Matylda Woliniewska clashed over these charges against the Polish women in general and the functionaries in particular. Matylda rejected the accusations out of hand as totally unfounded, claiming they derived from jealousy of the well-groomed Poles on the part of the Frenchwomen, who made no effort to maintain a feminine appearance, personal hygiene or tidy quarters, and were unable to adapt to camp conditions.[36]

Contentions of this sort are irrelevant to the question of whether or not a conflict existed between the two groups. In fact, the testimonies of Irena Seńko and her friends indicate that the allegations of Polish anti-Sovietism were justified. As regards collaboration, the claim appears to be overgeneralized and unwarranted. In all the Nazi camps there were functionaries who cooperated with the authorities, so that this charge can not be laid solely at the door of the Poles.[37] The issue of anti-Semitism will be considered in greater detail below. For the moment, however, these examples suffice to demonstrate the sort of 'international relations' into which the Jewish women were thrown on arrival in the camp, and the difficulties with which they were forced to contend.

New loves, old hate

The 1,200 Jewish women brought to the camp from Skarżysko in August 1944 did not constitute a homogeneous group, despite their shared experience. Internal division stemmed, first of all, from objective reasons. There had been three separate sectors in the Skarżysko camp, and the prisoners in Leipzig came from two them, those known as Werk A and Werk C.[38] In addition, the three distinct tiers that had characterized Skarżysko-Kamienna – the Radom, Majdanek and Płaszów groups – continued to exist in Leipzig.

Table 5.1 Distribution of Jewish prisoners in Hasag-Leipzig by place of origin

Place of origin	No. of prisoners	%
Radom District	254	21.2
Kraków	217	18.1
Warsaw	134	11.2
Łódź	65	5.4
Tarnów	44	3.7
Other	485	40.4
Total	1,199	100.0

Table 5.1 displays the composition of the transport of Jewish women in terms of where they came from. It shows that of these 1,199 prisoners, some 60 per cent came from towns in the Radom district (the 'Radom tier'), Kraków (the 'Płaszów tier'), Warsaw (the 'Majdanek Tier'), Łódź or Tarnów. The remaining 40 per cent were from around 260 cities and towns throughout Poland. Moreover, some of them were originally from Berlin, Vienna or Leningrad, and had been tossed by the vicissitudes of war into the Radom district or the camps of Majdanek and Płaszów, and from there to Skarżysko. The wide diversity of geographical and cultural backgrounds was, in fact, the primary cause of the internal division in this group. The Yiddish-speaking women from small towns, steeped in Jewish tradition and folklore, were known by those from the cities as 'Mezryczki' ('provincials', from the name of the town of Mezrycz).[39] A large number of the women from Warsaw were former Bund members who championed Yiddish culture, and others came from assimilated families. The prisoners from Kraków became a dominant group among the Jewish inmates, as many of them were high-school graduates or university students well-versed in the Polish language and culture. They also included

former members of the liberal Zionist youth movement Akiva, as well as a group of religious girls from the Beit Ya'akov movement.

While the population of Jewish prisoners was highly diverse in terms of origin and cultural background, there was little age difference among them – not surprising if we consider that the Germans chose those most fit for work, that is, healthy young women, for their labour camps.

Table 5.2 Distribution of Jewish prisoners in Hasag-Leipzig by age

Year of birth	Age	No.	%
1929–40	15 or under	28	2.34
1919–28	16–25	640	53.38
1909–18	26–35	389	32.44
1899–1908	36–45	118	9.84
1894–98	46 or over	17	1.42
Unknown		7	0.58
Total		1,199	100.00

As is apparent from Table 5.2, the large majority of Jewish women at Hasag-Leipzig (some 85 per cent) were between the ages of sixteen and thirty-five. The number of older women or younger girls brought to the camp with their mothers is insignificant. Hasag, like other German concerns, wanted their workers to be capable of the maximum effort.

The disparity of cultural background, education and age determined not only the heterogeneous character of the 'Skarżysko women', but also the manner in which they formed relations with the other groups. By way of illustration, we may consider the controversy over the transport of Hungarian Jews brought to the camp in December 1944. The entire group, including several women who had been put in with them at Ravensbrück (i.e. Jews from the camps at Pionki, Bliżyn and Kielce) were not housed in the large camp building, but in the wooden barracks in 'Drugie Pole' ('the Other Field') adjacent to it.[40] The Polish Jews evidenced a variety of attitudes toward the Hungarians. Maryla Perlberg-Reich remembers them as pleasant, cultured women who were very polite 'and never used bad language'. Others regarded the 'Madziary' as 'dirty and unpleasant'.[41] It is likely that the fact that the Hungarian language was totally incomprehensible to the Poles (and vice versa), and that they were quartered in separate areas, prevented these two groups from getting to know one another and developing any real relationship.

The Hungarian women also evidenced a range of different reactions to their new reality. Some, having experienced the horrors of Auschwitz and Ravensbrück, felt as if they had landed in paradise. According to Irma Neuman: 'Here they didn't beat us, there were only 40 women in the barracks, each one had her own mattress, a small stove burned in the middle of the room... roll-calls were only seldom held outside, and they were generally conducted inside the barracks.'[42] A friend adds: 'Treatment here was better and the food was normal, at least at first.'[43] But there were also those who complained of frequent roll-calls, beatings and particularly of overcrowding, because of which the women were only able to bathe once every three days.[44] There is no doubt that they had considerable difficulty adjusting, and often provided an excuse for a punitive muster.[45] 'They were scared to death. Up to now they had lived in their own homes, and suddenly they had been thrown into hell.'[46] The more sensitive prisoners sympathized with their plight, and Henryka Karmel dedicated one of her poems to them:

> O my brothers!
> A dog-like terror in your eyes...
> Helpless
> Hopeless,
> In fear you ask:
> How can we survive like this?
> O my brothers!
> Fear not.
> Everything passes here,
> Everything changes,
> Soon, very soon
> Your senses will dull...
> Don't worry
> It's unnecessary, not needed...

Woe to anyone who dreams here,
All you need here is a strong pair of legs
To drag you along on the gloomy days...[47]

(Henryka Karmel)

If such were the relations between two groups of Jewish prisoners, it is not surprising that it was hard for the Skarżysko women to carve out a place for themselves within the multinational structure of the camp as a whole. With the exception of the former Majdanek prisoners, for the great majority of them this was a thoroughly unfamiliar reality, since in their previous camps (i.e. Płaszów and Skarżysko), both the prisoner population and the internal administration had been exclusively Jewish. At Leipzig they encountered, for the first time, inmates of other nationalities and an internal administration entirely in Polish hands. Although they had little contact with the Czechs and Belgians, the presence of the dominant groups, the French, Russians, Ukrainians and Poles, was very keenly felt. A survey of the large number of testimonies available reveals a surprising unanimity among the Jewish women: the vox populi held that the French were dirty, the Russians arrogant, the Ukrainians uncultured, and the Poles anti-Semitic, and 'none could stand us, the Jews'.[48]

Was the picture really so unrelievedly dismal? There are in fact considerable discrepancies between the memoirs, in line with the personalities of their authors. Felicja Bannet-Schäftler, an educated woman who spoke French, often visited the blocks of the Frenchwomen and represents an objective view:

The ancient Gaelic culture prevails here as well: they are invariably polite, reserved, calm and smiling, although to a certain extent they suffer more than the others. On the whole, the Frenchwomen are petite and frail, from the intelligentsia, lacking in physical strength, they don't know how to push others out of their way, to demand what's coming to them, are incapable of both doing their work and tending to the cleanliness of the block and their personal hygiene, which is a major element of survival, in a way more crucial than food. Camaraderie and mutual kindness are very apparent in their quiet cultured block, while at the same time the untidiness of the block and the pallets is unsettling, and they themselves are usually uncombed and unkempt. Because of the lice, offensive remarks are frequently uttered, arousing hopeless protests... They are very pleased when they can speak French with a foreigner. They feel isolated, because few of the prisoners speak French well enough to carry on a comfortable conversation with them, and they themselves do not generally speak other languages. Only the Poles and a small number of Jews spoke French fluently.[49]

There were also other women from the 'Kraków intelligentsia' who visited the French block and received a warm welcome.[50] Lillian Lichtensztejn describes her close relations with Lise London, 'a wonderful woman', whose barracks she visited together with the *ka-elniks* Anna, Danka and Hanka. They told Lise of the terrible tragedies that had befallen their families and the *Erntefest* of November 1943, when all the Jews of Majdanek were exterminated. Appalled, Lise and her companions tried to ease their suffering by displays of friendship.[51]

Ilona and Henryka Karmel also spoke French and participated in get-togethers enlivened by songs sung by the Frenchwomen. They immortalized these moments as well:

Perhaps it was the charm of the unfamiliar song
Conveyed by the fair ladies of Paris here.
Or perhaps the haunting strains of the tango
Quavering in the memory of nights long gone.
But all of a sudden the prison walls fell
In an instant the Quartier Latin arose,
And the sun shone down on the pitch-black night
And jasmine and lilac gave off their smell.
The breeze wafted like a poem through the trees in the fall
In the shade of the boulevards, gardens and parks.
It was the blood of France that rhythmically flowed
The reddest of bloods, and the youngest of all.[52]

(Ilona Karmel)

The Frenchwomen won the affection of the Jewish prisoners from their first days in the camp. Several of the Jewish women had their children with them, daughters between the ages of six and thirteen and even one small boy. 'When the Frenchwomen found out we had children here, they gathered up their entire store of bread and chocolate and brought it to us. They hugged and kissed the children, played with them, fed them... It was the first time in years that anyone had treated our children as a treasure and a joy.'[53] Lise London also mentions the Jewish children who visited the French block, which was like paradise for them: a place where they were pampered, if not with food, then at least with songs and hugs. Many of the Frenchwomen found themselves in the camp for having hidden Jews, regarding it as their sacred duty to help their persecuted compatriots. 'We knew that some of them were Jews with Aryan papers who had been closely protected by their friends.'[54] The warm relations between the two groups were also apparent in the daily routine of the camp. 'If somebody made a courteous gesture, offering me a place beside her in the showers, in one hundred cases out of a hundred I could respond with "*merci*" and I would always be right'[55] (see Figure 5.3).

We must recall, however, that this idyllic picture of friendship relates only to a small group of French-speakers. Those unacquainted with the French language and culture made no attempt, nor would they have been able, to have any real contact with the French prisoners. None the less, there is no mention in any of their testimonies of bad or deceitful treatment by the Frenchwomen.

In contrast, there is evidence of an ambivalent attitude toward the Russians. On the one hand, some testimonies (such as the Felicja Bannet-Schäftler's journal) praise them for being good, kindhearted, willing to help and friendly, for maintaining their dignity in relations with the camp authorities, and for being true friends to the prisoners. On the other hand, they are accused of arrogance. There also seems to have been a degree of envy of their heroic status (the whole camp knew of their refusal to work in the munitions plants), and a sense of inferiority in comparison to the fighting Russian girls, a feeling tellingly reflected in Ilona Karmel's

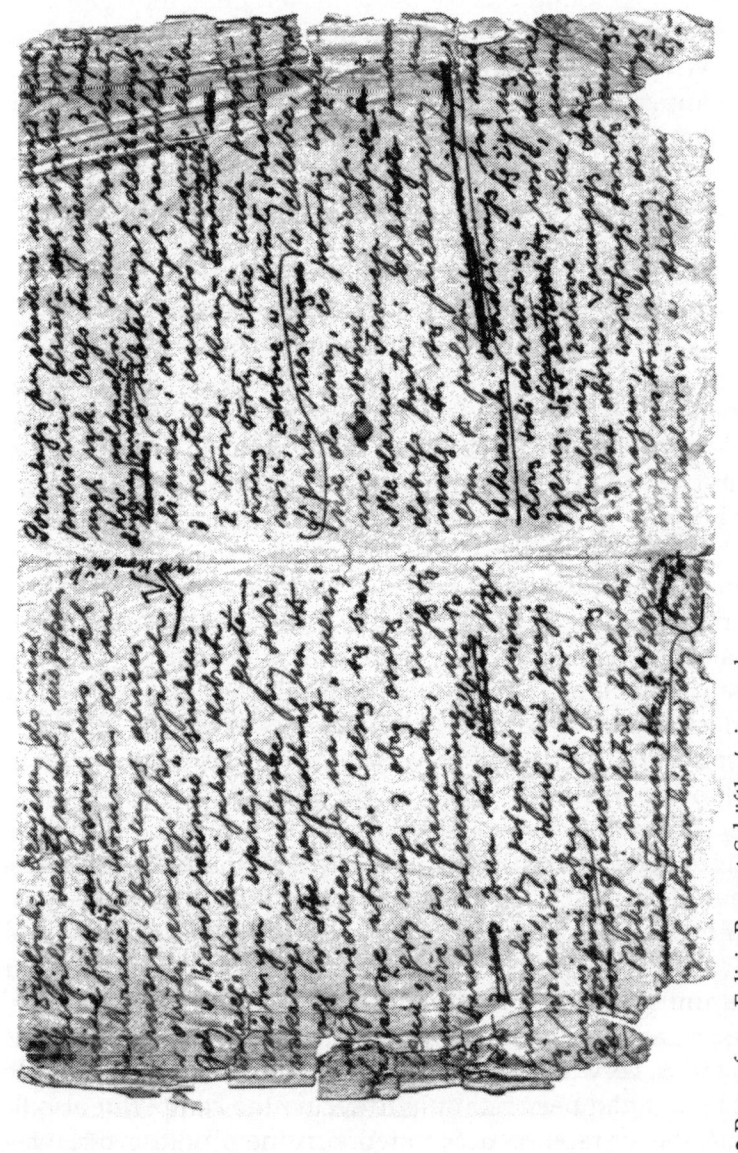

Figure 5.3 Pages from Felicja Bannet-Schäftler's journal.

Source: Bannet-Schäftler, 'Journal', YV, 0-33/4096.

poem 'The Dancer'.[56] However, there are also references to anti-Semitism, complaints such as: 'They always give us the thinnest soup.'[57] This charge even found its way into a ditty passed around among the Jewish women:

Tell me please, O lady grand,
Why your eyes are blackly sleek,
Your hips so full, so red your cheek,
Yet so tight-fisted is your hand.
Why do you water down the soup
And raise your voice in a rousing whoop?
Your curls tucked under a cap of white,
But meat in the soup – a long-forgotten sight![58]
(Rena Taubenblatt)

Relations with the Ukrainian prisoners were of a very different nature. The Jews were all only too well aware that the Ukrainians had conducted pogroms against the Jews after the First World War, repeating these actions a thousand times more brutally following the German occupation in 1941.

What the Bolshevik regime had erased from their memories, Hitlerism soon taught them. They beat us in the washroom, don't let us get to the faucets, shouting: 'Go away, dirty Jew!'... They take out all their anger for their suffering in the camp on the Jews, since after all, Nazi propaganda tags us as the cause of the war and of all the evil in the world.[59]

These accusations aside, the Felicja Bannet-Schäftler's journal depicts the Ukrainian women as hot-tempered, outstanding in their national solidarity and physical endurance, lending a helping hand to each other, and appearing as a united group, hostile to all other nationalities. It must be added that the women from Skarżysko had brought with them very harsh memories of the Ukrainian guards whose job it had been not only to secure the camp, but also to execute the groups of debilitated prisoners whose fate was sealed in selections.

The most complex fabric of relations was with the Poles, a

situation deriving from a large number of factors: the rise of anti-Semitism in Poland in the prewar years; bitter memories of Majdanek where the Jews had been the victims of beatings by Joanna Szumańska; and the experience of working together in the Skarżysko plants where many of the supervisory posts had been held by Poles who had made life miserable for the Jews by beating them mercilessly.[60] But while the Jews generally viewed the Poles as anti-Semitic, it should be recalled that this opinion was formed even before their arrival in Leipzig.

Was this attitude reinforced in the new camp? The very first encounter between the two groups did not bode well. Danuta Brzosko relates that when the transport from Skarżysko arrived, she met a few women who had been with her in Majdanek. 'Spontaneously, I ran to them and shouted: "Girls! How good to see you again! You're still alive!" The response I got was: "Yes? You're happy? If you'd returned Danzig [to Hitler] we'd all be alive!" Their words sent a chill through me and for a long time I couldn't talk with the Jewish women,' she concludes.[61] Malka Zuckerbrot seems to be referring to the same incident: 'When we got to Leipzig, the Poles were amazed that we were still alive.' Eda Lewin, who was also in Majdanek, adds: 'When we arrived at Leipzig we were greeted by the Poles with anti-Semitic remarks: "What, are you still alive?" '[62] Their sensitivity, stemming from obvious causes, led the Jewish women to the general opinion that at Leipzig 'the Poles displayed anti-Semitism'. "What is most surprising is that the same view is expressed by the chief poet of the Jewish group, Henryka Karmel, whose poems bear witness to her love of the Polish culture.[63]

What do the Polish women have to say? Some claim that 'the Jews keep to themselves, are frightened, and lack faith'.[64] This characteristic is also mentioned by the Jews themselves, who admit that their group 'kept to itself and was closed off from the others'.[65] This, however, was not unusual in the camp where, as we have seen, the different nationalities were kept apart. Indeed, it was not this fact that created the antipathy between the Poles and Jews. 'We had the feeling,' Irena Seńko confesses, 'that the Jews had grievances against us because we enjoyed better conditions.'[66] She admits that 'everyone was aware that of all the prisoners, the Jewish women suffered the hardest lot. They had the strain of the worst threat to their lives because of who they were.'

What, then, were the possibilities for co-existence?

It was the same as in any population operating on the principle of a steam engine, compressed by force and always under pressure. To the dangers inside the camp were added the external dangers [a reference to the shelling.]. Consequently, people behaved in different ways. There were individual, personal conflicts and group confrontations. There were instances of sacrifice, but also instances of ugly crudeness. In any case, I am unaware of any incidents of violent conflict between individuals or national groups.[67]

This view is extremely generalized and makes no attempt to explain whether the accusation of universal Polish anti-Semitism has any basis in fact. There can be no doubt that a closer look will reveal a much more complex relationship between the Polish and Jewish prisoners. There was constant contact between the two groups, and because they shared a common language, it encompassed every aspect of life in the camp. Thus it would be unwise to reach a final conclusion before examining life within the walls.

Notes

1. Testimonies of Maryla Reich and Jadwiga Landowska.
2. Brzosko-Mędryk, *Matylda*, pp. 45–52.
3. Testimony of Mata Hollender, YV, 0-3/987; Bannet-Schäftler, *'Journal'*, p. 20.
4. Testimony of Ewa Cukier, YV, 0-3/1664.
5. Letter from Danuta Brzosko-Mędryk, 14 May 1994, YV, 0-33/4239; Kornblum-Rosenberger, *Neder*, pp. 75, 77.
6. In German, *Zuckerbrot* is a type of cake. Testimony of Malka Hottner.
7. Bannet-Schäftler, *'Journal'*, pp. 21; 39.
8. KZ Bu, Verwaltung, An das Arbeitskommando Hasag Leipzig, 4 February 1945, ThHSA, NS 4 Bu, Vlg. 99, p. 47.
9. KZ Bu, Arbeitslager Leipzig, Betrifft Bekleidung der SS Aufseherinnen, Leipzig, 25 February 1945, ThHSA, NS 4 BU, VLG. 99, p. 314.
10. Landesausschuss der pol. Verfolgten in Bayern, München, 23 September 1947, YV, M-21/234.
11. Testimony of Paula Gimes.

12. The name Anneliese Giese appears on a number of lists; see also note 8.
13. Testimonies of Maria Lewinger; Paulina Buchenholz; Helena Zorski; and others; Bannet-Schäftler, 'Journal', p. 33.
14. Oświadezcnie, Matylda Woliniewska, YV, 0-33/4237.
15. Brzosko-Mędryk, Matylda, pp. 69-71.
16. Testimonies of Felicja Shahar and Maryla Reich.
17. Testimony of Paula Gimes.
18. Testimonies of Maria Lewinger and Felicja Karay.
19. Testimony of Genia Reiser.
20. Bannet-Schäftler, 'Journal', p. 39.
21. Bannet-Schäftler, ka-elniks bore the letters KL on their clothes.
22. Testimonies of Sonia Światłowska, Joanna Szumańska dossier, YV, M-21/4-89.
23. Letter from Dora Sroka to The Committee of Liberated Jews in Munich, ibid.
24. Ilona Karmel, 'Na dziedzińcu więziennym', ŻIH, sygn. 246, nr 38.
25. Bannet-Schäftler, 'Journal', p. 1.
26. See Plaul's welcoming speeches, Kornblum-Rosenberger, Neder, p. 72.
27. Oni pobjedili smjert', Izdat. Polit. Literatury, Moscow, 1996, p. 182.
28. Bannet-Schäftler, 'Journal', p. 2.
29. Ibid., pp. 2–3.
30. Testimony of Maria Lewinger.
31. Woliniewska, 'The Debate'.
32. Rohmer in Wormser-Migot and Michel (eds), La tragédie de la deportation, pp. 224–5.
33. Testimony of Irena Seńko. The expression 'stabbed us in the back' is a reference to the Red Army's invasion of eastern Poland after the Ribbentrop–Molotov Pact of August 1939.
34. Testimonies of Jadwiga Węgrzecka; Barbara Natanson.
35. Ricol-London, La Mégère de la rue Daguerre, pp. 324; 330; 365.
36. Woliniewska, 'The Debate'.
37. Compare the comments of Gilbert Dreyfus, Wormser-Migot and Michel (eds), La Tragédie de la Deportation, p. 211.
38. 'The Skarżysko-Kamienna Camp', Encyclopedia of the Holocaust, p. 1360.
39. Testimonies of Rina Cypres and Lilian Goldberg.
40. Testimony of Rywka Najberg, YV, M-I/E/2460/2526.
41. Testimony of Felicja Shahar.
42. Testimony of Irma Neuman, YV, 0-2/768.
43. Testimonies of Arnona Goldszmid, YV, 0-15/522 and Arenka Bonat, YV, 0-15/1289.
44. Testimony of Janona Pereny, YV, 0-15/506.
45. Testimony of Regina Kalman, YV, M-1/E/2370/2445.
46. Kornblum-Rosenberger, Neder, p. 79.
47. H. Karmel, 'Braciom węgierskim', Śpiew za drutami, p. 15.
48. Testimony of Bracha Bar Ilan.
49. Bannet-Schäftler, 'Journal', p. 2.
50. Testimonies of Felicja Karay and Helena Zorski.
51. Testimony of Lilian Goldberg; cf. Ricol-London, La Mégère de la rue Daguerre, pp. 344–5.
52. I. Karmel, 'Francuska krew', ŻIH, sygn. 246, nr 188.
53. Bannet-Schäftler, 'Journal', pp. 2–3.
54. Testimony of Bina Herstein.

55. Bannet-Schäftler, *'Journal'*, pp. 2, 10.
56. See note 24.
57. Testimonies of Sara Bojer and Halina Razowski.
58. The song, written by Rena Taubenblatt (Rina Fradkin), appears in her testimony.
59. Bannet-Schäftler, *'Journal'*, p. 3.
60. Karay, *Death Comes in Yellow*, pp. 155, 171.
61. Letter from Danuta Brzosko-Mędryk, 14 May 1994, YV, 0-33/4239.
62. Testimonies of Malka Hottner and Eda Jewin.
63. Testimony of Henryka Karmel-Wolfe.
64. Testimony of Jadwiga Landowska.
65. Testimony of Rina Cypres; Henia Buchman-Strelski, *We Remember*.
66. Oral testimony obtained at a meeting in Warsaw on 26 June 1994. Those participating were Matylda Woliniewska, Irena Pełka-Seńko, Jadwiga Węgrzecka, Danuta Debek and Felicja Karay (hereafter Woliniewska Karay *et al.*, meeting).
67. Testimony of Irena Seńko; cf. testimony of Ester Netzer.

6 Life in the Blocks

The Lagerverwaltung *at a crossroads in time*

Despite the shelling, the work stoppages and the punitive roll-calls, life in the camp went on as usual. Days passed slowly: the routine was always the same.

> Each morning it comes to meet me
> So mundane, just the same
> In the dim light of streetlamps
> Grey like a day in the rain,
> Vague, like the autumn,
> The dawn.
> Each morning it comes to meet me
> So mundane, just the same
> With the muted pounding
> Of brakes,
> The stench of poison,
> The blazing heat it pours,
> The factory floor.
> Each morning it comes to meet me
> In the unending toil,
> In the vain hopes,
> In the undreamable dreams,
> The graveyard – the day –
> So much the same, so mundane,
> On white pallets like coffins,
> The grave of pitiful dreams,
> So loathsome and sinister
> A dismal jail.[1]

(Henryka Karmel)

'A dismal jail' – Hasag-Leipzig, like all the Nazi camps, was like a tiny separate country in which daily life ran along two parallel tracks: the official track whose schedule was dictated by the plant management and the camp commanders, and the unofficial track ruled by the internal administration of the camp. As we have seen, the supervisors of various sorts had more of a direct influence on the life of the prisoners than all the SS overseers put together – a fact reflected most obviously in the camp argot. Nearly all the German terms for the different functions were reconstructed in Polish form, and no matter what country they came from, all the women were familiar with the terms: *Oberka*, *Aufzejerka*, *blokowa*, *sztubowa*, *grupowa* and others. At the same time, the functionaries were the first to incorporate German words into their Polish speech.

Their influence on social life was considerably more significant. Here a class of 'prominents' of a single nationality (with very few exceptions) controlled a multinational population of inmates, including over 2,000 'rank-and-file' Poles. As a result, they were the focus of social tensions in two separate contexts: within the Polish sector and with the prisoner population as a whole.

The internal tensions derived from differences in social status, education and mentality, particularly between the political prisoners and the others. Among the latter were women from the cities who had been picked up for trading in the black market or work-evasion, country girls arrested for not delivering the necessary quotas of agricultural produce to the authorities, and those who had been caught in a *'łapanka'*, a random 'hunt' conducted by the SS in the streets of occupied Poland in order to snare forced labourers.

The political prisoners, not all of whom held posts of authority, stood out on account of their superior education, their strong national consciousness and their attempts to conduct a variety of Underground activities. The overwhelming majority of them had been held in the notorious political prison of Pawiak. The Pawiak women (known as 'Pawiaczki' in the camp) had arrived from Majdanek as a close-knit group with experience in organizing surreptitious operations and, most tellingly, ardent ideological motivation. As political prisoners who had been active in the

Underground, they considered their incarceration to be just punishment from the standpoint of the German enemy, as well as a stage in their own struggle. The members of the group, who gravitated around the dominant personality of Matylda Woliniewska, belonged to the intellectual elite and bore the badge of their offence with pride – something that can not be said of the hundreds of other Polish inmates.[2]

The Polish women from Majdanek (the 'Majdaniarki') tried to use their connections and the support of the camp elder Joanna to secure assignments to the 'better' jobs. This is evidenced by Irena Pełka, who was aged nineteen at Leipzig. At first she worked in the plant, but when she complained to her friends of health problems, they had her transferred to the kitchen. When even this work turned out to be too strenuous for her, she approached the camp dentist, Nieszczyńska, who arranged for her to work in the infirmary. Several of Irena's friends enjoyed similar good fortune. As a rule, however, the exploitation of 'connections' of any sort did little to improve relations among the Poles. As in other camps, the 'privileged' inmates had greater access to sources of food, the clothing stores, the infirmary – all those places that were crucial to survival. Thus, writes Irena Pełka-Seńko, 'it was very easy to pass judgement on the functionaries in the camp, if only on the grounds that 'they have it better', 'they're so clean and well-groomed', 'they don't lift a finger'. Even Matylda is forced to admit that the functionaries were not very well-liked by the other Poles: 'After all, they were the "authorities" and the Poles don't like authority, or at least do not look on it favorably.'[3]

It was against this background that a serious rift opened between the 'productive sector' and the 'administrative sector'. The 'ordinary' Poles who worked in the plant were often treated contemptuously by their compatriot 'prominents', who tagged them with the highly pejorative nickname of '*fabrykantka*'.[4] This state of affairs was immortalized in a sketch written in the camp by one of the Polish inmates (the names of the characters are fictitious):

The camp mess hall at lunchbreak. Two Polish women enter, each carrying a bowl of soup. One, MARYSIA, *has been assigned to peeling vegetables* (Schällerei) *in the cellar. The other,* ZOSIA, *is a* 'fabrykantka'. *At the entrance to the mess hall,* ZOSIA *shoves* MARYSIA.

MARYSIA: Look out, you worm! Don't you have eyes?

ZOSIA: Well lah-de-dah! The grand lady! You think because they put you in the cellar you can thumb your nose at me, the *'fabrykantka'*?

MARYSIA: *'Fabrykantka'*! Well, well ... Where I come from, no decent woman was a *'fabrykantka'*. There was no difference between a whore and a *'fabrykantka'*! When I was forced to do it, I didn't have a choice! But when they kicked me out and all I could get was *Schällerei*, I volunteered for the cellar on the spot! Here I can get another bowl of soup without a coupon, here my feet don't hurt from standing at the machine. Here a person can maintain her dignity![5]

But this was only one side of the coin. The fact that the majority of official posts, even the most minor ones, were held by Poles spawned discontent throughout the prisoner population. Commandant Plaul encouraged this state of affairs, on the assumption that it was better for him for the prisoners' grievances to be directed against the 'Polish administration' than against himself. As Felicja Bannet-Schäftler writes:

There are a lot of Poles here who suffer as much as we do. They work hard in the plant, freeze in the cold and fall ill, their heads are shaved. But still they were hated because of the privileged status of the policewomen, because they control the office, the kitchen and the storeroom. It was forgotten that only a small proportion of the Poles who came from Majdanek enjoy this status.[6]

The animosity of all the other national groups toward the Poles as the collaborators with the German authorities took several forms. We have already considered the attitude of the Russians and Ukrainians, and as Lise London's accusations indicate, the French and Jewish prisoners formed a sort of alliance against anti-Semitic and anti-Soviet manifestations on the part of the Poles. This was clearly not the atmosphere they would have wished to prevail in the last months of the war.

The functionaries were undoubtedly aware of the danger: in relation to the other Poles, they had to maintain their connections with the 'masses' and promote a sense of national solidarity. Yet because of the differences in mentality and education, their attitude to them was condescending. There were also the weighty considerations of their special privileges and the desire to take advantage of their position of authority for personal gain. Thus various factors operating consciously and subconsciously shaped the behaviour of the functionaries toward the prisoners in general, and toward the Jewish women in particular.

From 'Niunia' to 'Kozunia'

'*Wstawać! Panie cholery, wstawać!*' Madam Eugenia Godlewska, the *blokowa* of Block 20, kept shouting: 'Get up! Rotten women! Get up!' She moved from bunk to bunk, hitting out right and left with the heavy board in her hand: 'Get up!'

The block lorded over by Madam Niunia (as her subjects called her) was the largest in the camp, with 600 Jews under her harsh rule. Ten women have already been singled out to go to the kitchen for the vats of 'coffee', and another morning has begun:

'It's 4 a.m.!'
The women call.
Today this group and that
For the coffee will go.
And the chaos begins
As they run to the shower
For the water has power
To chase sleep away!
Here's the coffee! And the 'coffee girls'
Sztubowa Ada, sztubowa Hania,
Both so good at the chore!
So why, tell me why
Are the portions so poor? ...
Here is Madam Niunia
Our patron saint!
She looks all around

And her voice resounds:
'Why aren't you dressed yet?
Why is she in her bunk with her shoes on?
If you don't obey my every command
In a roll-call you will stand!'
O madam, we all understand very well,
How much, how hard you have to work!
To rule here over this 'city of women',
Six hundred all told – no laughing matter at all!...[7]

(Gela Meiersdorf)

Gela's laudatory words of flattery for the *blokowa* Niunia give only a vague idea of just how notorious *'Panie cholery'* was. The words from her famous wake-up call (literally 'women cholera') soon became her nickname among all the Jews. The board she carried was no less infamous, although the subject of debate. Felicja Shahar claims it was for purposes of show alone, and recalls how Niunia would sometimes call out to her and her friend Ludka, both remarkably thin: 'Come here, little rats, and get some more soup. Otherwise you'll croak from starvation!'[8]

She was especially kind to 'her actresses' (all the women involved in cultural activities were housed in Block 20), and particularly fond of Fela Schächter for her recitations in Polish. However, when Niunia offered Fela and her sisters some canteen coupons, they refused out of solidarity with the inmates who did not enjoy her favor. For the same reason, these girls and a number of their friends refused to donate to the collection taken up by the *blokowa*'s two firm supporters (the 'donation' consisted of a ration of margarine, the accepted legal tender in the camp) to buy her a present. Among Niunia's accusers is Felicja Bannet-Schäftler, who describes her as coarse and vindictive.[9] After the war it was rumoured that Niunia was a Jew with Aryan papers, but Danuta Brzosko who knew her family, insisted this was not true.[10]

Niunia was not the only *blokowa* to gain immortality. Felicja Bannet-Schäftler devotes a section of her journal to 'Kozunia', who was apparently in charge of Block 19. Bannet-Schäftler prefaces her story with the remark: 'The Poles were a separate issue, and one that is very sensitive for us, Polish Jews. I would not like their actual behaviour to be distorted by the offenses and injustices perpetrated on us, and so will attempt to present only the facts in the most objective manner possible.' She knows little of 'Kozunia's' biography. Her first name was probably Maryla, but her family name is unknown. She is described as a short, slender blonde who had been an elementary school teacher in the region of Lvov before the war. She was incarcerated in Majdanek not as a political prisoner, but for trading on the black market. Bannet-Schäftler's journal portrays 'Kozunia's' bunk as the height of luxury, with a plethora of pillows and blankets, and she had many clothes which 'her' Jews sewed and mended in exchange for a slice of bread or a ration of soup.[11]

Figure 6.1 Striped dress (*pasiak*) of prisoner no. 648.

Source: Testimony of Luna Fuss-Kaufman, YV, 0-33/1819.

Where did these clothes come from? As we have noted, the women in the internal administration wore the same striped uniform (*'pasiak'*) as the other prisoners (see Figure 6.1). But unlike the rest, they also had additional clothes. The storeroom (*'kamera'*) in the camp held clothing, shoes, bedlinen, etc., that had been confiscated from the prisoners. Since most of the women came to Leipzig from other camps (Ravensbrück, Majdanek) where all their personal belongings had already been taken away, it may be assumed that most of the items in the *kamera* came from the Jews from Skarżysko, who still had some 'civilian' clothes with them when they arrived.

All the inmates, particularly the Jews, wore a single tattered dress for months on end, washing it over and over again and trying to pretty it up in any way they could. Although it was strictly forbidden, the more quick-fingered women 'organized', (i.e. stole) rubber aprons from the plant, shortening them and then fashioning belts from the remnants or selling them to other prisoners. Some succeeded in pilfering a few rags from which to sew collars. According to Bracha Bar-Ilan, the commandant turned a blind eye to these infractions, apparently pleased to see his 'subjects' so well-groomed. Yet despite their best efforts, the prisoners gazed in envy at the Polish supervisors dressed in good clothes in addition to their uniforms. Not surprisingly, the ditties they composed on the subject were rather sarcastic:

> In the *kamera*, the *kamera* new goods on the shelves,
> There are dresses there and coats as well...
> There they can deck themselves out
> All sorts of luxuries flaunt,
> In the dark, in the dark of the night...
> While just one tattered *'pasiak'* is all you get,
> And as for a belt, that you can just forget.[12]
>
> (Rena Taubenblatt)

At first the elegant 'Kozunia' addressed the women courteously, but she soon began to adopt the language of curses: 'Bitches, dolts, rotten women'. Until one day she was rewarded for her crudeness.

Once, when 'Kozunia' cursed the 'Jewish lepers', a response came from a very unexpected quarter. Tynia Tischowa, a well-mannered, cultured woman, planted a ringing slap across her face, for which she was sentenced to a 'personal punitive parade' in the courtyard. She stood out there in the freezing cold for three hours, and when she came back to the block, she didn't even notice that we were all staring at her in admiration.[13]

The name of the *blokowa* in the third block (probably a reference to Block 18) is unknown, but Bannet-Schäftler remembers her thus: 'She treated us like a cunning merchant would treat the customers he has to maintain good relations with even though he doesn't like them. The *blokowa* from Block 17 was a good, decent woman who was ready to help and her relations with the Jews were ideal.'[14] This is apparently a reference to Hanka Skowrońska, whose real name was Maryla Reich, and who was appointed to the job by Joanna.

Each *blokowa* was assisted by two women of the rank of *sztubowa*, and was entitled to choose two 'cleaners' (*sprzątaczki*). After the day shift had left for work, the women from the night shift, who returned at 6 a.m., remained in the block. Officially, they could go to sleep, but this was generally an impossibility, since at this time the cleaning was done, directed by the shouting of the *blokowa* and her aides. This was not the only way to make the prisoners' life miserable. Whenever a consignment of clean underwear arrived, the 'favoured' women got the best items and the others had to make do with underpants that didn't fit.

There is a wide range of opinions in the testimonies regarding the lower ranking supervisors and policewomen, but none maintain that they beat the prisoners with rubber stanchions, as Lise London claims.[15] On the contrary, Ester Netzer states unequivocally that the Polish supervisors treated them much better than the Jewish policemen in Skarżysko. According to Eda Fenik, Felicja Shahar, Ewa Cukier and others, they do not all appear to have behaved in the same way. Some are mentioned only by first name, such as Dora and Marysia from Niunia's Block 20. Maryla Reich has some good things to say about Nuna Michalska,

Wartarasiewicz and Halina Kielar. Danuta Brzosko speaks of the good relations between the Jews and Helena Bujakowska, a policewoman (*Lagerschutz*) in the 'Drugie Pole'.[16]

The most popular functionary, however, was Zina Bragińska, assistant to Joanna Szumańska, the camp elder. She was a middle-aged woman with dyed blonde hair, and was universally liked. Despite her high rank, no accusations were ever voiced against her. She was invariably ready to help. Indeed, she once arranged for one of the French women to meet with her father, incarcerated in the nearby men's camp, and even provided a loaf of bread so that the daughter would not greet her father empty-handed.[17]

'I always thought she must be Jewish,' states Towa Zilberberg. Since she and her friends still had relatives in Majdanek, she once summoned the courage to ask Zina if she knew the fate of that camp. She thus heard from her the horrifying news of the slaughter in November 1943 of all the Jews at Majdanek.[18] During the evacuation of Leipzig, Zina disclosed the truth to Maryla Reich: she was indeed a Jew, born in Lvov. Her real name is unknown.

Zina's secret brings us to the question of how the Poles treated those of their group suspected of not being of 'pure' extraction. According to Maryla Reich, there were a number of Jews with Aryan papers in the camp – a fact which came as a complete surprise to the women when it was revealed after the war. Others never disclosed their true identity. The Poles sometimes dropped remarks such as 'a Jewish aunt' (*Żydowska ciotka*) or 'that Jew pretending to be one of us'. But Maryla's Polish friends were loyal, and she never heard of any of them informing on a 'suspect' member of their group. Her own situation was particularly risky, because she was appointed by Joanna as *blokowa* in one of the Jewish blocks (most likely Block 17). When the Jews from Skarżysko arrived, some of them recognized her, among them Henryka Karmel who had been friendly with her before the war. At first Maryla was afraid to admit it was really she, but in time they renewed their friendship.

Despite the exceptions mentioned in the testimonies, all agree that the majority of supervisors 'were allergic to anything Jewish... When the Jewish children visited the

French block, the Polish *blokowa* grumbled that they were Jewifying (*zażydzają*) the block'[19] – an extremely serious allegation. The Jewish women complained of being treated with contempt and ridicule: 'The Poles liked to prove that they were superior to us,' according to Towa Zilberberg, made to stand in a personal punitive parade by some functionary.[20] Felicja Bannet-Schäftler contends that even when the supervisors prefaced their orders with 'ladies, please', this outward courtesy merely masked indifference or even hostility and disdain. 'The Poles in the office are upper-class women who take no notice of us at all and don't want to know us... In the blocks, the Poles treat us differently: Jews aren't allowed in Block 6. They are greeted with blows and cursing, and physically kicked out. Block 10 is calmer and more friendly, and the *blokowa* is very decent.'[21]

If we consider the various opinions as a whole, it appears that despite the differences and tensions that were the legacy of the past or were dictated from above, in the everyday reality of the camp certain terms for coexistence between the Jewish prisoners and the women of other nationalities were created. While Bracha Bar-Ilan contends very pessimistically that 'they couldn't stand us because we were Jewish', and the anti-Semitism reported even by prisoners of other nationalities could be seen in their support and approval of the vindictive treatment of the Jews by the anti-Semitic supervisors, the Jewish women in Leipzig were more spirited than before. They no longer accepted discriminatory practices without protest, and numerous fights and arguments flared up over this issue.[22] It was perhaps because of this that coexistence was possible: something which is evident in the 'Hasag Anthem' the Jewish women sang loudly for all to hear:

> Hasag is our father,
> The best father there is!
> He promises us
> Long years of happiness,
> In Leipzig – a paradise on earth!
> There's bread and butter, and salad green,
> Luxury homes are where we live,
> Four storeys high – and the pallets are clean,

From Hasag we get toilets and showers right here,
And they give us the clothes of prisoners to wear!
Chorus: The commandant's for
            Law and order, no more!
            That we calm our nerves
            Before we become
            A can of preserves...
We have Joanna, a fine lady indeed,
Who treats us in a 'model' way!
And Zina, a political prisoner too,
Who is nice to us each and every day.
            The cooks – excellent women,
            Such awful soup they make,
            You'll never find potatoes there
            Because the '*Jewrejki*'
            Are not to their taste.
The sanitary crew is ever on hand,
Ready to shave each and every head!
The *Schreibstube's* numbers are often wrong:
'*Blokowa*, you take care of this instead!'
            There's an entire SS squad to guard us here,
            Making sure we do not make our break,
            And the *Lagerschutz* women, the entire gang,
            Beating is a task they gladly undertake![23]

The anthem was a collective effort, with the 'finishing touches' performed by Rena Taubenblatt-Fradkin. It provides a pithy description of the features of the Leipzig camp, for better and worse. Dominated by the scathing chorus, it shows a total lack of trust in the German 'wonders'. Yet at the same time, it reveals a spirit of cooperation that bears witness not only to the women's ability to adapt to the new reality, but also their sardonic tolerance for their trials and tribulations, on the order of: 'Well, we've seen worse...'

Around the soup vat

Linka stood in the middle of the *Waschraum* in her underwear and started working: she spread two dresses out on the floor, hers and her friend Paulina's, and poured hot water over

Hymn więźniarek Hasagu

Hasag to nasz ojciec
Hasag to nasz tata,
Hasag nam zapewni
Szczęśliwe lata!
Daje nam raj tu w Lipsku całym,
Daje masło i ser biały,
Daje nam mieszkania komfortowe,
Daje nam prycze czteropiętrowe,
Daje klozety i łazienki
I więzienne te sukienki!
Refren   Bo komendant pragnie,
By wszystko szło tu składnie,
By uspokoić nerwy
Nim zrobią z nas konserwy...
Mamy tu Joannę kobitkę morową,
Która się z nami obchodzi "wzorowo",
Mamy także Zinę sympatyczną,
Też więźniarkę polityczną.
Mamy tu kucharki kobitki - takie!
Które nam gotują zupy byle jakie.
I kartoszków mało wydawają,
Bo Jewrejek nie uznają.
Sztab sanitarny jest zawsze gotowy,
Żeby nam wszystkim ogolić głowy.
A Szrajbsztuba wciąż numery myli:
"Blokowa, proszę zejść w tej chwili!"
Oddział SS pilnuje nas cały,
Byśmy przypadkiem stąd nie zwiewały,
Mamy Lagerszucek całą hordę,
Które dobrze walą w mordę!

Figure 6.2 'Anthem' of the Jewish prisoners in Hasag-Leipzig.

Source: Testimony, Rena Taubenblatt-Fradkin.

them. She didn't have enough soap, but she would have to make do. At least she had been able to borrow a strong brush. Patiently, meticulously, she scrubbed the dresses and then rinsed them in the sink, finally laying them over a warm pipe. She would stand there for several hours, turning and rearranging them until they were completely dry. The next day was Sunday, no work, so she had to take advantage of the opportunity. She had already showered and washed her hair, using a few rags she had 'lifted' from the plant as a towel. They were very fortunate that at least they could maintain some semblance of cleanliness in this place![24]

It wasn't so nice, however, to have to use this soap... What about the letters RIF? (It was rumoured they stood for '*Rein jüdisches Fett*' ...) No, that's not possible! But some girls are reluctant to use it.[25] They do their best to get hold of or even buy some other soap. But who can afford that? Here in the camp the prisoners do not even have any opportunity to earn some extra money. Some try. Oh, there's Hela Schächter! She's carrying two dresses, one is hers and the other belongs to her friend Helena Feig, a tall very skinny girl who doesn't have the strength to do laundry. Some industrious women wash a number of dresses in exchange for bread. The competition is fierce, particularly when it turned out that some of the Poles are also willing to pay a bowl of soup or a bread ration in exchange for laundry or tailoring and sewing jobs.[26]

Every now and then a miracle happened. Genia Grosswirt and Rachel Wierzbicki had been in Majdanek and Skarżysko together, where Rachel, the older of the two, often helped Genia and even saved her skin a few times. Here in Leipzig they were lucky enough to run into a Polish friend from Majdanek: a woman named Stefa. At their very first meeting, Stefa told them about the slaughter of the Jews in Majdanek in November 1943. She did a lot for Genia and Rachel, like getting hold of coupons and standing in line at the canteen to buy them things that were unavailable to the Jews, such as biscuits. Once she even bought them two flannel undershirts – treasure's that saved them from the perils of winter.[27] Stefa also taught them how to earn an extra food ration. From time to time, when Rachel was not on the night shift, Stefa would sneak the girls through the back door to the kitchen where they were put to work peeling vegetables. They were paid with a bowl of soup and a portion of bread. Sometimes they even managed to 'organize' some turnips or other vegetables which they shared with their blockmates.[28]

Others employed different means to improve their lot. Some (it is impossible to tell how many) managed to smuggle a piece of jewellery or gold into Leipzig by swallowing it before they got on the train. Indeed, a number of Polish women noticed the strange behaviour of certain Jews who seemed to be looking for something in the communal toilet. Testimonies do not reveal how or to whom these precious items could be sold. The accepted currencies in the camp were coupons or margarine rations. The coupons were highly prized, particularly when cloth or straw shoes showed up in the canteen. There were months when no coupons at all were issued to Jews, so they could only get them from other prisoners, obviously for a price.[29] Only a few lucky ones were able to get an odd job in the kitchen from time to time.[30] Those with an advantageous work-assignment could conduct a bit of 'trade' with the Ukrainians and Russians, if they had anything to sell. So what was a hungry woman to do?

> I'm hungry! – is what you hear everywhere
> I'm hungry! – each woman cries in your ear.
> So there's no choice – whoever can snatch
> A little extra food, hides it in some cache.
> Some sewing or laundry are willing to do
> In exchange for a sausage or two.
> Others sell rags, really nothing more,
> For a bit of butter in their pocket to store.
> Some for the price of a piece of bread
> Will clean the lice from another's head.
> While others the future know how to tell,
> And that is what they have to sell.
> To borrow a comb or some thread, let's say,
> Don't forget there's a price to pay.
> Thus, whatever they can get they are ready to trade
> As long as with some extra soup they're paid!
> In short, an interesting symptom, did you know?
> That here the art of barter flourishes so!

147

But I'm not skilled, it's not for me,
So I'm plagued by hunger more and more,
Each day in worse shape than the day before...[31]

(Gela Meiersdorf)

Barter was common in all the Nazi camps and served numerous purposes. Thanks to this trade, Leipzig prisoners with a variety of skills were able to support themselves. Some made belts from rubber straps, others fashioned comb cases from bits of plastic or barrettes from wires (see Figure 6.3). Most of the raw materials were pilfered, or 'organized,' from the plant. Barter helped the women to maintain a degree of personal hygiene, with some Jewish prisoners even willing to trade their bread ration for a handful of soap powder or a dense comb to help in the war against lice.

A number of women displayed considerable ingenuity. Lilian Lichtensztejn tells of the 'business' she and three of her friends conducted with the ladies from the *Schreibstube*. The foursome

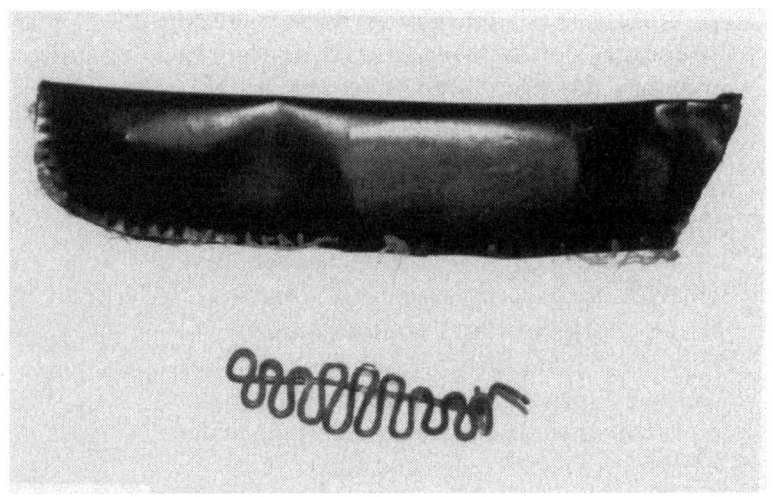

Figure 6.3 Wire hairpin and comb-case made by Malka Zuckerbrot.

Source: Private collection.

set up a 'workshop' making slippers. For raw materials they used old blankets they 'organized' in diverse ways and the cartons in which food rations were brought to the blocks. They cut the soles from several layers of carton glued together and covered them with blanket scraps. The tops were sewn from mesh cut out of old mattresses. The business partners were joined by a '*Mezryczka*' who skilfully embroidered the slippers using thread they got from the *Schreibstube*. The finished products were sold for bread, margarine, or jam.

Under the conditions of starvation in the camp, the most sought-after commodity was naturally food. Where did it come from? Some women managed to put a little extra aside thanks to the help of free workers in the plant. The more fortunate ones had a friend assigned to the kitchen. But the main sources of food supplements were the supervisors charged with distributing rations to the prisoners. The routine theft of food by supervisors plagued prisoners in all camps, including Hasag-Leipzig. Felicja Bannet-Schäftler relates that a *blokowa* and her two assistants would take for themselves a considerable portion of the supplies intended for the inmates: margarine, sausage, jam and especially bread. Whatever was left over was distributed to the 'riff-raff'.[32] There is no indication of which *blokowa* is being referred to here. Testimonies contain repeated complaints of hunger, particularly in the final months of the camp, but, with the exception of the Felicja Bannet-Schäftler no one points a finger specifically at the supervisors. Nevertheless, the phenomenon is immortalized in verses sung by the Jewish prisoners, such as the following 'indictment' of the *blokowa* Wanda:

> Such a doll and what a face!
> There is no one with her grace!
> She is Wanda, Wanda mine!
> Like an expert, well she knows
> Just how food allotting goes:
> 'You sit there and quiet stay,
> And be careful what you say!'[33]
> (Rena Taubenblatt)

Who was this *blokowa* named Wanda? Her identity is unknown, but from the verse it is clear that she was assigned to

Figure 6.4 Rena Taubenblatt-Fradkin.

Source: Private collection.

Block 20 (and is also mentioned in poems by Gela Meiersdorf), perhaps as Niunia's assistant or helper. And she was apparently skilled at the art of 'dividing up' the prisoners' meagre soup ration. But what the inmates had to resign themselves to in the case of foreigners, they were unwilling to accept from 'their own' supervisors. There was a storm of protest in Block 20 when Niunia appointed (as was common in other blocks as well) two 'helpers' to be in charge of doling out the soup.[34] The subject of the dispute can be learned from the poems and verses that began to circulate in the block, such as this 'tango':

> Why do we deserve it, why
> That the soup past us 'goes by'?
> Our bowls are never filled to the brim,
> Every tasty bit is whisked away by 'them'!
> But nothing in nature ever really gets lost,
> The soup adds 'padding' to them of course!
> On their hips it peaks

Puts colour in their cheeks
And so we ask out loud:
Might things still change somehow?[35]

(Rena Taubenblatt)

This ditty generated a prompt response in the form of Gela Meiersdorf's 'statement for the defence':

What can you do?
Almost everyone here suffers starvation.
The biggest problem – doling out the soup ration.
So there is a special group,
Whose job is to always complain and protest,
That it's unfair the way they distribute the soup,
And that 'certain women' are treated the best,
While less than their share get all the rest!
Some even say that the time has come
To tell the commandant what's being done!
But, dear ladies, please try to grasp
That control of the soup-vat is a difficult task!
And when things are so hard for everyone
It's best to try to get along.
Różka and Aśka also do what they can
To empty the vat to the very last drop
And fill our bowls up to the top.
So come on Jewish ladies all,
Let's give a cheer for our friends from the dining hall![36]

(Gela Meiersdorf)

It cannot really be said that this call for harmony was widely embraced. As hunger grew, so too did dissension among the prisoners. There were more instances of the theft of bread in the Jewish blocks. Even women who had hidden a piece of bread under their heads were astonished to discover it gone in the morning. Some even stole from their sisters or close friends, and the arguments and bickering increased.[37] It has been suggested that the situation arose from the heterogeneous nature of the camp's Jewish population, the lack of solidarity within it and the lack of a unified leadership. By contrast, visitors to Lise London's block were amazed by

151

the marvelous sense of solidarity that prevailed there, 'unlike what goes on among us'.[38]

Is it true that the Jewish prisoners lived beside each other but not together, as has been claimed? Admittedly, they produced no leaders of the order of Matylda Woliniewska or Lise London, but the fact is that these women were influential primarily in frameworks they themselves established and not in their national groups as a whole. Matylda organized an artistic troupe (to which we will return later)[39] and Lise set up an 'opposition committee' all of whose leading members were her communist friends.[40] Despite the friction, however, there was a much better atmosphere here among the Jewish women from Poland than in their previous camp.[41] The conditions for self-help were similar to those available to the prisoner population in all camps. They formed small groups composed principally of people who were related by blood, were from the same town, had belonged to the same party or movement, received the same religious education, been schoolmates, or simply shared the same pallet. In contrast to Skarżysko, where there had been both men and women, there was no possibility for couples (whether married or unmarried) to support each other in Leipzig, though there are a few veiled hints about lesbian relationships in some testimonies.[42]

Life in camp went on, as did the shelling which was growing ever closer. When air raids became more frequent, the kitchen would be closed before the prisoners were led down to the bunkers. As a result, no cooking was done at all and the starvation got worse.[43] 'At first, we didn't want to go downstairs at all, until the Commandant himself came and pleaded with us: "*Kinder*, why aren't you going down to the shelter? You're putting your lives in danger!"'[44] In the end, there was no choice:

Another air raid siren. The overseer's harsh whistle. Panicking, we race to the shelters, modern cages, excellently equipped, pipes, fans, gas masks in the cupboards, walls and ceiling of reinforced concrete. The height of twentieth century technology. It is a real pleasure to die in such luxury, so pampered! The overseers are so silly! They run around constantly from bunker to bunker counting us over and over again... 'Anyone who escapes during an air raid will be taken out and shot.' Idiots! Where would we go? Prisoners with no home, no family, remnants of human beings, survivors of the horrific storm... where would we go?...

The air raid is in full swing. *'Hallo, Achtung, Achtung!* (Attention, attention!).' There's a radio in the bunker, naturally! Reports of air battles interspersed with music. Such cynicism! 'There is fighting in the air over Hanover, Dresden and the surrounding area!' I strain my ears and my imagination goes to work: I hear huge explosions, thunder, noise and screaming – I see buildings collapsing on the people inside, ruins, parts of houses, stones and bodies flying through the air, flames. I can hear and see all this distinctly. 'Heavy shelling from the air over...' All accompanied by a gay, carefree foxtrot... And then again... *Achtung, Achtung!'* I'm enjoying every minute...[45]

The prisoners welcomed the thunder of each bomb. At last! Were they in danger? They sat in the shelters with a jumble of thoughts going through their minds. Would a shell fall on them too?

> For five long years death has lain in wait for me,
> Clever, treacherous and wily.
> And from its claws I have managed to run
> Nor have I been found by a bullet from a German gun
> Or carried on a train of death
> To that unspeakable end.
> So should I cringe at the engine's ring?
> At the roar of the airplane's silver wing
> And the fire that it starts to fling?
> For me a song of hope they sing,
> Their buzzing of liberty informs
> And the peace that always follows storms.[46]
>
> (Henryka Karmel)

One bomb landed on the camp. Fortunately for the prisoners, it happened before the night shift returned from work and the day shift happened to be standing outside on the other side of the building. The shell damaged one of the walls. Several women who were still on the stairs were injured, and one was killed.[47] According to Fela Blum, a few of the women tried to take advantage of the commotion and the hole opened in the bars of the camp fence: 'We started to run away, but we came right back, because we just didn't know where to go.' Towa and her friend Pola were heading for the gate when the guard stopped them, threatening to shoot them if they did not go back immediately. They did.[48]

Mila didn't heed the warnings and was brought down by a murderous bullet to the heart as she ran toward the breach in the fence. Her death was commemorated, painfully, sadly, in a poem by her friend Henryka Karmel:

> Freedom laughed in its beckoning way,
> Through the lips of broken bars,
> And like a whore with a wink it pointed
> Before eyes that were yearning for magical worlds.
> But when she ran toward it, drunken with love,
> A machine-gun was all the greeting she got...
> She focused her gaze with a look of surprise
> And only whispered, my freedom, why?...
> And gazed at her hands dripping with blood,
> As death silently closed her eyes for good...[49]
>
>   (Henryka Karmel)

Again there were a few days of quiet. Again they went to work. Again they returned to the camp. Again they got their soup... If they could only hold out! Not falter! Not be sent away with the transport!

The terror of selections

The first to go were the children, those who were newly born and those who were soon to come into the world.

There were very few pregnancies among the women from Majdanek and Ravensbrück, since those who had been pregnant had already given birth before being sent to Leipzig. When the Jewish prisoners from Skarżysko arrived, however, the authorities faced a different situation. With no separation between the sexes at Skarżysko, there were several pregnant women on the transport,[50] as well as a number of children between the ages of four and thirteen. Table 6.1[51] contains the names of children who arrived in the camp alone or with their mothers. According to Zacharia Zweig, his daughter Sylvia was about 11 years old at the time, but the date of her birth was apparently falsified in order to make her appear older. Similarly, the date of birth of other children may not necessarily be accurate.

For the first few weeks, the children accompanied their mothers to work. Shortly afterward the SS authorities announced that mothers wishing to be released from work in the plant could register at the office. They would be assigned to jobs in the camp to enable them to care for their children, whose rations would also be bettered. Believing these promises, the women, including Helena Zweig with her daughter Sylvia, reported to the office. They were assigned to *Stubendienst* (block services) and the children were given milk and other food supplements.[52]

Table 6.1 Children at Hasag-Leipzig Camp

Name	Year of birth	Place of birth
Szajbe, Henryk	1940	Koprzewnica
Lerman, Wigdor	1939	Skarżysko
Frydberg, Frajda	1939	Jędrzejów
Ajzenberg, Szlame	1937	Skarżysko
Lerman, Helena	1937	Skarżysko
Grzenis, Halina	1936	Łódź
Florensztein, Sala	1935	Łódź
Birman, Rena	1932	Skarżysko
Weitz, Edyta	1932	Leipzig
Blumel, Genia	1931	Łódź
Feichler, Henryka	1931	Kraków
Praszkier, Fela	1931	Łódź
Zweig, Sylwia	1931	Kraków
Boroniec, Zofia	1930	Warszawa
Frejlich, Cela	1930	Radom
Thaler, Rachela	1930	Kraków

The same directive contained the requirement that girls up to the age of sixteen were to register and would be given improved food rations as well. 'I had the feeling,' Fela Blum states, 'that this wasn't their real aim so I decided not to tell them my correct age. I advised my friends to do the same.'[53] Her survival instincts did not let her down. One evening, all the children and their mothers were gathered together and issued with tattered clothes instead of their striped camp uniforms. They were told they were being transferred to Ravensbrück, where mothers were allowed to keep their children with them. Pregnant Jewish prisoners who could no longer hide their condition, along with the sick of other nationalities, were sent on the same transport.

According to information received from Dr Seidel, after the pregnant women and young children (precise number unknown) were registered, they were transported to Auschwitz on 17 September 1944.[54] Additional sources also appear to refer to this group. Zacharia Zweig, Sylvia's father, was sent from Skarżysko to Buchenwald with his son Jurek (then four years old). He learned in October 1944 that the names of his wife and daughter were on the list of the transport of 28 September 1944 intended for Auschwitz, not Ravensbrück. After the war, a study of the Buchenwald file revealed that, according to the system used in the concentration camps, every transport from one camp to another came with its own file, with the prisoner cards of a transport intended for extermination cancelled (turned around) in the file of the camp from which it had originated. Among such cards, Zweig found those of his wife and daughter. In both cases, reference appears to be to the same transport that was recorded on a later date in the Buchenwald file.

It is not clear whether this is also the transport referred to in the Auschwitz '*Kalendarium*', according to which 72 Jewish-Polish pregnant women and their children arrived from Hasag-Leipzig on 29 August 1944 and were all sent to the gas chambers.[55] There may have been more than one transport, as indicated by the discrepancy in the dates, or one of the entries (28.9.44 and 29.8.44) might have contained a typing error. Whatever the case, such occurrences, mentioned in numerous testimonies, made it clear to the Leipzig prisoners that the danger of a death transport constantly hung over their heads even in this 'paradise'. Officially, it was invariably announced that the prisoners were being transferred to Ravensbrück, which accounts for the indication of this destination in the testimonies.[56] The victims were of two types: women selected during roll-call and the gravely ill taken from the *Revier*.[57]

The selections were conducted by Commandant Plaul accompanied by several SS officers in the presence of the *Oberka* and Joanna Szumańska. Prisoners whose exhausted or pale appearance might place them in jeopardy used make-up to try to put a 'healthy' colour in their cheeks. They bought lipstick and blusher from the German women in the plant, and, according to Felicja Bannet-Schäftler, paid a very high price for them: three bread rations or three 'fingers' of margarine. The makeup had to look natural; otherwise the Commandant could detect it and beckon the unfortunate woman with the words '*Du Aufgetackelte komm auch*' (You floozie, you come too). One woman caught redhanded in the act of putting on makeup was shot dead on the spot.[58]

The numbers of the women who were chosen were recorded as 'removed' (*abgestellte*), that is, unfit for work. 'Until they were taken to the transport, they wandered around the blocks like ghosts. They were given smaller bread rations. Some cried in desperation, while others accepted their fate serenely, even trying to smile... Our total inability to influence our fate is so awful. The cars awaiting them stand on a railway spur, waiting for the locomotive. We pass those death trains on the way to work...' From March 1945 no more public selections were conducted. Those who were 'not needed' simply disappeared without ceremony.[59]

The selection of patients from the *Revier* is not proof that the camp hospital was merely a corridor to the next world. On the contrary, it made a significant contribution to ensuring that the prisoners remained in a tolerable state of health, since it offered the opportunity for a few days rest. Although the supply of medications was limited, cases of pneumonia, influenza or diarrhoea were generally cured. In the winter, the inmates were bothered particularly by arthritic and rheumatic pains, and the Jewish women, especially the older ones, were often afflicted by erysipelas in the legs.[60]

Work accidents were also very common. Miriam Eitan, who broke her arm, was unusually lucky when Commandant Plaul sent her to the city hospital where she got as much food as she could eat.[61] Less serious injuries were referred to the *Revier.* Here the Polish doctor Maria Pilichowska and the nurse Sawicka performed minor surgery and always had a long line of patients waiting for their attention. The following sketch, written by one of the Polish prisoners, Maria Antoniewicz, is not only a satire on the infirmary and its medical practices, but also includes a reference to the primary threat – transport.

At the Revier[62]

The infirmary, patients seated on a bench waiting for the doctor and talking among themselves. A doctor's aide is seated at the desk.

AIDE:	Quiet please!
POLE:	Yes… quiet! You stand by the machine for 12 hours, and then you wait here for the redeemer!
BELGIAN:	(*stretching her leg*) Oh, it hurts so much! *La jambe!*
UKRAINIAN:	(*rubbing her head*) Don't whine, my head is killing me. The machine bangs away all night, and when I get back to the block, instead of lying down to rest I have to wait here for the doctor for hours…
AIDE:	What nonsense! You think I don't know what the plant is like? What are you complaining to me for? Do I force you to work? You don't want to work at the machine, tell them to give you a piano. What do I care!
JEW:	Ooh! Can I go in yet? I have such an annoying problem, I can't sit for very long. Right away I get dizzy.
UKRAINIAN:	Go to hell with your problem! Look at her, damned house louse! She can't sit, but she can run around the blocks doing business. That doesn't make you dizzy?
JEW:	What do you mean run around? What do you mean doing business?
FRENCHWOMAN:	*Mesdames – donnez un peu place pour moi –*

	je suis malade... j'ai fievre.
UKRAINIAN:	(*making room*) *Pojaluysta, madame!* (*turning to the Jew*) *Ubiraysia k chortu!*

(*The Polish doctor enters*)

DOCTOR:	Does everyone need dressings?
BELGIAN:	(*showing her the afflicted leg*) *Je suis malade, la jambe...*
DOCTOR:	What, what??? Tell me what's bothering you, quickly.
FRENCHWOMAN:	*J'ai mal...* (*stretching out her hand*) *La main...*
DOCTOR:	*Lajamb, lamae...* what a mess! Oh dear... – Ah... (*seeing the* BELGIAN'S *leg*) – (*to the aide*) That needs a dressing... (*turning to the* FRENCHWOMAN *with the sore hand*)
AIDE:	(*turning to the* FRENCHWOMAN *harshly*) Give me your hand... What are you hiding from? I said give me your hand!
FRENCHWOMAN:	*A... J'ai mal...*
AIDE:	*Mal, mal...* it hurts... you all make such a fuss over every little thing... it hurts. I'll stick my finger in and twist it around and you'll know what hurting means. (*starts to dress the* FRENCHWOMAN'S *head – the patient resists*)
FRENCHWOMAN:	*Non, non... pas la tête... c'est la main...*
AIDE:	Look at her! Who knows best what hurts you, you are me? I've seen enough wounds like these! What are you afraid of, you're not going to die! (*The patient walks out hopelessly with a bandage around her head*)
DOCTOR:	(*examining the leg of the* BELGIAN *and asking in Polish*) Does this hurt?
BELGIAN:	(*looking at her, not understanding*)
DOCTOR:	What are you staring at? Hurt? *Kranken... maladi?*
BELGIAN:	*Niks verstehen,* no understand.

DOCTOR:	What the devil, I don't understand! This Tower of Babel is a real mess. I talk to her in French, German, and she just stares at me... *nu, nu gut werden, maladi, ich sehen,* it'll be allright... (*turning to the* UKRAINIAN) What's your problem? Your heart? Wait here! (*to the* JEW) What's this? Your finger got cut off? It's scandalous! You need diachil and a compress!
AIDE:	There is no diachil.
DOCTOR:	Then maybe vaseline... or some other junk, what difference does it make.
JEW:	Can I get some time off work?
AIDE:	Of course not! Time off? What an idea! You don't need two hands to work. One is enough. Get out of here, or I'll send you to the *Revier!* (*The patient runs off in panic*)

(*The other (Russian) doctor enters*)

DOCTOR B:	*Kto do menia?*
UKRAINIAN:	Me!
DOCTOR B:	*Chto bolit?*
UKRAINIAN:	My heart! I can't breathe, I feel sick!
DOCTOR B:	(*examining her*) *Nu, nu, nichego, nichego, nado rabotat!* You have to work, otherwise – there'll be a transport!
UKRAINIAN:	But I'm really sick – I could die!
DOCTOR B:	*Da, da... moshno segodnia, moshno zavtra...* (Yes, yes, maybe today, maybe tomorrow...) You can never tell with the heart! So a transport now?
ALL PATIENTS:	What? A transport! (*they all sing*) Transport is the magic word – curing all pain, And wounds and burns, sending us running Back to the plant again! So we ignore our ills and we hide our pain,

> Because, to go on a transport – Oh, you
> have to be insane!
> So bravely we will suffer bunker, *Revier*,
> and lice,
> Because a transport – O my God – we're
> out of here in a trice!
>
> (*All run off stage*)

The threat of a selection and transport hung over everyone. Ewa Cukier mentions the Polish doctor (probably a reference to Dr Maria Pilichowska, although this is not certain) who gave her a warning before one selection, thereby saving her life. She relates that the selection took place after the visit of the Hasag general manager, Paul Budin, who announced that he had no intention of paying for sick prisoners.[63] The life of Paula Gimes was saved by 'her' supervisor.[64] Felicja Shahar describes a similar event:

Once I was very sick with an ear infection and I was in the hospital. I slept most of the time because of the fever... From time to time, the doctor touched me gently and affectionately. That hand was so loving, warm and patient, like a mother's. It was the hand of a Polish doctor who took care of me in a manner we weren't used to in those terrible times. She kissed me, fed me, once even brought me an apple and called me 'daughter'. Her behaviour toward me was astounding, almost frightening. I couldn't understand how, under those conditions, someone could be so good to me and so full of affection... One night, the doctor ran in and like a madwoman started dragging me out of bed and screaming: 'Get out of here, fast! Get dressed and go back to the block, you're well, go to work!' She shrieked hysterically, put my clothes on me, and sent me to the block. I was terribly disappointed. How was it possible that I couldn't even trust her any more? I loved her so much... I was barely able to work. When we got back at night, I found out that all the patients had been taken out of the *Revier* in death trucks. That night my doctor found me in the block, led me into a side room, kissed me and asked me to forgive her, saying: 'You see, daughter, none of those patients is still alive'... I didn't even know her name. I can never forgive myself...[65]

The testimonies of Jewish inmates also contain a considerable number of grievances against the *Revier* staff for lack of proper treatment and a degrading attitude. In Block 20, the Jewish women heartily sang 'The *Revier*' to the tune of 'Titina, Titina':

> Once a girl got very sick
> She went to the doctor quick
> To the *Revier* was sent
> They will check her there I bet.
>> They knew her: 'She's a Jew!'
>> They diagnosed her too:
>> 'Such filth, the smelly dope,
>> She's never even heard of soap'!
> O dear doctors, hear me well,
> One secret I will tell:
> You can't blame the Jews, oh no,
> If it's medicine you don't know.[66]
>> (Rena Taubenblatt)

In reality, the situation was somewhat more complex. In general, without a doubt all patients received some care at the *Revier*, and in serious cases a free pallet and appropriate treatment could always be found there, even for a Jew.[67] Swayed by negative talk of the place, Lilian Lichtensztejn was afraid to go even when her breast was inflamed. Eventually, she had no choice. When she told the doctor which block she was in, the woman was amazed: 'What? You're Jewish? With a face like that?' (Lilian was a blue-eyed blonde). In the end, both the treatment she received and the doctor's behaviour toward her were very good.

The prisoners also fell prey to death by natural causes. 'They died so quietly, as if they weren't suffering at all, just asked me to hold their hand for a minute,' Jadwiga Landowska remembers sadly.[68] Several of the younger girls contracted tuberculosis, among them the lovely Ela Bornstein from Łódź who had been a dancer.[69] Irena Pełka became very friendly with her, and describes her death several days before the liberation of the camp with profound grief. Death also took the youngster Kiri, and when the siren sounded, she was not even able to go down to the shelter without the help of Irena, who was always there to support her.[70]

Some women who had been brought to the camp in the early stages of pregnancy had disregarded orders and not registered. Hanka Kurtz worked in the plant throughout her entire pregnancy, and was lucky enough to receive a great deal of help from her German manager.[71] Fela Herling was able to hide her pregnancy for eight months, but since she appeared to be plump and healthy, she was assigned the harder tasks. Until one morning a woman in her block went into labour. As a result, it was announced at roll-call that if all the pregnant Jewish women did not report, the entire block would suffer collective punishment and the offender would be hanged. Herling reported, and three weeks later gave birth to a son in the *Revier*. She was placed on a transport list, but the train could not be sent out because the Front was now too close, and thus she was saved.[72] The night before the camp was evacuated, Hanka Kurtz gave birth to a daughter, and both mother and child survived. The fate of the other woman, Mirka (last name unknown), who gave birth is not known. At around the same time Różka Millstein also had a child and remained in the camp after the evacuation thanks to a bribe the Polish prisoners gave to the SS overseer.[73] Two testimonies refer to the tragic case of an anonymous Jewish mother who killed her infant in order to avoid a transport.[74]

Nor is it clear which birth is the subject of this story told by the young Ida Kelberg: 'One night a woman went into labour... It was a profound experience for me. The other prisoners gathered around her and a few Christians knelt down and started to pray... I heard that the baby survived the war. The prisoners hid him... The child was a symbol of the freedom that was coming soon...'[75]

Notes

1. H. Karmel, 'Moje Życie', *Śpiew za drutami* p. 13.
2. For the incident of the market stallholders, see Chapter 5.

3. Letter from Matylda Woliniewska, 19 April 1994, YV, 0-33/4237.
4. From the Polish for 'factory'.
5. Excerpts from a sketch by an unknown author; in the papers of Matylda Woliniewska, YV, 0-33/4237. For the problem of the 'whores' and the prisoners who worked in the plant, see Chapter 4.
6. Bannet-Schäftler, '*Journal*', p. 5.
7. Excerpts from a poem by Gela Meiersdorf, 'Collected Poems'.
8. Testimony of Felicja Shahar; cf. the testimony of Tema Hertz, YV, 0-33/3269.
9. Testimony of Maria Lewinger; Bannet-Schäftler, '*Journal*', p. 38.
10 Letters from Henryka Karmel, 6 March 1980, private collection; information from Danuta Brzosko-Mędryk.
11 Testimonies of Maryla Reich and Sara Shalem; Bannet-Schäftler, '*Journal*', p. 29.
12 Testimony of Rina Fradkin.
13 Bannet-Schäftler, '*Journal*', p. 29; testimony of Sara Bojer.
14 Ibid., p. 5.
15 Ricol-London, *La mégère de la rue Daguerre*, p. 329.
16 Letter from Danuta Brzosko-Mędryk, 14 May 1994, YV, 0-33/4239.
17 Ibid.; see also: Ricol-London, *La Mégère de la rue Daguerre*, p. 353.
18 Zilberberg, *Mama, Your Prayers Have Been Answered*, p. 236.
19 Ricol-London, *La Mégère de la rue Daguerre*, p. 346.
20 Zilberberg, *Mama*, p. 236.
21 Bannet-Schäftler, '*Journal*', p. 5.
22 Testimony of Lilian Goldberg.
23 The original text of the 'Anthem' is contained in the testimony of Rena Taubenblatt-Fradkin (see Figure 6.2).
24 Testimony of Paulina Buchenholz, p. 44.
25 Testimony of Malka Hottner; Kornblum-Rosenberger, *Neder*, p. 75. The letters RIF on the soap stood for the National Office for the Supply of Industrial Oils (*Reichsstelle für industrielle Fettversorgung*). The claim that the Nazis produced soap from human fat has long been found to have no basis in truth. It was the misinterpretation of the letters to mean '*Rein Jüdisches Fett*' that gave it its bogus credibility.
26 Testimonies of Eda Jewin; Helena Kurzman; Bannet-Schäftler, '*Journal*', p. 5.
27 Genia Shechter, *Lost Youth* (Hebrew), (Tel Aviv: Ministry of Defence, 1997, pp. 107–9).
28 Ibid., p. 108; oral testimony of Rachel Danziger.
29 Testimonies of Maria Lewinger and Hanka Kornfeld.
30 Testimony of Sabina Rozenblum, YV, 0-3/3572.
31 Gela Meiersdorf, 'Collected poems of'.
32 Bannet-Schäftler, '*Journal*', p. 18.
33 Testimonies of Rina Fradkin, '*Na blokowąWandę*'.
34 Testimony of Henryka Karmel.
35 Testimony of Rina Fradkin, 'Na dwie kapomanki'.
36 Gela Meiersdorf, 'Collected Poems'.
37 Testimony of Bracha Bar-Ilan.
38 Testimonies of Lilian Goldberg, Rena Cypres and Henia Strelski.
39 See Chapter 7.
40 Ricol-London, *La Mégère de la rue Daguerre*, p. 336.
41 Testimonies of Luna Kaufman, Helena Zorski and Lilian Goldberg.

42 See Chapter 5. Testimonies of Maria Lewinger, Pauline Buchenholz and Helena Zorski. See also the testimony of Lilian Goldberg.
43 Testimony of Fela Witosz, YV, M-1/E/2487/2568.
44 Testimony of Maria Lewinger.
45 Testimony of Ela Margulies-Timberg, Margulies-Timberg Collection.
46 Henryka Karmel, 'Rozmyślania w schronie przeciwlotniczym' (excerpts), *Śpiew za drutami*, p. 22.
47 Testimony of Irena Seńko, p. 15; Kornblum-Rosenberger, *Neder*, p. 78.
48 Zilberberg, *Mama*, p. 243; testimony of Felicja Blum.
49 H. Karmel, 'Na śmierć Mili' (excerpts), Margulies-Timberg Collection.
50 Testimonies of Genia Reiser, Eda Jewin, Fela Rapp, YV, 0-33/1803.
51 The list was compiled on the basis of the prisoner file, YV, JM/3963, 3964 and probably does not include the names of all the children.
52 Testimony of Zacharia Zweig, YV, 0-3/2192.
53 Fela Blum, *We Remember*, p. 22.
54 'Frauenaussenkommando Hasag-Schönefeld', Dr Irmgard Seidel, Gedenkstätte-Buchenwald, private collection.
55 Danuta Czech, *Kalendarium*, p. 61.
56 Testimonies of Sara Bojer and Fela Rapp; cf: Kornblum-Rosenberger, *Neder*, p. 77.
57 Testimony of Pola Goldweiss, YV, M-1/E/2113/1892.
58 Testimony of Luna Kaufman.
59 Bannet-Schäftler, '*Journal*', pp. 28, 39–40.
60 Testimonies of Rina Fradkin and Luna Kaufman.
61 Testimony of Miriam Eitan.
62 The sketch is contained in the writings of Matylda Woliniewska, YV, 033/4237.
63 Testimony of Ewa Cukier.
64 Testimony of Paula Gimes.
65 Testimony of Felicja Shahar, pp. 7–8.
66 Testimony of Rina Fradkin.
67 Testimonies of Malka Hottner and Eda Jewin; Genia Reiser.
68 Testimony of Jadwiga Landowska.
69 Testimony of Eugenia Różycka, YV, 0-33/712.
70 Testimony of Irena Seńko.
71 Testimony of Henryka Karmel.
72 Testimony of Fela Herling, YV, M-1/E/1987/1810.
73 Oral testimony of Rachel Asa.
74 Testimony of Jadwiga Landowska; Ricol-London, *La Mégère de la rue Daguerre*, p. 350.
75 Testimony of Ida Buszmicz.

7 Man Cannot Live by Bread Alone

After Work

Another week has passed. The November days are getting shorter, heralding imminent winter. It is hard to stand for roll-call in the cold and the wind. It's good they got it over with quickly today. Rena, Hela and Malka have already showered. The bread and margarine they got for supper is a distant memory. They sit on Rena's fourth-storey pallet... What are we going to do tonight? It's too early to go to sleep; there's too much noise still. Rena is deep in thought. Maybe she's composing a new song? No, this time, perhaps out of boredom, she starts humming a familiar melody and Malka and Hela immediately join in:

> *Es geht alles vorüber,*
> *Es geht alles vorbei...*
> Melancholy day follows melancholy day,
> Despair and tears are all they have to give,
> Their anthem – endless labour,
> And tomorrow – you may no longer live...
> Each of us has weathered many storms,
> So smiles you will not see here about,
> But still you must believe, believe heart and soul
> That over evil, happiness will win out.

Why do they have to sing now? Anka is exhausted. She didn't feel well today and she wants to rest. But how can you sleep in this anthill? All that talking, shouting, noise... and then they start singing! Are they giving out extra bread or soup? What do they have to sing about?... O God, there they go again...

166

Everything passes after all,
Hell, heaven and life,
And when sad December is over,
The days of May will again arrive.
The sun will shine again for us,
And wipe our tears away,
Joy in our hearts will blossom again,
Like a spring lilac at the end of the day... [1]
                                    (Halina Nelken)

The singing stops. But still Anka cannot fall asleep...
Muted screams suddenly came from the pallet across the way.
What's going on there? She can see a few girls – they climbed
onto Riwka's pallet, were holding two blankets over her...
and were beating her! Really hard! Why? Anka didn't want to
get involved. It was only later that she found out what it was
all about. Halina, a heavy smoker (the prisoners were strictly
forbidden to smoke) had got her hands on a cigarette at the
plant and wanted to savour it in the toilet. She asked Riwka
(not her real name), who worked alongside her, to watch her
machine for a few minutes. Apparently, Riwka couldn't
manage both jobs, and when Halina was gone she informed
on her to the supervisor. That earned Halina no more than a
severe beating, but Riwka's act has enraged the women and
they have decided to try her as an informer. They wrote up the
indictment, read it out to her... and gave her a beating. [2] The
affair did not have much effect on the block, since there were
no informers at Leipzig.

Even after that business is over, still Anka cannot go to
sleep. This time the noise is coming from the hallway. She can
hear rhythmic steps, as if someone were dancing... and
singing! (What is this, a labour camp or an opera house?) The
song doesn't sound familiar. Anka hardly has time to make it
out before the shaved head of her neighbour Rachel appears
at the foot of her pallet: 'What are lying here for? Come on!
The Frenchwomen are having a party! Come on!'

She has no choice. Sighing deeply, Anka climbs down from
her third-storey bunk and goes out to the corridor. She cannot
believe her eyes: inmates from all the neighbouring blocks are
crowded around, laughing and clapping their hands, and

there in the middle... have they gone crazy? A long line of women, each wearing a hat! They are not of this world! They have everything is: feathers, flowers, birds, ribbons and chains, hats of every shape and colour. There is a romantic turban with grapes on the side, over there a cardboard model of the Eiffel Tower; a tall Spanish comb adorned with black lace; a cage with a sleeping white bird inside... They are dancing a lighthearted *'farandole'* through the halls, now ringing with gaiety and singing...[3]

> *Au clair de la lune, mon ami Pierrot,*
> *Prête-moi ta plume, pour écrire un mot...*

They burst into the Polish block, snaking between the pallets as they sing:

> *Ma chandelle est morte, je n'ai plus de feu*
> *Ouvrez-moi la porte, pour l'amour de Dieu!...*

The whole camp is in an uproar: 'Look at what that one's got on her head! It's a swan! It almost looks real!'; 'Did you see Denise's hat? Like from the time of Louis XIV. Where on earth did she get all those coloured ribbons?; 'Good Lord, we see them every day and they look so wretched, skinny, unwashed... and then all of a sudden, look what happened to them! What a hat can do for a woman! They look like pretty butterflies!' But where are the overseers? Have they all disappeared?

The SS overseers on duty that night have not disappeared at all. They are standing apart, as amazed as the prisoners, and... clapping like everyone else! Incredible, but that's the way it is: a woman is a woman... The gay *'farandole'* winds through the Ukrainian block on its way to visit the Russians. They are still singing:

> *Sur le pont d'Avignon,*
> *L'on y danse, l'on y danse...*

The patients in the *Revier* want to see it too, so the procession makes its way to the top floor, bringing jollity and singing. The dancers come back downstairs and into the Jewish block, where nobody knows what the festivities are all about. Anna, who speaks French, hastens to explain: tomorrow, 26 November, is Saint Catherine's day – *La fête de Catherinettes* – a popular holiday dedicated especially to simple women and unmarried maids. It is the custom to wear funny hats and dance in the streets to folk tunes, drinking and making merry. The lines of dancers passes before a 'jury' who decides who will have the first prize. The winners are the girls who have made their hats into *le train de la paix* (a train of peace). The singing, noise and laughter echo throughout the camp long into the night.[4]

Some of the Jewish prisoners gaze at the merry dance with envy... They are celebrating as if the war was already over! Oh yes, the French had something to be happy about. Paris had long been liberated and they would have somewhere to return to. But what about them? They wanted so much to join in, to dance too! But could they? Would they be accepted?

O sisters, let's dance, let's dance and be gay!
Paris is dancing, drunken today,
Drunken with champagne and liberty...
   Listen, O sisters, to the thrilling heartbeat
   And let's go, come on, let's tap our feet.
   The dance will tread under all suffering and pain
   For those who are free although they are slaves.
   Paris is dancing, drunken with freedom,
   So let's all dance, come on now, come!
But I just stood there at the side,
Hoping that way to hide my eyes
And the dark curls upon my head
And hear only the beating of my heart
Love is all it yearns for...
And no more...
   So take my yearning heart and soul
   And my hands in your frenzied dance, grab hold
   So in silence my heart with you can flee
   In the gay song of youth,
   Paris, Paris, Paris.[5]

(Henryka Karmel)

'The Hat Parade' was a major event for the whole camp. The Frenchwomen, who up to now had kept to themselves, isolated, had earned universal affection. Felicja Bannet-Schäftler recalls that she had visited the French block a short time before and did not understand the meaning of the feverish activity going on there. 'There was everything imaginable there! Flowers made from paper and rags, all sorts of little objects tastefully fashioned... figures carved from bread... it's no chance that France dictates *haut couture!* We learned here what that meant.'[6]

The question of which national group was the first to initiate cultural activities was the subject of heated debate. The Poles claimed that as they had arrived before the others, they were the first to begin organizing performances.[7] From the testimonies, however, a somewhat different conclusion can be drawn. Cultural activities were introduced simultaneously by the four large national groups: the Poles, French, Jews and Russians, in mid-autumn 1944, as part of the process of adjustment to a new reality. Despite the relatively good conditions at that time in the Leipzig camp, it took about two months for a prisoner to become acclimatized. The non-Jewish women who arrived from Majdanek or Ravensbrück had a hard time adapting to the totally unfamiliar work in the munitions factory. On the other hand, the Jewish women from Skarżysko for whom this aspect of camp life was not new, found it difficult to adjust to the international character of Leipzig, so utterly different from their previous experience.

It is possible to identify several typical features of cultural activity in the camp from its inception:

- It emerged in response to the challenge posed to the organizers by the prisoner population. 'Despite the hunger, cold, and hard labour, the whole camp was thirsty for a word of comfort, although each national group organized activities only for itself.'[8]
- The large majority of performances or gatherings were associated with religious or national holidays.
- Activities were of two kinds: the first everyday and spontaneous, and the second organized, initiated individually or collectively, and demanding planning and preparation.

- The most common activities were poetry or literary readings.
- Although in essence, these were underground activities, particularly in regard to the organization of shows, neither the internal administration nor the German commanders forbade their existence or punished the inmates involved.
- A certain degree of cooperation between the different national groups in respect to the organization of performances did take place, but it was extremely limited. On the whole, it was passive cooperation exhibited through invitations to guests of other nationalities.
- Lack of testimony makes it impossible to determine whether these principles applied to the smaller groups as well, such as the Greeks, Slovenians, Czechs, etc.

Autumn gatherings

'We tried to celebrate every holiday in some manner, and every "artistic" gathering was a festive occasion for me, and not just for me,' recalls Ester Nessel from Block 20. But how could the Jews possibly think about holidays in the autumn of 1944, with nearly all of Europe *'Judenrein'*? When Rosh Hashanah (the Jewish New Year) came, the date marked under the auspices of the Red Cross, there was great disappointment. 'We saw them unloading boxes from trucks bearing the sign of the Red Cross,' relates Rut Kornblum, 'but we didn't get a single one... The SS women ate Swiss chocolate, dried fruit, and all sorts of other treats which were actually meant for us.'[9]

Yet despite the hunger and the let down, the inmates still wanted to maintain a holiday atmosphere. After work, they gathered in the small hall next to their block for the traditional *'Oneg Shabat'*. The practice had begun at Skarżysko, where they would get together in the evening for readings, talk and community singing, except that there had also been men at their former camp. Where were they now? Here there were only the girls of the Kraków group: Rut Kornblum, the Schächter sisters, Rena Taubenblatt, Hela Feig, Malka Zuckerbrot, Helena Brunnengraber, Eda Lewin, Ester Nessel, Tamara Shapiro, Anna Hauser and others. And, of course, Henryka and Ilona Karmel. They were indispensable.

The core of the group was made up of former members of Akiva, the Zionist pioneering youth movement popular in Poland before the war. In its heyday, the Kraków branch had produced Mosze Imber's outstanding choir, which had featured prominently in the 'farewell concert' at Skarżysko singing their marvellous songs in Hebrew, Yiddish and Polish.[10] Now the same songs were being sung within the walls of the Leipzig camp at an '*Oneg Shabat'* in honour of Rosh Hashanah:

> *Kineret, Kineret, elayich,*
> *Nimshekhet kol nefesh meaz...*
> (Kineret, Kineret, to you is drawn
> Each soul since time long gone...)

The women opened the programme with sad songs of yearning, but on that Rosh Hashanah in 1944 in Leipzig, they shared a fervent desire to return to the days of happiness and memories of home:

> The Holy Days, the happy days of the past!
> The days painted in red and autumn gold!
> My tormented heart cries out for you,
> Reawakened longing – hope for you we hold...
>   The Days of Awe with no fear! Days holy and pure,
>   Today I call to you, the prayer I sing!
>   Like on a silvery morn, in September mists,
>   The old rabbi's call to '*slichot'* did ring...
> Days of a father's hand and a loving stroke,
> Days of a magic tale that ended too soon...
> Today I call to you in my yearning song
> That with passion I will always croon.
>   Days of tears so pure in a holy calm,
>   How bitter the despair and the sigh of pain I feel!
>   May the mercy of forgiveness descend on me,
>   In these days of terror so real...
>   *Slicha, slicha, slicha...* [11]

> (Henryka Karmel)

Henia's poem came to an end, but the words still echoed and the melancholy thoughts still lingered. Could there be a better way of following this elegy than with Hasidic tunes? Rut, Malka and the Schächter sisters started off, the familiar melodies running into each other in a rousing beat. Next they sang Hebrew songs: *'Horat Ha-Galil'*, *'Od Lo Nootka Ha-Sharsheret'*. Why not dance a *hora*? The 'lookout' positioned near the door reported that 'the coast was clear'. But it was nearly curfew. They had better call it a night, in case that damned SS overseer showed up... They ended the evening with sentimental songs, popular Polish love songs, the man who left – would he return? After all, they each had someone: a husband, a lover, a boyfriend...

> Some day I'll come back, beneath your window stand,
> And you'll ask, 'Who's there?' And I'll say, 'It's me'.
> One has already come, and another too,
> But mine has not returned and the pain won't leave,
> O where are you, my own love true... [12]

(Anon.)

The lookout sounded a warning – the duty overseer was coming. They had to get back to the block. Quickly they scattered.

The hardest time for them was Yom Kippur. When the plant authorities learned of the nature of the Day of Atonement and the fast, they issued a directive stating that it was permitted to fast, but the women could not take food out of the factory to eat later. Eda and some of her friends decided not to fast. At first Paulina did not want to give up her soup, but she was persuaded by her friend Linka.[13] Malka concealed an apple she got from 'her' German, saving it to break the fast with.[14] There were also a few surprises: apparently in honour of the holiday, the overseer Annelise gave Sara Bojer back a picture of her family that she had confiscated.

On the eve of Yom Kippur there was unusual excitement in the Jewish blocks.

Today after the evening roll-call we didn't linger. We have to get washed, get our rations and eat them as fast as we can. Tomorrow we won't take the coffee or the soup in the plant. We'll all fast, even the women who didn't observe the holy day in ordinary times. This time it's a sign of the solidarity of resistance. In the evening, we greet each other, or more precisely, embrace and weep. Everyone is crying. What can we possibly wish for ourselves? That next year we'll meet in freedom? We have no hope of seeing Hitler defeated; we don't even dare dream of it. Our *blokowa*, 'Kozunia', watches all the emotion here in astonishment.[15]

A few friends gathered on Helena Brunnengraber's pallet to hear her poems. (She wrote beautifully.)[16] Today they want something special in memory of their loved ones who are gone: the mother murdered in the ovens of Auschwitz or Treblinka or Belzec...

> I'll weep no more –
> So I have promised myself.
> Inside I lock my grieving heart, frozen like ice.
> Two threatening fists I'll raise up to the sky.
> Then my soul through the bars will fly,
> And I will shout, so loud I'll shout,
> That I am free, that no more tears will come out.
> But for you, saintly one, I have buried some deep,
> To fall on my knees at your ashes and weep,
> Like a small child, to weep...[17]

In Niunia's block, the women wished to greet the holiday in a special way. 'That night was the only time we all got off our bunks and sang songs in Yiddish and Hebrew. This time our brutal *blokowa* Niunia didn't say anything or hit us.'[18] Late at night, when it seemed as if things had quietened down, they suddenly heard singing. 'It was Dziunia Rebenstock. She had a beautiful soprano voice that filled the huge hall with the exquisite notes of the prayer.'

They all held their breath as they listened, remembering their home, their family gathered around the holiday table, grandparents, parents, brothers and sisters... Here almost everyone was all alone. A ringing chorus of prayer resounded from every corner: 'Hear O Israel, the Lord is God, the Lord is One!'[19] There were no memorial candles to light and not everyone knew the prayers, but Ilona was there to pray in the name of them all:

In my house no memorial candles will glow,
For millions would have to burn,
To mark all the days of mourning in the year,
For the dead who will never return.
    In my house no memorial candles will glow,
    For there's not enough time for them all to light,
    My life is one long memorial day,
    Each moment in mourning burns inside.
Why do I need lamps of tears and grief,
When with such deep mourning my heart is afire,
It burns like a bonfire so great and so sad
For me, for you, for the joy expired.[20]

                                        (Ilona Karmel)

It would soon be November, with its frost and rain. The month began with the Christian *Zaduszki*, the memorial for the dead. On the first of November, singing could be heard in all the Polish blocks as the prisoners raised their voices in the prayer for dead. They were joined by the Christian women from other blocks.[21] Every inmate there, no matter what her nationality, had someone to pray for: a husband who had fallen in battle, a son tortured in a Gestapo dungeon, an elderly mother who had died in a distant homeland, a sister who had died of typhoid in Majdanek... The prayer played an important role in the search for consolation. Even among the Frenchwomen, an especially large proportion of whom were left-wing political prisoners, there were those who tried to organize religious activities. Madame Caden arranged a daily evening prayer for the Catholics in Block 12. 'Every Sunday at six in the evening we gathered in the shelter and conducted an Underground mass. Madame Caden played the role of parish priest. How spontaneous and fervent were our prayers in those dark caves!'[22]

That same cold November, the Poles decided to organize a performing troupe they called the 'Bunkerkommando' (see Figure 7.1). Matylda Woliniewska was the initiator, manager, and director of the group. According to one of its members, it was a 'resistance group' the aim of which was to strengthen the spirit of Polishness and patriotism and to promote Polish culture and folklore. The performances were designed to help

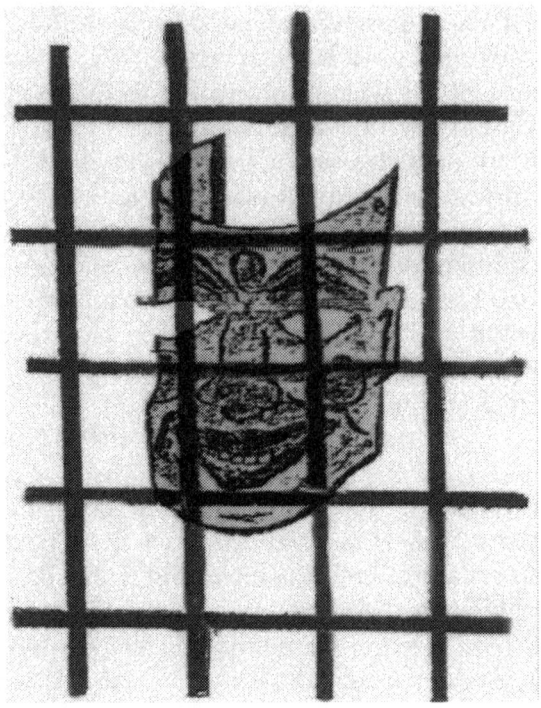

Figure 7.1 Emblem of the 'Bunkerkommando'.

Source: Private collection.

the population of prisoners bolster their faith, to raise morale, and to bring a little light and joy into the bleak life of the camp... 'We wanted to prove to the prisoners of other nationalities that we were... a part of a cultured and courageous nation.'[23]

Such challenges were Matylda's guiding light, but she added a number a practical aims as well. She regarded cultural activity as a means of preventing serious social clashes between the functionaries and the rank-and-file prisoners and helping the individual inmates maintain mental stability.[24] Moreover, there was a rumour circulated among the Polish women from the latest transport (arriving in September 1944) that Matylda, so looked up to by the other prisoners, was a communist,[25] and although this had no basis in fact, it could widen the rift between the 'veterans' from Majdanek and the 'new girls'. And so, it was decided that the first 'concert' would be held in honor of Polish Independence Day on 11 November.[26] Joanna Szumańska, the 'camp elder', was invited to the first rehearsal in the hope that she would give her blessing to the enterprise. It was clear to Joanna Szumańska, who knew Matylda from Majdanek and was well aware of her extraordinary influence on the others, that by giving her approval she herself would gain status in the prisoners' eyes.

The performance was organized by an 'executive committee' composed of 'Majdanek women', including, in addition to Matylda, Maria Antoniewicz, Stefa Błońska, Jadwiga Elżanowska, Maria Dworakowa and Sabina Łukomska. Some of the younger women, such as Danuta Brzosko, were also among the 15 'performers'. The programme consisted of pieces from the works of the greatest Polish poets on the struggle against the country's occupiers, along with battle songs from every war. It concluded with concentration camp songs.[27]

The first performance was meant only for Polish prisoners, but with the support of Joanna Szumańska, which brought with it the cooperation of the entire internal administration, the second concert was to encompass a wider sector. This time Poles who had not come from Majdanek were also pressed into service to perform. Most of them were factory workers for whom this was on the order of a 'step up'. The programme included folksongs and dances from all regions of Poland which the troupe wished to perform before prisoners of other nationalities as well. When news of the 'concert' spread through the camp, so many people showed up that it almost had to be cancelled because of the pressure of the crowd. According to Danuta Brzosko, Frenchwomen, Russians, Jews and Belgians were invited. In order to make things more comprehensible to the guests, a number of programmes in French were distributed. She recalls that as a result of this show, the 'Bunkerkommando' became celebrities throughout the camp.[28]

It should be noted that the testimony of Jewish prisoners makes no mention whatsoever of the 'Bunkerkommando' or

Polish 'concerts' in November, 1944. Although this cannot be seen as evidence that no connections existed between the two groups, the fact is that the French performances are mentioned, that is, they were attended by Jews. Moreover, it is unlikely that the Frenchwomen's 'hat parade' was inspired by the Poles' cultural 'concert', as Matylda believes.[29] If there was any influence at work here, it may have been of a different kind: the Frenchwomen realized that public yet 'controlled' cultural activity would not incur the wrath of the camp authorities.

The December festivities

Everyone in Block 20 knew that on Sunday, when they were off work, there would be a 'song night'. Usually they gathered in small groups of close friends in a corner of the block or on the bunks. There on the pallet of Towa and her friend Pola were all the members of Beit Ya'akov, Blimka, Rena Finkelstein, Rosa and others. They reminisced about their life at home and at school, with familiar melodies sometimes punctuating the conversation.[30] A different group gathered around Fela Shahar and her neighbours. Here they listened to the recitations of works by the Polish poet Adam Mickiewicz: Ludka knew 'Lilie' by heart and Fela recited 'Powrót taty' (Father's Return). To round off, they all wallowed in sentimental tunes.[31]

Halina preferred the poems of Julian Tuwim, accompanied by gastronomic memories.[32] Things were quite similar in Rena Taubenblatt's 'salon', with the added interest of a new ditty about anything and everything in the camp. What could be more popular than recalling mama's culinary arts, and what, how, and when they used to eat! Hit songs about the spring and love were 'revised' by Rena, and they could hear the familiar melody of 'What a Girl Dreams Of'. What? Not of love this time...

> What does a girl dream of
> When she awakes at night
> Her stomach growling yet...
> What does she hope,

What does she think,
What does she dream to get?
  The bowl of soup to eat,
  The coffee hot and sweet,
  The bread she'll clutch in her hand
  Better than the arms of a man...[33]
                 (Rena Taubenblatt)

The *blokowa* Wanda, looking for a way to enhance her reputation among her colleagues, decide to make use of Rena's talent for entertaiment. One Sunday she invited a group of functionaries to the Jewish block, where Rena performed a programme of 'requests'. She sang them all, the songs about the kitchen, the *Revier*, and more. The Hasag Anthem was received with the greatest delight, with the audience joining in on the chorus. According to Rena, the guests could not stop laughing and did not take offence at all.

Serious literary evenings were generally held in the hall near the *Schreibstube*. They were organized by the Schächter sisters and other women from the Kraków group, and the audience gathered round them. The featured pieces were

Figure 7.2 Henryka Karmel-Wolfe.

Source: Private collection.

Figure 7.3 Ilona Karmel-Zucker.

Source: Private collection.

invariably poems by the Karmel sisters. All the Jewish prisoners were familiar with the girls and their mother, Mrs Karmel, who had been through two camps, Płaszów and Skarżysko, with her daughters and was now here in Leipzig with them. She was exceedingly proud of her talented children and their poetry. Arguments would sometimes break out among the audience as to which of them, Henryka or Ilona, was the better writer. Henryka usually read her own poems, but Ilona's were generally recited by Fela Schächter, who also 'specialized' in the poems of Julian Tuwim, particularly the famous 'Ptasie radio' (Radio of Birds).[34] Excerpts from the journal of Maria Schächter, started at Skarżysko and continued at Leipzig, were also sometimes read out at these evenings.[35] Occasionally, Rut Kornblum read her lovely poems. She recalls these moments in her book, *Neder:*

At that time I wrote a lot of poems full of yearning for freedom, for flowers, for an open field, for little things like riding the tram, simply crossing a street alone, not under

Figure 7.4 Maria Schächter-Lewinger.

Source: Private collection.

the watchful eyes of the SS: things that were light years away from us, poems about events, love poems and satiric poems. I wrote them in a hardbacked notebook I was given at the Commandant's order. I also wrote in it those of the old poems I had written that I remembered. The poems were very popular among my friends...[36]

Another group gravitated around Gela Meiersdorf, who seemed to have no social contact with the women of the Kraków group, perhaps because of the age difference (Gela was born in 1902). Her friends included her bunk-mate Malka (family name unknown), a seamstress by trade who had a lovely singing voice. There was also little Haneczka, the orphan, for whom Gela felt a maternal instinct, even dedicating one of her poems to her:

> All alone, no father or mother,
> Frightened, hopeless,
> Hungry and barefoot,

181

A poor Jewish girl.
She stands at the side,
Only tears in her eyes,
Don't cry, Haneczka, have no fear!
You will survive, the whole world is yours,
You will get through this hell, despite the pain,
And you'll find your brothers and sisters again.
    Your life will be happy and gay!
    But when you are grown-up,
    Your mind may recall the days,
    When your friend 1123,
    Wiped your tears away,
    And comforted you in your grief.[37]
                  (Gela Meiersdorf)

The mood in the camp changed in December. There was excitement everywhere in anticipation of the Christmas holiday. It was whispered that the Frenchwomen were preparing 'something special'. The Poles were also getting ready for a grandiose Christmas show – the traditional *Szopka*. The pervasive atmosphere inevitably affected the Jews as well. The public performances staged by the French and the Poles had opened new possibilities for them too. Thus it was only natural for them to ask: What about us? We have a holiday too! Hanukkah! Maybe we ought to put on a show for the whole block?

The women from the Kraków group got together and decided to organize a public 'concert' for Block 20. The first problem they had to overcome was, of course, the *blokowa*, Niunia. Would she give her permission? Niunia seems to have been persuaded that as it had already been done in other blocks, why not put her 'realm' on the map as well. She had often enjoyed listening to the poems of the Karmel sisters. Once her permission was obtained, a date was set.

This was probably the show referred to by Danuta Brzosko-Mędryk, who speaks of seeing one in the 'huge block' of the Jews. She claims that it was organized in response to the urgings of Matylda, with whom the writers and directors, the Karmel sisters, consulted.[38] Considerable 'poetic licence' seems to have been taken with this story, as according to Matylda's own journal, she met the Karmel sisters for the first time 'the day before the camp was evacuated'[39] (i.e. in April 1943). There can be no doubt that the performance was the brainchild of the Kraków group.

Thus, early in December 1944, the festive evening arrived. A table covered in white paper was positioned at one end of the block and an improvised *menorah* with actual candles placed upon it. (Malka Zuckerbrot and some of her friends had 'organized' the candles from the factory.) Behind the table was a cardboard set with rocks and palm trees. A lookout was stationed outside. The audience had already taken their places, with the heads of hundreds of women peering out from every pallet. Several guests from the Polish blocks stood near the door. It was time. One of the women lit the first candle of Hanukkah and recited the traditional prayer. The group on 'stage' began 'Rock of Ages' and all the women immediately joined in, the singing growing louder and stronger. Then they sang some more familiar, well-loved Hanukkah songs.[40]

Ilona Karmel took centre stage. Not only was she a poet, but she was also very well-versed in Jewish history. She told the story of the Maccabees, how far away in the Land of Israel, over 2,000 years ago, the Jews had suffered under the Seleucids and all the harsh edicts and torments inflicted on them by Antiochus Epiphanes. And then Judah Maccabee and his brothers rose up and declared war on the tyrant, routing him and emerging victorious. And when Jerusalem was liberated and they came to reconsecrate the Temple, a miracle happened.

The entire audience breathed a deep sigh... O God! Could there be a miracle for us too? They sang another Hanukkah song of joy and happiness, but there was no joy and happiness. Still, it was better to sing together than to curl up in a corner and cry. Quiet everyone! They're going to recite something – a song of praise to Judah Maccabee written especially for the occasion by Ilona Karmel:

Judah Maccabee! Judah Maccabee!
No soldiers no blood in your war did you spare,
Fighting with a mallet, the few against the many there,
While we fled like frightened sheep.
You spilled your blood, while we spilled pitiful tears...

Please listen, remember, and understand:
Our fate is allied with the wanderer's staff
A hundred times heavier than the bayonet.
Hear and forgive us, no one is to blame
Those who grabbed the staff – forgot their friends.
For no uprising has come from bondage so harsh
For so long our lives have had no end.

Ester, a few years younger than Ilona, was struck by the fact that this was the first time in her life she had ever heard such an idea... Their slavery had gone on too long to give rise to rebellion. 'But I understood that we had not always been a nation of wanderers and there were heroes in our history too! We had also had a land and a country once!'[41]

Judah Maccabee! Judah Maccabee!
You fought the Temple doors to open.
We must fight to rid our hearts
Of rust and in your footsteps follow.
We can not march ahead like you,
For us no Book of Books, no miracle awaits
Only the dull day and long road to redeem us
And the fevered blood flowing through our veins.
Each part of the road – like a page from the Book,
A sacred letter – each and every stone.
Each blow of the hammer like a flash of truth
And the sound of the metal, the cry of the heart.
Those who point the way there,
In courage, in truth, go, follow the road
Proudly – like a mallet in the blazing sun
Like you to be – Judah Maccabee!

The recitation resounded throughout the block. The women listened intently: 'To be like you – Judah Maccabee! Could they? Would it ever come true, and, could they ever be in the Land of Israel?'

Judah Maccabee! Judah Maccabee!
Like oxen the plough we must draw.
Plodding ahead on the rocky earth

In sleepless nights and arduous days.
Bowing our heads down to the ground,
Lips trembling as we plant a kiss.
Gulping each secret, straining to hear
For like you we must always be
And rebel... can you hear us Judah Maccabee?[42]

The applause was thunderous. A few more poems were read and the evening ended with community singing. It was not easy to fall asleep after such an experience. The Kraków group was thrilled: we did it! Niunia, listening quietly, had not interfered, but now she called lights out. They had to work tomorrow. The 'bondage so harsh' was not over yet...

The rest of the camp was still seized by the atmosphere of holiday preparations. Even the Italians organized a 'family' concert and invited a number of Poles. The women's choir was awe-inspiring, as they accompanied themselves with small bells they must have made in the plant.[43] Matylda also tells of a show put on by the Greek women.[44]

What did the Russians do? The whole camp knew that they kept to themselves and were highly organized. The most popular of the 'prisoners of war' was Yefrosinia Chapaynikova, an army medic around forty. Imprisoned together with the younger women, she had been through quite a lot, and was like a mother to them and beloved by everyone.[45] The Russians sang on the way to work, and in the camp, where they would stand near a window that looked out on the street as people gathered to listen (until it was boarded up).[46] Now it was learned that they too were planning an evening of folksongs and dances, and had even borrowed costumes and props from Matylda for the purpose. But this time they really surprised everybody by putting on part of Chekhov's *Cherry Orchard*. The 'authors' knew the entire text by heart. The acting and direction were extremely professional. Among the props they had managed to obtain were even a top hat and a silver platter. The whole 'Bunkerkommando' was invited to the play, which earned rave reviews.[47]

The Polish Christmas concert, the *Szopka*, was held in the large bunker, with enough room for over 2,000 people. It now housed a stage, made of tables bound together with boards, costumes and props. Matylda had recruited a whole army of seamstresses, shoemakers and painters to make all the items necessary. They found old clothes in the camp storeroom, including Jewish capotes, red down quilts and other 'treasures' from which they made the stage-set and costumes for all the actors. The plant was also a source of supply, providing pilfered cables, paper, paint, bits of aluminum, etc. To their credit it must be said that most of the women in the 'Bunkerkommando,' which boasted 70 members at its height, worked in the factory and only gathered in the shelter for rehearsals, under the energetic direction of 'Mata' (as Matylda was called) and her assistants after 12 hours of backbreaking work and the evening roll-call.

Matylda's personality and influence can be deduced from an excerpt from the poem 'Bunkerkommando':

> At the head, of course, Matylda must go,
> Quietly, calmly... through her glasses she peers
> How vital it is that she always be there!
> Why? Naturally, for the sake of the show!...
> She wants us, in spite of the war
> To be rid, for a while, of all of our woes,
> So we don't think only of suffering and pain,
> Why don't we put on a couple of shows!...[48]
>
> (Maria Antoniewicz)

Folklore groups from all regions of Poland appeared in the *Szopka*, bringing imaginary gifts to Baby Jesus with their songs and dances. There were also groups representing the cities, such as Warsaw, Kraków and others, each appropriately costumed and presenting a patriotic text. There was nearly a catastrophe in the middle of the programme when several SS overseers appeared and were not overly pleased by certain parts of the performance. The day was saved when Joanna and Zina 'escorted' the German women out of the hall.[49] The *Szopka* was the talk of the whole camp. Even several Jews seem to have been invited, since they were able to report on what had gone on there.[50]

Rather odd rumours circulated among the Frenchwomen. As far back as the autumn, they had received the news that the Allies in the west had already captured the region of Alsace and the Soviet Army was advancing in the east. They had cherished the hope that they would be able to celebrate Christmas at home with their families. But these hopes were scattered on the winter winds and they slowly came to admit the terrible possibility:

> Ladies, softly it must be said
> That we will spend Christmas here instead...

Nevertheless, their spirit was not completely broken, and they decided to celebrate the holiday in suitable fashion. A Christmas committee was set up and determined that the programme would include an extract from a ballet, a choir and a play. Rehearsals began, with the entire French block feverishly at work on the preparations: there was an elegant dress to be sewn, peasant trousers to be stitched and papers of every sort and colour to be fashioned into stage-sets.[51] And then they were ready with their first surprise...

One evening after roll-call, the doors of the French block were thrown open to visitors for an exhibition of 'cakes'! Arranged on tables were artistic creations made of 'dough' mixed from bread, margarine and jam. The results were incredible! An Egyptian pyramid beside a palace, a farmyard full of animals, works of 'modern art', a bouquet of flowers, human figures, famous buildings and statues, a basket of fruit, even the Eiffel Tower! The doorway was crowded with curious prisoners who came in – and couldn't believe their eyes. Naturally, in response to personal invitations, the SS overseers also arrived, and gazed at the exhibit with undisguised amazement. If anyone had not known what France was famous for, she found out here. Even the Commandant came to see, and was so impressed by the Eiffel Tower that he ordered extra rations of bread and jam for the whole block as a reward.[52]

Christmas arrived. The enormous bunker was again turned into a theatre hall. Over 400 French and Belgian prisoners, as well as several hundred inmates of other nationalities, sat all mixed together on the floor. It was very hard for the 'security services' to stop the flood of women pushing through the doors. The entire camp had been abuzz with talk of the French

Christmas show, and everyone wanted to see it. The curtain went up. It began with a ballet performance entitled 'Love Throughout the Generations', with appropriate costumes to represent each period. Next the choir came on stage, and the 'men' and women danced. Each piece was applauded thunderously, with the audience roaring: 'Encore, encore! You have to do it again!'

After the intermission came the play: an act from *Don Juan* by Molière. The inmates used a text smuggled to them by French prisoners of war employed in the plant. The audience had no idea that Dona Elvira's glittering gown was made from the silk lining of an old coat, and Don Juan's trousers from SS-issue long johns stolen from the laundry line! The actors displayed extraordinary talent and vitality, 'and if the great author could have risen from his grave, he would have been very moved to see his play performed that day in the cellar of a concentration camp... What a lesson in courage and friendship was learned that Christmas', wrote Odette Dugue, 'and what a joy it was to see a smile on the exhausted faces, a smile of life, in spite of all the suffering!'[53]

The grand concert

Among the enthusiastic audience at the French 'concert' were members of the Jewish prisoners' Kraków group. Not only did the performance make a huge impression on them, but it also raised quite a few questions in their minds: How had they pulled it off? How had they made the incredible costumes and sets? 'What's wrong with us Jews?' grumbled Maria Schächter (known as Mania). 'We put on our own shows at Skarżysko under much worse conditions, so why not here? There must be some of us just as talented as the French or the Poles! We have to do something, something special!'[54]

But it was easier said than done. It was perfectly clear that this time permission from Niunia, the *blokowa*, would not be enough. They would need 'connections'. As we have seen, a number of the Polish functionaries were already familiar with the literary talents of Ilona and Henryka Karmel and were great fans of their work, even 'commissioning' a special poem for a friend's birthday or some other occasion. They were typically amazed to discover that the poets were Jewish, and treated their products with considerable reverence: 'These poems must be saved.' Some actually tried to smuggle them out of the camp themselves.[55] The Schächter sisters also used the connections they had developed with the 'powers that be' over the course of six months. And perhaps Niunia put in a good word for them, too. Whatever the case, behind-the-scenes negotiations proved successful and approval was granted, along with the promise of a certain amount of assistance, particularly of a technical nature.

Notwithstanding, it was clear to the entire Kraków group (now joined by Zosia Borowski and Halina Zuckerman) that a nationalistic-Zionist show would not go down well and would, moreover, be incomprehensible to the other nationalities. For technical reasons, folk-dancing such as the Poles had presented and classical plays such as the French had performed were out of the question. But the new year was coming! They finally decided to organize a New Year's Eve show for the whole camp, something that would suit an

Figure 7.5 Helena Schächter-Zorski.

Source: Private collection.

international audience, that everyone could understand. As Maria Lewinger notes in her memoirs: 'We knew how hungry they all were for the word, for art or something approximating art.'

The Karmel sisters and Rena Taubenblatt took upon themselves the literary side of the evening, while Maria Schächter and her sister Helena were in charge of organization and production. The programme was to include dance groups, a recitation, sketches, and a play. 'To get the materials for the costumes and sets, we did what everyone else did: used every opportunity to pilfer them from the plant by way of "organization".' The most efficient 'vehicle' for transporting them back to the camp was tall, thin Hela Feig: 'We stuck all the stolen materials under her *pasiak* and tied them on tightly, and then we marched arm in arm (so that nothing should fall, heaven forbid!) through the camp gate, avoiding the watchful eyes of the SS men.'

The show was to be called the Alexander Jazz Band in honour of a famous group in prewar Warsaw. Naturally, the women knew most of the songs by heart, and if they got stuck they could always call on Rena's excellent memory. Maria Schächter presided over rehearsals, and often had to chew out the band: 'That's not jazz! It's lousy! It has to be full of power, noise, fire! Not wailing!' But the poor women, who could only rehearse after 12 hours of work and the long-drawn-out evening roll-call, never complained. They lined up obediently once more and did it all over again...[56]

Meanwhile, others were preparing songs, and Ilona Karmel was writing the play *The Adventures of Socrates in a Concentration Camp*, hunched over a table pretending to be hard at work in the plant while her neighbour, Ester Nessel, actually did her job. Ester did this quite willingly, not only eager to help out the celebrated Karmel sisters, but also to give Ilona time to prepare the 'lecture'. As always, her writing was to be accompanied by a lengthy dissertation, this time on the subject of Greek mythology. The play was rehearsed in the washroom, where the costumes, sets and even confetti were being prepared in the evenings as well. The sewing and craftsmanship were overseen by Helena Schächter, who also ran roughshod over the girls she was trying to turn into ballerinas. She was joined by Eda Millstein, diligently rehearsing her solo dance. Fela Schächter lay on her bunk memorizing new poems. Hunger, cold and roll-calls were all forgotten amidst the feverish preparations.

The night before the show, Malka Zuckerbrot suddenly came running in panic to where Maria was lying on her pallet, wailing in desperation: 'You won't believe what happened! The se-e-e-ts... the confe-fe-fe-fetti...'[57] When they went down to the cellar they were stunned to discover that someone had ruined the sets, smearing the paint and strewing confetti about everywhere. 'We didn't know who did it. They said maybe the Poles or the Russians, or maybe a cat...'[58] With considerable effort, the damage was repaired and everything was ready for the big night.

Probably inspired by the prize awarded the Frenchwomen for their 'cake' display, it was decided at one of the Kraków group meetings to charge an 'entrance fee' in the form of a margarine ration – proof that the organizers had no idea what to expect. The 'concert' was to be held in the enormous bunker where a stage had been set up. As soon as the doors were opened, the first ten or 20 or so prisoners handed over the 'entrance fee', and then the dam broke. The protests of the guards at the door were lost in the flood of prisoners pouring in. The Jewish women really could not complain, since the same thing had happened at the other shows. Everyone wanted to see it; everyone wanted to hear it! Especially something as big as this!

According to the testimony of Malka Zuckerbrot and Rut Kornblum, the Commandant himself was invited, along with the overseers. The camp officers sat in the first row of the hall, the last inch of which was filled with thousands of prisoners crammed in. It was so packed that even Joanna Szumańska could not push her way inside. It was time: on stage, the *emcee* (compère) appeared.[59] The five girls in the Alexander Jazz Band were in place, each decked out in evening clothes (i.e. a jacket, bow-tie and black top hat), all made of the cardboard used to cover the windows in the black-out. The chorus line started its dance to the song:

Come on and hear...
Come on and hear...
For many many years and more
The great sounds of jazz reached our shore...
Sung by a cowboy under the skies,
Then westward to the cities arrived,
New York, Chicago, and from there –
To the old world here...[60]

The huge crowd began swaying to the rhythm. This was music! It brought with it the spirit of the outside world, the spirit of freedom! The dancers linked arms, their hips swaying and their feet tapping to the wild beat:

> *Melodią tą kołysał jazz,*
> *Wiał saksofonów smętny ton...*
> (The jazz thrilled us with its melody,
> The saxophones blew to its lovely sounds...)

Thunderous applause. The next act was already lining up on stage. This time in long white dresses with paper ornaments. Helena Schächter, who led the ballet corps, had also made the costumes. The charming ballerinas twirled to the music of Strauss's waltzes sung by the choir. They left the stage to a riot of applause. Now it was the turn of Eda Millstein, covered in black shoe polish for her chimney sweep dance. It was no surprise that she was such a fine dancer: after all, she had been a dance instructor.[61] She was followed by the second number by the Alexander Jazz Band, now singing 'Rumba Negra'. The 'little black boy' danced and sang:

> Faraway in the jungle the village stands,
> There the black man lives with Jimmy his son,
> From a distant land a man once came,
> And brought little Jimmy a saxophone!
> But so short the night,
> And so short the day,
> When Jimmy on that
> Saxophone does play!
> *Oh, Rumba negra, Rumba negra!*[62]

The audience refused to let the dancers go: 'Encore! Encore!'
But the show must go on, and the main attraction was still to
come: *The Adventures of Socrates in a Concentration Camp.*[63]
Frenzied activity on stage and the buzz of intermission in the
hall. And again everyone fell silent. Before the drawn curtain,
two characters appeared: Saint Peter, the gatekeeper of
Heaven, and the Greek philosopher Socrates (played by Maria
Schächter), dressed in a white sheet.

SOCRATES: O Saint Peter, save my soul!
            The shouts of my wife I can no longer bear!
PETER: What are you talking about?
SOCRATES: Xanthippe! Can't you hear?
            Always fights and bouts,
            Complaints and shouts,
            Hell would be easier to sustain,
            Than up here with her to remain!
PETER: If your suffering is so hard,
            Toss out your obligations, pard!
            Why to Hell in a hurry be?
            Go instead to Germany!
SOCRATES: Good bye – I will take your advice!
            To earth I return in a trice!

*(The curtain opens to reveal barbed-wire fences, barracks,
a watch-tower, and barred windows)*

SOCRATES: *(looking right and left in awe)*
            Wherever I look,
            Only barbed wire I see!
            Fences here and fences there,
            On every side of me!
            And the style is very odd,
            I do not know this façade,
            No loggia or column anywhere,
            Only barbed wire and bars here…

*(He goes in through the gate and sees prisoners lined up for
a roll-call. In front of them is the BLOKOWA [probably played by
Helena Schächter]. One of the prisoners walks toward SOCRATES)*

SOCRATES: What Amazon is coming near?
                She looks like my wife, I fear...
                She seems full of pep and sass,
                Walking quite fast,
                Maybe she's a nicer lass?
PRISONER: A new inmate has arrived
                I don't know how he came today,
                How am I supposed to record him,
                So he won't get in our way?
BLOKOWA: Come here fast!
                Over here you!
                Run and get the *Schreibstube*!
                If you do not record this man,
                Like all the others
                You'll soon stand
                In a penal roll-call too!

(*She shoves* SOCRATES *rudely*)

SOCRATES: This behaviour I can't grasp!
                Why does she give my face a slap?

(*He sees a line of prisoners in front of the coffee vat. One of them is carrying a cup of coffee. He thinks it is a trophy*)

SOCRATES: Congratulations to the victor, glory, honour and more!
                That is a trophy you are holding, for sure?
PRISONER: No, it's coffee, plain white coffee!
SOCRATES: White coffee? That must be
                The nectar marking victory!
                Might there be a few drops for me?
PRISONERS: Stand in line, no tricks, you specimen
                Before you feel a hand across your face again!

(*Several overseers appear and push him into line*)

OVERSEER: Get a move on, it's time to work to go,
                Everyone in line, don't be so slow!

Keep in line, no talking too,
Or there'll be another penal roll-call for you.
SOCRATES: Where are you taking me, lovely Amazon?
Is Zeus to glory leading me on?
CHORUS: Close your mouth, not another word say,
Or they'll throw you in the bunker right away!
SOCRATES: (*Musing*) To a pot of rotten stew
This country I'd compare,
Without the barbed-wire fences
It wouldn't have a prayer!
They hold it tight
Just like the fear forlorn,
Hidden among the fences
That reveal the thorns!
They are like the jaws,
Of wild dogs![64]

(*As the play proceeds, Socrates undergoes a series of adventures
in the factory. Back at roll-call in the camp*)

SOCRATES: For what crimes have you put me here, O Zeus?
Am I of hunger and thirst my life to lose?
CHORUS: (*sings*) *Cicho, sza, i nic nie gadaj chłopie!*
Cicho, sza, Neue Ordnung jest w Europie!
Tak jest i tak ma być, cicho sza, nie gadaj nic!
Be still, man, no complaints, desist,
Here in Europe a 'new order' exists,
That's how it is, and should be too,
So be still, no more complaints from you!
SOCRATES: O Saint Peter, I can barely persist,
I shall return – even my wife is better than this!

The adventures of poor unfortunate Socrates were greeted
by waves of laughter. Here in the camp, not even his wisdom
could help him! The play received thunderous applause. The
actors took their bows, thrilled that it had all gone without a
hitch. And the show went on. A 'clock' appeared on stage.
There were 12 holes in the clock-face, with a woman's head in
each. Slowly they revolved, reciting in unison:

195

Some say another year has passed,
Four months times three.
But I say it has only been days
And nights too long for me...
For each day was once twelve hours long
And sixty seconds each minute made,
Seven hundred minutes in a night
Each one – so full of pain... [65]

(Henryka Karmel)

'The Clock' affected the mood of the audience. The atmosphere turned sombre, as if everyone had suddenly remembered where they were. Fela Schächter came on stage to recite a new poem by Ilona Karmel, 'Living Robots'. The audience fell silent:

From the Oder to the Rhine – from Berlin to Vienna!
From the end of the earth to the edge of the world!
A new message shall ring out like thunder
Through the ether on the air and sea:
Living robots! Living robots!
A marvellous invention! The height of genius and
   simplicity!
Living robots! Raise your voice in rousing cheer!

There was no need to explain. It was clear she was talking about all of them, the slaves of Hasag! About the Jews, the Poles, the French – all of them! The audience sat frozen, gulping down each word. Their spines shivered; their hands clenched...

Hallo, hallo! Hallo, hallo!
Come closer! Gentlemen, just look!
A hundred per cent profit! Clean! No joke!
The look of normal people they have got,
But have no fear! Human he's not!
Asks for nothing, doesn't cost a dime,
Just keeps working! Hard, and all the time!
Even twenty hours he'll work and no rest need,
With amazing dedication and at full speed!
For a spoonful of soup and a piece of black bread,

He'll keep working fast, full speed ahead!
Herr Kommandant, Herr Ingenieur,
Herr Direktor, Herr Werkführer!
For our plant – the golden age is here!
Hurray for the robots! Let's give them a cheer!

The words pierce the women's hearts... that's just what we are, isn't it? Day shift, night shift, backbreaking toil in stifling halls beside machines dripping hot grease. Every day we drag ourselves to work for miles, in the rain, heat, or frost. The damned Germans are proving their patriotism at our expense, trying to defend the Reich with our hands... And they don't even give us food to appease our hunger...

The gentlemen asks if there are problems too?
Yes, sometimes that can happen too,
When his soul – or his heart, for instance – comes awake...
But that's nothing serious, a small mistake!
And fixing it is really a snap!
Just give him a shove or a simple slap,
Deny him food – and he's right as rain!
Back at work, and speeding again!
Any delay or hold-up is made up in a twitch,
In short – it's a machine without a hitch!

That's what they want, for us to have no soul, just work, without uttering a word... They wouldn't have given permission for this 'concert' either if it weren't for the air raids on Leipzig. They're so scared, those heroes, 'the German master-race!' They're always the first into the bunkers... But when will there be an end to our torment? O Lord, when we will be free?

But all of a sudden one day – this you must know,
The robots will stop – the machines won't go...
And the sound of longing will burst from within,
They will come alive and everybody will listen
To the sobs of despair, the pain and tears,
And they will move! Those whose yearning has stung
     them for years!

Through the cities dead and the empty streets,
Like a raging storm, the hordes will stamp their feet,
Walking soberly, beaten, lost,
In the madness of the untamed, the madness of the saint,
Before the world they will stand – tens of thousands
    strong,
Consumed by hatred, compassion long gone,
And on their lips, that black from suffering have become,
A cry – like gushing blood – will burst: freedom!!![66]

(Ilona Karmel)

The room went wild. Hundreds of prisoners rose, cheering, applauding thunderously, weeping and shouting… Yes, we will be free, and we will show them, our 'masters'!

An 'astrologer' now came on stage carrying a large telescope. He pointed it at the sky and predicted what the coming year held for the various national groups, each represented by a couple performing an appropriate song. As soon as they started the Polish song 'It's Time to Go Home' ('Czas do domu, czas'), the Polish inmates joined in spiritedly.[67] Then there was a number for the Frenchwomen. The Russians didn't give the performers a chance to present one for them, and instead began singing 'Moskwa maja'. Finally, on behalf of the Jews, the chorus sang 'Anu Olim Artza' (We are Going to the Land of Israel).

For the finale, all the performers gathered on stage for a rousing chorus:

> *O Nowy Roku z radością cię witamy!*
> *Ty pewnie wolność dziś przynosisz nam!*
> Oh New Year, a joyous greeting we sing!
> For us, freedom and liberty you bring!
> For ever more, the bars of shame obliterate,
> And before us open the prison gate!
> > Of camps and barbed wire we have had our fill,
> > From sorrow and despair our hearts are frozen still,
> > But the smile of freedom our faces will illuminate![68]

(Henryka Karmel)

The song ended and the clapping finally died down.

Slowly, the crowd dispersed. Talking and shouting could still be heard along the long corridors. The women returned to the blocks as the supervisors attempted to restore some order to the camp. It would soon be curfew. But it was hard to stifle the excitement, and voices continued to come from the bunks until late into the night. Who would have thought that the Jews were capable of organizing such a performance!

'As a result of that "concert", we Jews gained a lot more prestige,' writes Helena Kurzman. And Malka Hottner adds: 'Anyone who was at that show will never forget New Year's Eve 1945.' Maria Lewinger recalls:

> After the show, I became famous throughout the camp. Whenever I went by, they would clear a path for me and whisper 'Socrates is coming, Socrates is coming'... The performance was a much greater success than we even imagined. We won respect and glory in the whole camp. A little while after that, one of the Polish supervisors, Anita, asked me to write a few texts for her in exchange for bread and margarine. But I refused, because she was known for her cruelty to the Jews.

And Maria's sister Fela remarks: 'I suddenly became famous. No one ever struck me, and sometimes I even got extra soup.'[69]

It was probably because of the Grand Concert that a 'rebellion' broke out among the members of the *Bunkerkommando*. The young women were sick of always singing patriotic folk tunes, and they also wanted to dance to the beat of modern music. As a result, Matylda agreed to organize a Carnival Concert which, not surprisingly, was a great success.[70]

But then it was back to routine, and they had to get up the next day and plod through the snow to work. Again they stood by the machines and toiled and toiled: the living robots, the slaves of Hasag...

Notes

1. Letter from Halina Nelken, private collection.
2. Testimony of Halina Razowski.
3. *La farandole:* a French folkdance performed in a long line. Testimonies of Bina Herstein and Felicja Karay; Ricol-London, *La Mégère de la rue Daguerre*, p. 356.
4. Brzosko-Mędryk, *Matylda*, p. 66.
5. Henryka Karmel, 'Tany,' (excerpts), ŻIH, sygn. 246, no. 166.
6. Bannet-Schäftler, *'Journal'*, p. 3.
7. Brzosko-Mędryk, *Matylda*, p. 56.
8. Testimony of Irena Senko, pp. 13–14; cf. H. Klein, 'The Search for Identity and Meaning Among Holocaust Survivors', *The Nazi Concentration Camps*, (Jerusalem: Yad Vashem, 1984), p. 428.
9. Kornblum-Rosenberger, *Neder*, pp. 76–8.
10. Karay, *Death Comes in Yellow*, pp. 221–2.
11. H. Karmel, 'W Rosz Haszana,' *Śpiew za drutami*, p. 26. *'Slichot'* is the name of the Jewish prayer for forgiveness that is recited during the days preceding Rosh Hashanah.
12. Testimony of Malka Hottner.
13. Testimonies of Eda Lewin and Paulina Buchenholz.
14. Testimony of Malka Hottner.
15. Bannet-Schäftler, *'Journal'*, p. 23.
16. Henryka Karmel speaks of Helena Brunnengraber's poems in her testimony. Their fate is unknown.
17. 'Mojej matce', in M. M. Borwicz (ed.), *Pieśń ujdzie cało*, (Warsaw: Centralna Żydowska Komisja Historyczna 1947), p. 273. (The author's name is given mistakenly as Helena Blumengraber instead of Brunnengraber).
18. Testimony of Mala Hofnung-Sperling, YV, 0-33/4652.
19. Letter from Shoshana Adler, 3 May 1992, private collection.
20. I. Karmel, 'Rocznice', *Śpiew za drutami*, p. 67.
21. Brzosko-Mędryk, *Matylda*, p. 56.
22. *Kommandos de femmes*, p. 212, n. 1.
23. R. Stramik, 'Los zakładniczki', in Teodorowicz (ed.) *Nadzieją była wolność*; cf S. Demidowicz, 'Związek pięciu stworzeń', in Chojnowski (ed.), *Dla Ciebie Polsko*, (Olsztyn, 1988), p. 49.
24. Letter from Matylda, Woliniewska, 19 April 1994, YV, 0-33/4237.
25. Brzosko-Mędryk, *Matylda*, p. 76.
26. Poland won its independence in 1918 following the First World War, after having been divided among Russia, Austria-Hungary and Germany for 123 years.
27. Brzosko-Mędryk, *Matylda*, pp. 56–60; see also Letter from Matylda, Woliniewska, 19 April 1994.
28. Brzosko-Mędryk, *Matylda*, p. 65; testimony of Jadwiga Landowska.
29. Letter from Matylda Woliniewska.
30. Zilberberg, *Mama*, p. 237.
31. Testimony of Felicja Shahar.
32. Testimony of Halina Razowski.
33. Testimony of Rina Fradkin.
34. Testimony of Felicja Karay.
35. Maria Schächter-Lewinger's journal was destroyed in circumstances that will be related below.

36. Kornblum-Rosenberger, *Neder*, p. 75, the book does not include the poems of Rut Kornblum-Rosenberger because her notebook was lost during the death-march, p. 83.
37. G. Meiersdorf, 'Haneczce', in Borwicz (ed.), *Pieśń ujdzie cało*, p. 275.
38. Brzosko-Mędryk, *Matylda*, p. 77.
39. Letter from Matylda Woliniewska, 19 April 1994.
40. Testimonies of Maria Lewinger and Malka Hottner.
41. Testimony of Ester Netzer.
42. I. Karmel, 'Makabi', *Śpiew za drutami*, p.72.; testimony of Felicja Karay.
43. Testimony of Jadwiga Landowska.
44. Letter from Matylda Woliniewska, 19 April 1994.
45. Oni pobjedili smert', Izdat, Polit. Literatury, p. 182.
46. Testimony of Maria Lewinger.
47. Brzosko-Mędryk, *Matylda*, p. 67; Letter from Matylda Woliniewska, 19 April 1994.
48. 'Bunkerkommando', writings of Matylda Woliniewska, YV, 0-33/4237.
49. Brzosko-Mędryk, *Matylda*, p. 70.
50. Testimonies of Maria Lewinger; Felicja Karay and Ester Netzer.
51. Bernadac, *Kommandos de femmes*, pp. 206–10.
52. Testimonies of Luna Kaufman, Helena Zorski and Henryka Karmel.
53. Bernadac, *Kommandos de femmes*, pp. 210–11.
54. Testimony of Maria Lewinger.
55. Testimonies of Henryka Karmel and Eda Jewin.
56. Testimony of Maria Lewinger.
57. Testimony of Felicja Karay. (Malka Zuckerbrot tended to stutter when she was excited.)
58. Testimonies of Rina Fradkin and Henryka Karmel.
59. No single description of the entire 'concert' exists. The following is reconstructed from several testimonies.
60. Testimony of Felicja Karay.
61. Testimony of Eda Jewin.
62. The words are derived from the testimony of Rina Fradkin.
63. The text of the play is derived from excerpts in the testimonies of Maria Lewinger, Rina Fradkin and Ester Netzer.
64. This section was reconstructed on the basis of the poem 'O kraju niemieckim' by H. Karmel: ŻIH, *sygn*. 246, nr 103.
65. H. Karmel, 'Rachunek', *Śpiew za drutami*, p. 38; in some unknown manner, this poem also reached Auschwitz as the work of 'an anonymous woman': see Mark Ber, *Megilat Auschwitz* (The Hebrew) Auschwitz Scroll, (Tel Aviv: Sifriat Poalim, 1978), p. 23.
66. Testimonies of Malka Hottner; Felicja Karay and Maria Lewinger.
67. Testimony of Rina Fradkin; letter from Shoshana Adler, 3 May 1992.
68. The song appears in the testimony of Ester Netzer.
69. Testimonies of Felicja Karay, Maria Lewinger and Helena Kurzman.
70. 'The Carnival Concert', Matylda Woliniewska Collection, YV, 0-33/4237.

8 Freedom Draws Near

The Front moves closer

One evening, a small group of women was gathered around the table in a corner of the block. Ester Nessel and Fela Zilberstein were there, along with a few others. On the table was a large sheet of paper covered with figures and letters. A tiny bowl had been readied. They were going to have a séance. It was time:

We put our fingers on the bowl, and when it started to move, we called on the spirits. There was Theodore Herzl, and then the late Polish leader Józef Piłsudski. We even called up the spirit of the Polish poet Adam Mickiewicz. 'We asked them all the same question: When will the war be over?' The bowl spun from letter to letter. We followed it with bated breath. And it always showed the same date: 8–9 May.'[1]

Other inmates looked for the answer in cards.

Some of the women really believed; others just played with the hope. But the shelling went on. There were nights when there was no point trying to get to sleep: twice they had to run back and forth to the shelters. By now, it was all merely part of camp routine, but there were also some surprises. Every now and then fliers were tossed from the planes.[2] Of course they were not allowed to pick them up, but sometimes they did. One was a pamphlet about Hitler's declaration: 'Give me ten years and Germany will be unrecognizable!' (How right he was!) The flier contained a list of the German cities that had already been destroyed and occupied by the Allies. 'Our hearts were filled with joy when we read the fliers. We knew now that the war was drawing to a close. But – would the Germans allow us to remain alive?'[3]

Figure 8.1 Playing cards smuggled into Hasag-Leipzig by prisoners.

Source: Private collection.

On 27 February 1945 English fliers rained down on the camp claiming that Germany would be obliged to compensate the nations that had suffered under its occupation and would be required to repay the entire cost of the war.[4] It was the talk of the camp, particularly among the Jewish inmates: even if we survive the war, will the Germans ever be capable of making amends for their atrocious crimes? What kind of compensation were they talking about? No reparations could ever atone for murder and torture; there were some crimes you could not put a value on:

> And who will restore the years I have lost,
> My youth, my eyes' sparkle, my laugh so gay,
> Bright dreams conceived in pain,
> Like a distant sound that dies away.
> Who will return the peace to my home,

The aroma of the Sabbath and holiday delights,
Who will compensate for my torment so dread,
The tears in the sleepless nights...
Write this, gentlemen, under the heading of 'lost':
Laughter, love, happiness, dreams.
Perhaps they'll return my youth that has past,
Perhaps the price of tears they'll redeem...[5]

(Henryka Karmel)

Many voiced the opinion that no compensation of any kind should be accepted from the Germans; rather, vengeance should be exacted at all costs. This brought an immediate response: could any sort of revenge possibly approximate the immeasurable scope of the Holocaust? True, the Allied planes were destroying Germany, but that was part of their own war, not something they were doing in the name of the Jews! Would Jews even know how to take their revenge? This became a central issue in the impassioned arguments that broke out whenever the women got together. Everyone was waiting for the Day of Judgement:

And when the day comes for revenge
The sky in clouds will hide its head,
The sun will fade in distant mists,
Fearful of the voices of vengeance so dread...
   And when the day comes for revenge
   The earth its turning will cease to perform,
   The sea will silence its echoing sighs,
   At the sight of the fury erupting like a storm!
And when the day comes for revenge
The universe will halt in place,
Worse than death the terror then,
Like a *shofar* the wind will rage
When the day comes for revenge...[6]

(Ilona Karmel)

Not all the prisoners were capable of comprehending the full significance of the apocalyptic picture. Those who gathered in less 'sophisticated' circles, who were used to expressing their feelings in a more prosaic manner, sought solace in poets like Gela Meiersdorf, who articulated their hopes in her own inimical way:

> Maybe, God willing, there will come a day,
> When from this camp we are finally free
> And can live a life of freedom and liberty.
> Then to all we will tell
> Of the German brutality,
> How they beat us endlessly,
> How in the wind and storm and rain,
> We stood in roll-call hours on end,
> On our knees, they did command,
> And our hair shaved by their hand.
> Yet if we survive somehow,
> On all that we hold dear we vow,
> Our revenge on them will come,
> With no mercy, until it's done.[7]
>
> (Gela Meiersdorf)

The will to survive was invariably linked with the hope of locating other family members. Some even tried looking for them in other camps using official channels, through the mail. In theory, the prisoners were allowed to correspond with the outside world, and permitted to send and receive two letters or postcards a month. Even food parcels were allowed. But the Jews had no one to write to. Ela Wachtel, however, knew that her husband was in Buchenwald, and in February 1945, she sent him a postcard:

My dear husband!
I wish to know how you are: are you well? Everything is okay with me. I am working and I am well. Please, write me. Love and kisses. Yours,

Lusia

The postcard was returned to sender, together with the note: 'There is no Wachtel Simche in Buchenwald camp' (*Im K. L. Bu sitzt nicht ein* [Wachtel Simche] – see Figure 8.2).[8] On the other hand, Sara Albirt, the daughter of Elias Albirt, the former 'camp elder' of Skarżysko-Kamienna and now in

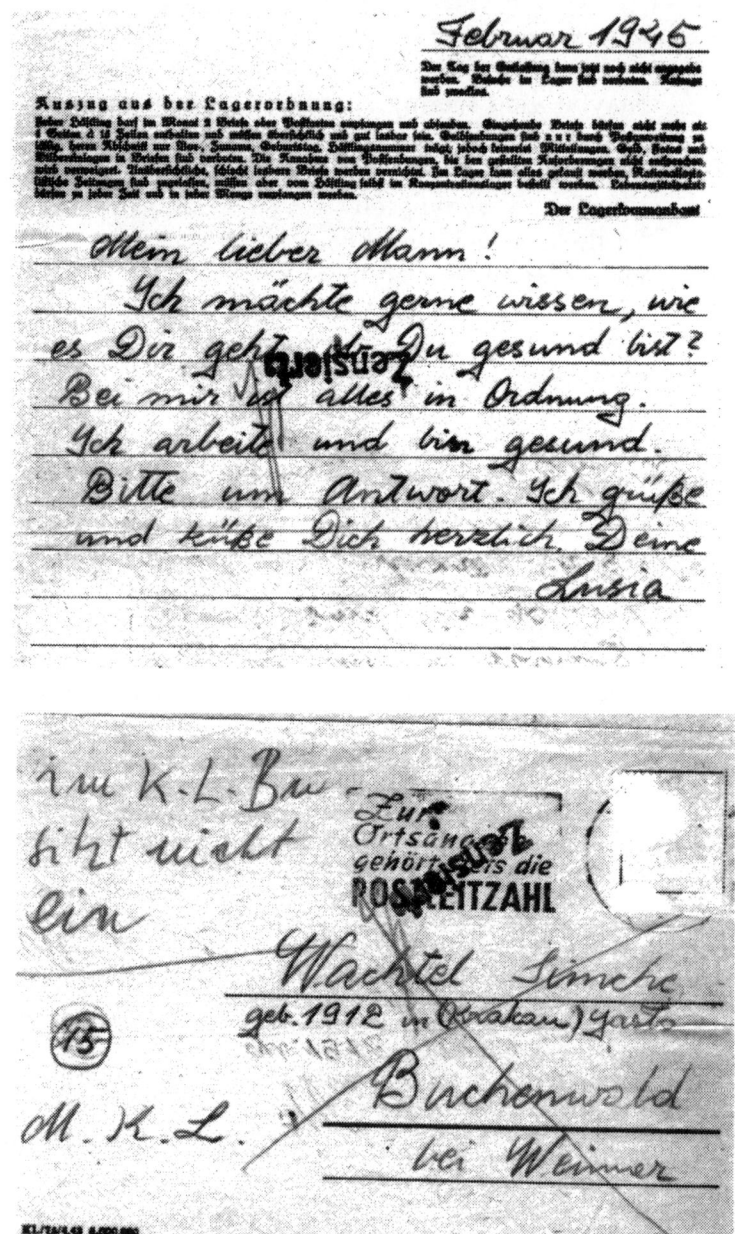

Figure 8.2 Letter from Ella Margulies-Wachtel to her husband at Buchenwald, written on an official Leipzig Camp form.

Source: Margulies-Timberg Collection, YV, 0-48/47d-3.

Buchenwald, was blessed with a miracle. In early January, she received letters from her father, and later even two parcels.[9]

The inmates with no chance of such joyous events went on with their 'ordinary' lives. What could they do to keep up their spirits but get together in the evening and console each other? Some optimists even kept up their language studies, as did Sara Shalem, who taught herself English and instructed two groups in Hebrew. She used plenty of Zionist songs in her lessons, too, believing that 'all this contributed a lot to raising morale'.[10] Hanka Brandwejn, who arrived in Leipzig with her two sisters, also organized 'get-togethers' on her bunk where they preferred popular Polish songs that had suddenly taken on new meaning, such as: 'Only in a mother's heart does love live forever', or 'How quickly life goes by'.[11]

There were quite a number of educated women among the Jewish prisoners who could tell stories of faraway places, their travels and studies. Anna Hauser, known for her wit, always had a rapt audience. 'That helped me a lot to increase my education,' recalls Luna Kaufman. 'We wanted to maintain the sense that we were cultured people whatever the cost, because the conditions we lived in were created to break our spirit. There was no way we could change the physical situation, so at least we fought for our souls.'[12] Heated arguments sometimes broke out in the wake of school-day memories: What good were all the lovely things the teachers taught us now?

You taught us to look for ideals
In the words of the writers and poets,
To soar on the wings of poetry
And strive to plumb life's secrets.
    With the word *'humanus'* you charmed our souls,
    You commanded us kneel before the great lofty pearls!
    Thus now it is so hard to bear our torment
    Thus now I am helpless, alone in the world.
You should have rushed out in secret
To teach us how with both hands to grab life!
And to strike a sharp blow, right between the eyes
A blow to life – boldly to triumph!
To teach us to shout out loud, to be heard

To break through each barrier with the force of the flood,
To trample the others, so we won't be trampled,
To accustom our eyes to the terror of blood!
Why did you plant vain yearnings in our soul,
O wise, learned teachers wherever you may be!
As you fostered the truth did you really not know,
There is no place in this world where humans can be?[13]

(Henryka Karmel)

Had the women lost all belief in universal ideals? Now that these Jewish youngsters had had a taste of 'real life' in the most appalling sense of the word, now that they were left with no family and no home and were forced to fight constantly just to survive for one more day, did they become cynical, did they lose forever any hope for a better world? Although it is hard to give a short answer to such a complex question, without a doubt, it would not be a simple yes. Without hearing one of the most popular poems written in the Leipzig camp, 'To the German People', it would be impossible to appreciate just how surprising the response of these young people was.

The poem is associated with a dramatic incident that remains etched in the minds of the survivors. As usual, one Sunday a group of prisoners gathered for an evening of poetry in the hall next to the block. And as usual, a few Polish guests were present. At the request of the audience, Fela Schächter recited:

Hey you – are you asleep???
The old world is collapsing with a roar,
The day of freedom is coming and calling to you!
Can you hear it?
How it throbs and bangs to the beat of the 'Marseillaise',
The red star is burning so bright,
By its power, Soviet tanks burst through!
You don't want freedom? O but it will come!
And as a gift it will bring life to you!
But you, you fools, are you asleep?

There was deathly silence in the hall. Everyone was listening with rapt attention. All of a sudden, the

Commandant walked in! 'We all held our breath. The Commandant didn't speak Polish, but... how would Fela react? We were scared to death! How well I remember that moment! She went on as if nothing had happened. I remember her clenching her fist so tightly.'[14]

So – arise!!!
Prepare your feverish hearts for the day,
To the 'Marseillaise' rhythm they will beat as one!
Open wide the gates of your soul
Like a lover opens the door for his love to come.
    Do you not want freedom, the gift of God,
    Do you suddenly avert your eyes from his light?
    Are you frightened by the flag as red as blood?
    The world is lying in blood of a red more bright!
So – arise!
Forward march! The workers in front!
For on every corner in Germany
Is a Bastille, being torn down this very day!
With fists of steel on its gates we pound,
And shatter as well its barricades!
Forward march! Who is brave enough to lead the way
In holy frenzy, a frenzy so fine
To raise the flag '*Fraternité, Egalité*'!
    And then all together, large and small,
    Of marble and steel the building we'll raise
    And engraved in gold for ever more:
    The one and only, the eternal, '*Fraternité*'![15]

(Henryka Karmel)

The Commandant left without a word. 'For several days afterward's we were still afraid the incident would not end well. There was also the fear that someone would inform on us. It was said that if she recited poems about the Russians coming to liberate us, they would kill her for it.'[16] The poem does not appear in the collection entitled *Śpiew za drutami*, but it has been preserved in several testimonies.[17] Many years later, Felicja Shahar, who still remembered the occasion clearly, wrote to the reciter of the poem: 'We saw you clenching your fists and we heard your loud voice... We were terrified! It was an act of supreme courage on your part!'[18] To the reciter's great fortune, no one informed on her and no trouble ensued from the incident.

Where is home?

The days of March 1945 passed slowly. Starvation was worse again. Although the younger women were the most severely afflicted, the older prisoners (thirty-five and over) also showed clear signs of emaciation. Anna Hauser was barely able to walk. The petite figure of her friend Roza Bauminger was even tinier than usual. Henia and Ilona Karmel watched with increasing alarm as their mother's strength dwindled. Despite her condition, she kept trying to trick her daughters into taking her bread ration on the pretext that she 'got it from someone in the factory'. Once when Ilona caught her out, she literally force-fed the bread to her mother. As she knew all too well, there was still a danger of 'silent' selections aimed at weeding out the sick and debilitated.[19]

Every rumour sent shivers downs the spines of the infirmary patients. Beds were set up in the cellar for the ones who could not walk on their own so as to save the nurses the trouble of having to carry them downstairs each time the air raid siren went off. It was whispered that the Germans intended to blow up the camp. What would happen to them? Nobody knew. Meanwhile, anyone still in good enough health dragged herself to work. In the plant, the Germans were edgier than ever; in the camp, the overseers took out their anxiety on the prisoners. 'Routine' life went on... another day, and another. Would they make it?

The inmates banded together to improve their chances of survival. Those who were alone formed their own 'camp families'. Felicja Blum, Towa Zilberberg and Henia Strelski did this, as did many others. Regina Ohrenstein, whose ward Edyta had been sent away on the children's transport,[20] joined forces with other young women all of whom came from Kraków, among them Fela Goldwasser and Rywka Jucker.[21] The members of these 'camp families' shared not only their rations, but also memories, hopes, and poems:

How good after so many years it will be,
To return to the land of our past,
To sense the familiar smell of a homeland,
In our own home to live free at last.
Yes, we have a home, a home that is ours,
So pain and tears behind you cast,
For from afar for us it waits,
How good to be free in our own home at last.[22]

(Anon.)

This simple, anonymous poem invariably triggered a debate over the painful question: 'If we live to see liberation, where will our home be?' Opinions were divided, ideological differences that were reflected in the poems of the Karmel sisters. Ilona expressed faith in Zionism, believing her home to be linked with the eternal Jewish nation, despite assimilation:

I have been won over by the mighty power
Concealed in the chain of black letters,
Seduced by the melodic sorrow of the prayer,
And the divine majestic call of the *shofar*.
I have been sworn for eternity by the glow of Sabbath
    candles,
Commanded to defend and preserve them for evermore,
For 'your home is here!'
I have been blinded by the brilliant white of the holy texts,
Like the wind I soar as I recite the words:
'*Shema Yisrael!*'
I have been bewitched by the charms of the ancient prayer,
Conquered by the legend of the Maccabees for all eternity,
Like angels they surround me,
Confound my steps and bind my thoughts,
Like a wall they stand before my dreams...
'Remember, your home is here!' – they call to me...[23]

(Ilona Karmel)

The 'Zionist faction' included former members of the Akiva youth movement, representatives of nationalist religious Zionism led by Malka Hottner, former students of Beit Ya'akov, and quite a few assimilated Jews as well whose hopes of living a peaceful life in the Diaspora were crushed by the Holocaust. Nevertheless, many educated women had not yet found a solution to the question of identity. They had a profound appreciation for Polish literature and poetry on the one hand, and a dread of the anti-Semitism that put paid to any chance of social integration on the other. These mixed feelings are very aptly expressed in Henryka Karmel's poem 'To Poland', which even the *blokowa* Niunia found moving:[24]

> You wouldn't let me love your open fields
> Your houses of prayer or your cottage homes –
> The clear pure water of the Visla,
> Or the echo that through the hilltops roams.
> You wouldn't let me love the sea waves
> The Ojcow rocks or grotto caves
> You heeded not, O Poland, my loving cries,
> Scorned and mocked, unheard my longing sighs... [25]

What comfort remained to ease this despair? Only memories of their family home, a carefree childhood, relatives, holidays. As Passover drew near, the Kraków group decided to arrange a 'Seder' of sorts. When they had all gathered in their customary spot, one of the Polish prisoners asked to join them. How odd! The Polish block had organized its own religious ceremony in honour of Easter, with hundreds of inmates clustering around a symbolic tomb of Jesus.[26] What did she want here? Rena Cypres eventually convinced her to go away so as not to raise suspicions that she might herself be Jewish.[27]

The 'Seder' began with singing. For *matzot* they had sliced beets, and for wine, 'coffee' set aside from breakfast. Henryka Karmel and Rena Taubenblatt recited the main sections of the Haggadah from memory in Hebrew and in Polish (How very appropriate were those words written thousands of years before!). Now they were brought up to date. Instead of Egypt, there was Germany, and SS officers instead of Egyptians: 'We were slaves to pharaoh in Egypt... and now we are slaves to Hasag in Nazi Germany, and they afflicted us and imposed upon us hard labour... Hear, O Lord, and bring all the plagues down on Germany, may they be punished with blood and fire and pillars of smoke!' (The air-raid siren sounded. Blood and fire and pillars of smoke!) 'Hear, O Lord, the cry of your nation and bring us out of accursed Germany, from darkness to light, from bondage to freedom, and lead us into the Land of Israel!' No prayer had ever been uttered with deeper feeling. And then they sang: 'We were slaves, and now free men, free men ... '[28]

Next, Ilona read out her story *'Talith'* (prayer shawl). It had a tragic prologue:

Once, when crates of rusty ammunition arrived at the plant, the German supervisor gave us rags to clean them with. Ilona also got a scrap of white cloth. Suddenly we saw her turn as pale as a ghost. She held the rag out to us and whispered, in shock: 'Girls, do you know what this is? It's a *talith*, look, you can still see the blood stains on it! Like the stains on my father's *talith* when they murdered him ...' She didn't want to use it to clean the ammunition. And now we were listening to the story about her father, how he prayed on holidays, wrapped in his white *talith*.[29]

The religious women tried their best not to eat unleavened bread during the Passover holiday. Towa Zilberberg traded her daily bread ration to a Polish prisoner in exchange for a small bag of rice, and 'cooked' two spoonfuls each day in a can on the radiator.[30] Those who had no other way to celebrate the holiday, sang the famous 'Slavery Tango': 'Freedom calls, of freedom I dream'.[31] The time had not yet come for them to have to worry about going home ...

Expulsion from Paradise

In the early days of April 1945, transports from other camps closer to the Eastern Front began arriving in Leipzig. One held a group of women prisoners from Auschwitz that had been sent to Ravensbrück, from there to Malchow, and two months later to Leipzig.[32] Among the women who came, there was also Halina Nelken. After recovering from their astonishment when receiving the thick soup, a few of the 'new ones' were recruited by the Polish *Blokowa* to clean toilets. 'Why them,' writes Halina, 'they are slaves like us, and yet they mock the "Jewish work" of exhauted women?' When Halina fell and became soiled with excrement, she said to the Polish women, that this was a good sign: she would survive the war and receive great honour. The embarrassed *Blokowa* took Halina to the shack to clean up. On her way back, Halina met a group of Polish women, who were discussing a celebration for 3 May. (On 3 May 1791, the Polish *Sejm* [parliament] approved the first liberal constitution.) Halina, an expert in Polish literature, offered the amazed organizers plenty of literary suggestions. As a result the *Blokowa* invited her to participate in the show. (However, the camp was evacuated in April.) This incident resulted in the friendship between Halina and the *Blokowa*, and they even met after the war.[33]

The inmates were still being marched to the plant every day, where it was rumoured that the city would be surrendered to the Allies without a fight and that the factories would continue to operate, and so the authorities pretended that work was proceeding at full swing. The labour itself no longer had any purpose: the only thing that mattered was to delay departure of the *Volkssturm* (civil guard) for the front for as long as possible. The camp was pervaded by an 'eleventh-hour' mood. It was said that the Americans were only 12 kilometres from Leipzig. Would they get there in time to liberate the prisoners? Who would strike first, the Allies or the SS? From some unknown source the rumour spread that Commandant Plaul had opposed the order to exterminate the prisoner population before the city was occupied. Others claimed he had efused to transfer the women to Dachau.[34] Tension was high; no one really knew anything for certain.

Matylda Woliniewska suggested they establish a prisoner committee representing all nationalities. It would be charged with maintaining order in the camp, preventing any incidents of kangaroo courts, looting, or anarchy, and conducting negotiations with the Germans and the Allies 'who are moving so slowly!'[35] The Poles voiced the loudest objections, the French agreed to set up a network of liaisons, and the Russian prisoners of war, who were already very well organized, were unsure what to do. 'On 12 April, I spoke with the Karmel sisters (I knew them previously only by their poems) who were chosen by the Jews to represent them,' Matylda relates in her memoirs. 'They opposed my proposal to vest responsibilities in "rebellious elements" in order to force them to toe the line. In their opinion, such functions should only be granted to women of moral authority.'[36]

All attempts to organize themselves were undermined by the rapid progress of events. The women assigned to the sewing shop noticed that the overseers were frantically at work on civilian clothes. In the air raid of Tuesday, 10 April, a bomb fell on the camp wall, damaging the water and electric mains, killing one Russian and injuring several Jewish women, among them Dora Glücksman, who remained in the cellar with the other casualties. The following day there was again heavy shelling nearby. The camp air raid siren was out of commission, and it was obvious that preparations for evacuation were being stepped up. Yet when several of the functionaries asked the *oberka* for permission for the women to hang on to their winter coats, she replied that they had to be stored away for the following winter![37]

It was 12 April. The factory was closed down, and all its supplies, including shoes, soap, etc., had been emptied out by the workers. Tension in the camp was very high. The inmates had received no bread for three days! They were barely able to stand for lack of sleep and nourishment. That night, the floodgates burst: hoards of prisoners descended on the food stores, breaking down the doors, screaming and fighting among themselves. Each woman grabbed whatever she could find; all the potatoes and beet went, since there was no bread to be had. Chaos reigned. Neither the local police nor the SS officers could bring the rioting masses under control. The next day, a Friday, the entire camp was made to stand in a penal roll-call for two hours.

On the night of 12 April, several men managed to escape from a nearby prison camp before its evacuation, reaching the 'Drugie Pole' and sneaking into the women's camp where they were hidden by Polish inmates. Their whereabouts were known to only a very few. This escapade saved their lives, as the entire men's camp was burned to the ground after evacuation of the last 100 prisoners. It was not the only incident of this sort. The Germans locked 330 prisoners in a barracks in the Tekla camp in Leipzig before splashing it with benzine and setting fire to it. What were they planning for the women here? Several inmates reported seeing cables stretched around the camp. Would they blow them all up at the last minute?[38]

The evacuation began on 13 April 1945. An extra bit of food was distributed, but things were still so chaotic that some women got double rations and others got none at all. They were given margarine and a spoonful of canned goods here and there. The lucky ones got bread. In the evening, the first groups were organized for departure. The evacuation was to take place in stages. The Jews were lined up separately in two groups.[39] The first group was sent out, with the second following some time later. The overseers scurried around to the very end, dragging out everyone they could find: 'Fast! Out! *Schneller!*' It was no longer possible to make a precise count of each group of prisoners as they left.

They marched out of the camp. 'We passed the railroad tracks. Cars were standing there, looking empty. But were they? In the last selection they had again weeded out the sick and the debilitated. But the front was so near now that there was nowhere to send them. They had been left in the cars to freeze to death.'[40] They walked on. Matylda was in one group of Poles, carrying the whole of their 'precious cargo': the texts of the 'Bunkerkommando'. Danuta Brzosko-Mędryk and most of the Polish women from Majdanek were with her. Joanna Szumańska and Niunia were there too. The French block marched close by. The Russians had been lined up separately. All of a sudden, Commandant Plaul's car appeared in the street. He rode slowly past, reviewing the ranks, making sure that everything was proceeding according to plan.[41]

The sick, those who had just given birth, and several women from the internal administration, among them Zina Bragińska and Maryla Reich, remained in camp. At the last minute, Maryla had approached the Karmel sisters and Rena Taubenblatt, proposing that they stay behind with her and hide, but they were afraid to risk it and refused. Irena Pełka, however, took her up on the offer, and the two women hid in the cellar. A few dozen others concealed themselves anywhere that seemed safe. A commando of 200 women, including several dozen Jews, spent two more days clearing out whatever was left in the camp. As Genia Grosswirt remembers it, the Poles and French were charged with cleaning the canteen and kitchen, while the Jews were sent to tidy up the blocks. It turned out to be a lucrative assignment, since the women were able to squirrel away extra food. The cartons of food and wares remaining in the canteen were loaded onto wagons and sent out two days later with the commando to join the groups that had left earlier.[42]

The question of their impending fate gnawed at the prisoners who had stayed behind. With no commanders left, Zina Bragińska continued to run the camp. Shortly afterwards, the Americans arrived in trucks and took them all to a hotel in the centre of town. But the sick were left there with two nurses, Irena Pełka and Elzbieta Panczyszyn. Two days passed and there were no more medicines and no food. Suddenly, American journalists appeared to 'liberate' the single American prisoner from the camp. She was the wife of a French general in de Gaulle's headquarters. It was only thanks to them that ambulances were brought to take the patients to a German hospital. The few other women still in the camp were transferred into town. Some time later they received the shocking news that the camp building had been blown up.[43]

Those remaining in Leipzig had no idea what had happened to the prisoners who had been evacuated. They marched on and on endlessly. The streets were quiet, with not a single living soul out on them, and – how strange – no shelling. All around them were ruins and destruction, hardly one building left intact, and here and there fires burning. Flanked by overseers and armed SS officers, the prisoners marched in rows of five, each wrapped in a blanket, constantly prodded to go faster, for the guards were afraid of an air raid – '*Schneller!*'

The dull thud of hundreds of wooden clogs broke the silence of the night. They were marching to an unknown destination, an unknown future. Expelled from paradise to set out on their final path, on the march to freedom...

The Death-March

I marched along with all the others. In a bag I held on to as tight as I could were all my possessions: a few lumps of margarine, a rag that served as a towel, a comb and hair pins I had made from wire. We walked. They led us down streets and roads and even forest paths. Rain mixed with snow began to fall. We had left Leipzig so long ago – how many days had we been walking? Three? Five? Ten? Kilometre after kilometre went by, and we had no idea where we were... I was terribly hungry and thirsty. It was worst at night. The cold pierced to our bones; our blankets had long ago become soaking wet. They kept changing the guards and making us go faster and faster, not letting up. They hardly gave us any time to sleep. We walked day and night. The girls dragged me along, because I would doze off as I walked... I dreamt there was suddenly a wall in front of me and I couldn't get through... It was horrible...

So it was for Malka Zuckerbrot, who only eight months before had sat on her pallet in a clean dress, thrilled to be feasting on a thick slice of bread spread with salad... When was that? It felt like years ago. Now there was only rain, snow, sun, more rain, and walking, walking, walking. The SS overseers had taken off long ago, leaving the guards who fired on anyone who could no longer keep up. The way was lined with corpses, some of them male, that had been shoved into the ditches on the side of the road. A feeble dying man lay in one, and as they passed, an SS officer remarked: 'Look at him. He's about to die and he might have been a free man tomorrow.'[44]

At first, each national group marched separately, then they were all mixed in together, and eventually were divided again. They covered about 30 kilometres a day. Periodically, the guards stopped to rest in a building along the way, while the women lay down in the mud at the side of the road. Thousands of women in striped dresses black with dirt and covered in lice, their faces as pale as ghosts and their eyes revealing the terror of death. 'And so we dragged ourselves down the roads, like phantoms from another planet'.[45]

The food they had been given for the march was soon gone.

> When we passed fields of crops, we threw ourselves on
> them, hoping to find a potato, a carrot, a beet. The guards
> would fire on us, and several women were invariably left
> lying there... The lucky ones ate the vegetables – raw
> obviously. We walked for maybe more than a week before
> we got any food. It was a Red Cross ambulance that gave us
> porridge without salt or butter. It saved our lives, because
> we couldn't digest anything else. We didn't understand
> why we weren't free if the Red Cross was in Germany.[46]

Still, many of the women fell ill with dysentery. Regina felt
the disease sapping her strength and was sure her end was
near. Those who spent too much time in the bushes at the side
of the road were pistol-whipped if they were lucky enough
not to be shot on the spot. Unexpectedly, one of the
supervisors who noticed Regina's distress ordered her on to a
wagon. What could have awoken such humane feelings in the
heart of the callous *Aufzejerka*? Could it have been fear? 'They
were afraid of the shelling. They pushed in among us and
covered their heads with rags so they couldn't be identified
from the air.[47]

How much longer would this nightmare go on? On 17
April, the line halted in a pasture near a woods. There were
Jewish, Polish and French women there, maybe 2,000 in all.
They grabbed at the nettles and ran to the trees to gather wood
for a fire. But there was a fence around the woods and the
shooting started immediately.

> Lord, so many were wounded! They were bringing another
> one... a Polish girl shot in the back. There was nothing we
> could do. We left her at the side of the road. We got to the
> Elba River, but the bridge had been blown up so the
> Germans waited for the ferry. It took a very long time
> because we were such a large group. In the meantime,
> Commandant Plaul showed up and started organizing
> supplies. They brought potatoes and rice from the villages
> nearby, and the really fortunate women even got a spoonful
> of some canned goods. But there wasn't enough food for all

of us. We tried to light a fire, without waiting for permission this time. Again they started firing on us. Our departure from that place was punctuated by the groans of dying inmates . . . [48]

Romualda Stramik recalls:

We moved like sleepwalkers. We no longer noticed the corpses lining the road or the shots being fired. I barely dragged myself along on the edge of the group. In the first light I saw some young man lying in a ditch and a woman kneeling beside him and staring at him helplessly. Suddenly she let out a shriek: 'Is that you, my son?' The man raised his head and called: 'Mama!' and fell back again. I heard two shots. I got back in line and crawled along with the rest of the women . . . The Germans kept changing the direction we were walking in. They wanted to fall into English or American hands. They were terrified of the Russians. [49]

Why didn't the SS simply kill all the prisoners? Romualda Stramik's contention that 'they kept us walking in order to finish off as many as possible' seems unlikely. The real reason would seem to be much simpler. First of all, the SS were never given the order to kill the prisoners, and their ingrained discipline made it impossible for them to take upon themselves the responsibility for such an action. Second, to the very last minute they remained fearful of being recruited to 'defend the Fatherland' against the Russians, and thus preferred to keep the prisoners alive. In the end, Plaul ordered that the women be divided up into smaller groups of 200–300, and sent each in a different direction. 'From time to time, American planes circled overhead, and then the SS officers would conceal themselves among us, even putting on the prisoners' striped uniform.' [50] Their attitude to the inmates never changed. They killed as many as they could. There were however, one or two exception.

One of these was an old guard called 'Dziadek' (Grandpa) who kept assuring the women that the front was getting very near and they would soon be free. [51] But the others were different. 'It's hard to understand what made them guard us so closely, not taking their eyes off us even now, when they knew for certain what was really happening at the front.'[52] Tired and hungry themselves, the guards often begged food from houses along the way, but refused to allow the local population to feed the prisoners. And if they got any beets or potatoes, they wouldn't hand them to the inmates; they would throw them on the ground the way you feed dogs, just to enjoy watching them trample each other to get to them.

The civilians treated them no better.

The German farmers would flee in terror when they saw us coming. In general, they were hostile toward us. Several times I saw written on the walls of buildings: 'The Jews are our misfortune' (*Die Juden sind unser Unglück*). They were afraid to come out of their houses. At most, they would set buckets of water for us along the road, but the SS men with us would knock them over on purpose.[53]

Did the Germans feel a sense of guilt at the sight of this parade of starving skeletons staggering through the mud and snow? Was the phrase that appears in several testimonies going through their minds at that time: *Das wird unsere ewige Schande sein!*' (This will be our eternal disgrace!)[54]

These testimonies are also confirmed by German sources. The German journalist Heiner Lichtenstein relates:

It was in April 1945. I was in a wagon, riding with my mother from our farm toward Leipzig; ruins everywhere... On the edge of the city we passed a group of women being quickly marched along the wall... I couldn't see who they were. I only remember that they were all wearing striped dresses [KZ uniforms]. My mother, horrified, refused to look at them, and said: 'The world will not forgive us this disgrace for a thousand years!' I was thirteen, and didn't ask what she meant...[55]

The condition of Eda's group got progressively worse. She herself learned to sleep as she walked, her friends propping her up on each side. Then they would switch. Fela Schächter got excruciatingly painful tendonitis in one leg, and if it hadn't been for her sisters supporting her weight, would have ended her life in a ditch. Anna Hauser grew so weak that one day she simply sat down and couldn't get up again. Her friends managed to gather a few twigs for a fire so they could heat up some water with a couple of crumbs of margarine for her. When the damp twigs wouldn't catch, Maria Schächter decided to sacrifice the journal she had written in Skarżysko and Leipzig, the sketch 'Behind the Great Curtains', composed after the Grand Concert, and some other texts.[56] The fire caught and Anna's life was saved. Human life was worth more than commemoration. How many died along the way? No one can say for sure. In some groups where 150 had started out, only 65 women were still alive two weeks later.[57]

In April 1945, thousands of prisoners from every camp were walking along the roads of Germany. The women from Leipzig encountered several groups of men, no less emaciated and debilitated than they were. Miracles sometimes happened as well. On one occasion, Rut Kornblum and her friends halted not far from a small group of men when all of a sudden they heard one of them call out her name. Startled, she approached and was told by a prisoner she had never seen before that he had been in Mauthausen with her father, who had asked him to call out her name whenever he saw a Jewish woman. And imagine! He'd already found her! Rut wept with joy. Her father was alive! There was now more reason than ever to keep up the struggle to survive. Lola Adler was blessed with a similar miracle when she ran into a group of men from Gross Rosen and one of them brought greetings from her father.[58] And on they walked. Another day, another night.

> We completely lost all sense of time. To this day I can't understand the mysterious power that kept us going. Was it the will to live that had become so deeply rooted in our hearts? Once when we were crawling alongside a dirt road, airplanes overhead tossed fliers on us. They said in several languages: 'Hold on, we will soon come to liberate you.'[59]

But maybe they should follow the advice of one of the SS guards: 'Try to escape when you get near the front!'[60] But who had the strength to run? And where would they go?

222

April was almost over. The first to take off were the SS officers. Halina relates:

> One night we heard that the guards had run off. The girls didn't know what to do. So we decided to split up from the rest of the group and set out on our own. There were six of us, including me, Wanda Blay and Stella Kestenbaum. When we saw a house, we went in and the Germans we met were very frightened. Nevertheless, they let us wash and gave us hot soup. But that night the head of the village came and declared that we couldn't stay there and would have to go to a refugee camp. On the way we met a group of Poles who took us to an abandoned villa. There we found food and clothes and were reborn. Finally, our torments were over.[61]

Not everyone was as lucky. Some groups realized that they were walking in circles because all the German escape routes had been cut off. Near the town of Strela, the guards let a group of 300 rest in a barn, but when they tried to chase them out again in the morning, the Russian prisoners among them convinced the others not to comply. The SS men dragged 12 women outside, slaughtered them, and threatened to burn the barn down, but they had run out of time. By morning, Russians soldiers had already reached the town. The story of Commandant Plaul also ends in Strela: he was taken prisoner by the Russians, although several Jewish inmates appealed for his release on the grounds that he had treated them well.[62] Their pleas were ignored, and his fate is unknown. In the final accounting, however, Commandant Plaul could enter his tolerable treatment of the prisoners in the 'credit' column.

In some instances, the Death-March went on for more than two weeks. Liberation was met in a variety of strange circumstances. Several women were captured by a Ukrainian company near the Elba, and were only saved from drowning at the hands of the soldiers at the very last minute when some Russians showed up.[63] Those who escaped along the way were helped by Polish labourers or prisoners of war from various countries. At one point, Irma Neuman and a friend of hers decided to leave the Jewish group and join the Russians.

The Germans kept them walking for another whole night until they finally let them rest in a hay barn. They kept them there for three days, bringing them a little soup and some potatoes from the local farmers.

We were getting more and more apprehensive from minute to minute. You could actually feel it in the air. All of a sudden, there was great excitement among the Russians. When an SS man came in and announced that we would be moving out soon, he was met with mocking laughter, and ran out. Fifteen minutes later, an armored car with Russian soldiers showed up, and the women nearly tore them apart in their elation.[64]

Apparently, some of the SS officers thought it judicious to hide from the prisoners their intent to flee, and they all seem to have employed the same stratagem. They locked the women in a barn somewhere, changed into civilian clothes, and took off. That was what happened, for example, to Malka Zuckerbrot and her friends. When they finally got the door open, they couldn't believe their eyes: the SS were gone! They were afraid to leave the barn until hunger got the better of them and they went out in search of food. A few German deserters passed and tossed them some dry bread. One of the women threw it back, shouting: 'You had better save every crumb now; you're going to need it!' It was only in the early morning of 23 April that Russian soldiers appeared and gave them the first bread they had seen in two weeks.

In the chaotic conditions, each of the groups found itself in a different place on the day of liberation. Some of the fortunate ones got a bit of help from the local farmers in the form of food or old clothes.[65] A transit camp for refugees of all types was set up in the city of Oschatz, and some of the Jewish women went there for lack of any alternative. Matylda also found her way there with a group of other Poles. As they were doling out food, one German woman was heard to remark to another: 'Look at the evil in the eyes of those women!'[66]

The Schächter sisters were liberated near the village of Olganetz.

When the Americans came, they sent our group (which included Eda Lewin, Tamara Shapiro and Hela Feig) to the house of the village elder, which turned out to be a villa with every comfort. The head of the village put us in the attic, because we were covered with lice. No one offered us fresh clothes or blankets. They brought us soup in buckets, as if we were cows. We lay there like that for several days. When there were Americans around, we got salt in our soup. When they left, there was no salt. Everything changed when the Russians came. They kicked the head of the village out of his beautiful house and told us to stay there and rest. That's when we heard the great news: the war was over! We stayed in Olganetz for about a month: a period immortalized in a sketch by Maria Schächter called 'We Make a Little Occupation'. Her sister Hela made us all our first dresses from the curtains and bedcovers. We didn't go out looting the German houses with the Russian soldiers like other groups did.[67]

Immediately after liberation, some quick-thinking women, assisted by the Russians, started searching for food, clothes and even jewellery in the German houses. 'It was hard for me to grasp,' Gela Meiersdorf observes, 'how most of them managed so quickly to erase everything we had been through in the recent past and act so pragmatically and rationally.' Luna Kaufman, also liberated at Olganetz, refers to similar instances. It was, in fact, a common occurrence, and indeed there was no reason to take pity on the Germans who had raped and pillaged all of Europe. But there was a difference in mentality at work here: most of the prisoners gave no thought to material advantage. Their immediate concern was solely for their physical well-being. The women were in extremely poor condition after the Death-March, and many of them got worse as a result of improper nutrition right after liberation. A large number fell ill, and several lost their lives.

Relations with the Russian soldiers constituted a complex problem. At first, only the German women were at risk of being raped, and were occasionally saved through the intervention of prisoners. Sara who escaped from the death march with her two sisters, reached a village where no one was willing to help them. Finally, a German woman invited them into her home on condition that 'we tell the Russians of her kindness. We agreed, and she gave us food and clothes. When the Russians came, they raped and murdered the whole village, but thanks to our intervention, they didn't touch that house'.[68]

In time, as the former inmates began to look normal again, rape became a threat for them as well. The various testimonies reveal the whole range of possible behaviour toward them on the part of the soldiers, from aid and compassion with no request for 'compensation', particularly from Jewish soldiers and officers, through impromptu associations formed for the purposes of joint looting, to accusations on the order of 'you helped the Germans produce weapons to be used against us'. A number of more serious couplings were even forged on the assumption that it was better to ally yourself with one man who could assist and protect you from the others. The argument, 'We liberated you, so why not?' was often heard. There were also cases of brutal rape by drunken soldiers, ending, in a few rare instances, in murder. Rut Kornblum reports a variety of incidents, and quotes a soldier who apologized for his comrades' behaviour, asking for understanding.[69]

The most critical problem now facing the ex-prisoners was where to go and what to do. They had no homes. It is a theme which recurs constantly, in one form or another in testimonies: 'Liberation found us unprepared and helpless'; 'No one was waiting for me and I had nowhere to go'; 'I didn't know what to do with myself'. The former Jewish prisoners of Leipzig chose one of three alternatives, as did other Jews: (1) some returned to Poland to search for family members and remained there; (2) others seized the first opportunity to go to the United States; and (3) thousands were dispersed among the camps for displaced persons where they awaited their chance to immigrate to Palestine.

Hasag's final days

What was the fate of the Hasag concern?

With the occupation of Eastern Germany by the Soviet Union and the inception of the new regime, the Office for a New Industrial Order (Amt für Betriebsneuordnung) was established in Leipzig in mid-1945. Three 'commissary trustees' were appointed to manage Hasag property: Max Walther, Erich Beck and Rudolf Oswald, with the latter two serving as commercial directors. According to the procedures initiated, all three were listed as official agents of the company in the Commercial Registry of Leipzig factories.[70]

In view of these new circumstances, Max Walter, the head of the factory committee, wrote to the administrator of the Commercial Registry on 18 February 1946 requesting that he implement the following changes:

1. All previous members of the board of directors (including two more bank managers, Gruber and Jagman, in addition to the original five) were to be erased from the registry since 'some can not be located and some are no longer entitled to occupy their positions after the transfer of the Hasag company to trusteeship (*Treuhandschaft*)'.
2. The names of four managers were to be erased:
   • General Manager Paul Budin – missing as of 3 March 1945;
   • Hans Führer – arrested;
   • Dr Georg Mumme – deceased;
   • Gustav Hessen – dismissed from office.[71]
3. The names of 27 former procurists (authorized agents) of Hasag were to be erased, leaving only three in place (see Figure 8.3).[72]

This document raises a number of intriguing questions. First, the transfer of Hasag to a trusteeship might suggest an intent to disband the company, but if so, why were commercial managers appointed? Although we do not know what the Office for a New Industrial Order planned to do with Hasag, the fact is that the company was omitted from the Commercial Registry in 1947, that is, it ceased to exist at that time.[73]

The second question relates to the fate of Paul Budin. Why does the document employ the vague term 'missing' (*vermisst*)? According to records revealed at the Leipzig trial in 1948, at the end of the war, just before the Allies entered the city, Budin blew up the main Hasag plant in Leipzig together

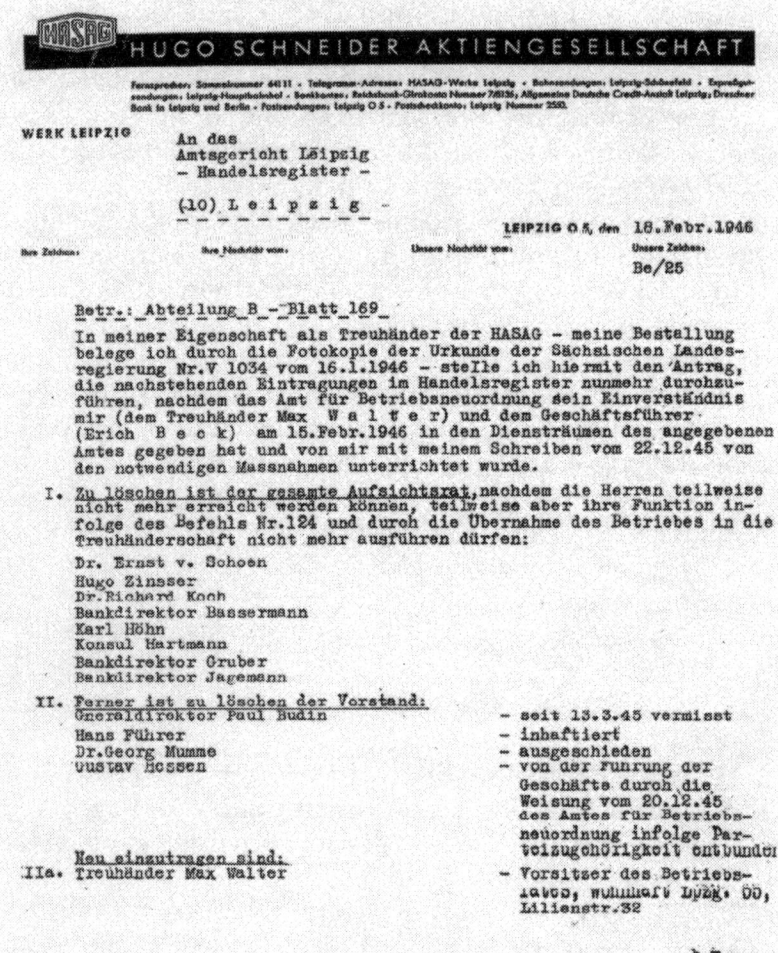

Figure 8.3 Letter from Max Walter, official agent of Hasag to the Leipzig Commercial Registry, 18 February 1946.

Source: StAL, AG Leipzig, HRB 169.

with the administration building. 'Budin and his wife were presumably killed in that explosion.'[74] The date of Budin's disappearance cited in Walter's letter (13 March 1945), fully a month before the evacuation of the camp and occupation of Leipzig, thus raises certain doubts. Did Budin indeed commit suicide, or did he escape in time and arrange for the explosion in order to cover his tracks? The truth has yet to be discovered.

The list of Hasag procurists is no less perplexing. How is it that the managers of the company, without exception all Nazi Party members responsible for the death of thousands of Jewish prisoners in the Hasag camps in the *Generalgouvernement*, were not put on trial immediately? After Budin's disappearance, one of them, Gustav Kuhne, even planned to take over management of the Leipzig plant and resume production. He approached a large number of employees with this proposal. It was only due to the chance involvement of two upright Germans, Karl Herold and Martin Giesel, that Kuhne was brought to trial in 1948, together with 25 other Hasag managers from the Skarżysko factories.[75]

In contrast, as far as we know, German managers of the Hasag-Leipzig plant were never indicted for their brutal treatment of the prisoners. Similarly, neither Wolfgang Plaul, nor the *Oberka* Käthe Heber and her various assistants (whose beatings remain etched in the memories of the survivors), ever faced trial.

Many of the Hasag prisoners lived to see liberation and were subsequently scattered throughout the world. A considerable number of them rebuilt their lives, with the past now only a dim distant memory. But not all were so fortunate.

It was during the time when we were wandering from place to place on the Death-March. After one stormy night, one of the groups started trudging through the mud again. After an hour, we were given a few minutes to rest, because the women didn't have the strength to move. We sat down on the grass by the road, utterly exhausted. We couldn't see anything because of the mist in eyes we couldn't keep open... Suddenly, German tanks appeared to one side of us. The panicking women tried to get up, to move... Three didn't make it. The tank rumbled over their bodies, leaving behind shredded human beings lying in a pool of blood.[76]

Those three were Mrs Karmel and her daughters, Henryka and Ilona. Their mother was killed on the spot. Miraculously, the two girls survived. The tank took one of Henryka's legs and one of Ilona's.

The appalling news, which in mysterious ways spread like wildfire among the Leipzig prisoners, fell like a blow from above. Wherever they went, wherever they looked, the ghastly prophecy rang in their ears:

Through the cities dead and the empty streets,
Like a raging storm, the hordes will stamp their feet,
Walking soberly, beaten, lost,
In the madness of the untamed, the madness of the saint,
Before the world they will stand – tens of thousands
    strong,
Consumed by hatred, compassion long gone,
And on their lips, that black from suffering have become,
A cry – like gushing blood – will burst: freedom!!!

Notes

1. Testimony of Ester Netzer.
2. Testimony of Sara Fajszewicz, YV, M-1/E/1797/1655.
3. Testimony of Paulina Buchenholz.
4. This is referred to in H. Karmel, 'Ulotki' (excerpts), ŻIH, *sygn.* 246, nr. 125.
5. Ibid.
6. I. Karmel, 'A gdy nadejdą zemsty dni', *Śpiew za drutami*, p. 67.
7. Gela Meiersdorf, 'Collected Poems'.
8. Letter from Ela Wachtel, Margulies-Timberg Collection.
9. Testimony of Sara Albirt, YV, M-1/E/2210/2072.
10. Testimony of Sara Shalem.
11. Testimony of Hanka Brandwejn-Ezer, YV, 0-33/3420.
12. Testimonies of Luna Kaufman and Felicja Karay.
13. H. Karmel, 'To the Professors', in Karay, *To Face Death Alone*, p. 36.
14. Testimony of Malka Hottner.
15. H. Karmel, 'To the German People', ŻIH, sygn. 246, nr 102, cf. the testimony of Ester Netzer, which states that the writer is Ilona Karmel.
16. Testimonies of Lea Muskatenblut and Malka Hottner.
17. Testimonies of Ester Netzer and Felicja Shahar (Margulies-Timberg Collection).
18. Letter from Felicja Shahar of 29 November 1992, private collection.
19. 'Al pat lehem'; *Al Ha-Mishmar* (19 June 1961), p. 3.
20. This may be a reference to Edyta Weitz; see the list in Chapter 6.
21. Oral testimony of Regina Ohrenstein-Haubman.
22. Author unknown, in the testimony of Malka Hottner.
23. I. Karmel, 'Mój dom', (excerpts), *Śpiew za drutami*, p. 58.
24. Testimony of Felicja Karay.
25. H. Karmel, 'Do Polski,' (excerpts), *Śpiew za drutami*, p. 40.
26. Stanisława Demidowicz, 'List z Buchenwaldu', *Gazeta Olsztyńska* (26 December 1993), p. 10.
27. Testimony of Rena Cypres. ('Seder' – the festive Passover meal.)

28. Testimonies of Henryka Karmel, Rena Fradkin and Ester Netzer.
29. Testimony of Malka Hottner.
30. Zilberberg, *Mama*, p. 242.
31. 'Niewolnicze tango', testimony of Felicja Blum.
32. Testimony of Margalit Gross, YV, 0-3/1761.
33. H. Nelken, *Pamiętnik z getta w Krakowie*, p. 328. According to a common belief in Poland if somebody becomes accidentally soiled by excrement they will have a good future and enjoy great honour.
34. Testimony of Sara Bojer; Kornblum-Rosenberger, *Neder*, p. 79.
35. Brzosko-Mędryk, *Matylda*, pp. 80-81.
36. Letter from Matylda Woliniewska, 19 April 1994.
37. Ibid.
38. Testimony of Irma Neuman; Brzosko-Mędryk, *Matylda*, p. 79.
39. Testimony of Hela Beitner, YV, M-1/E/313/197.
40. Testimony of Ewa Cukier.
41. Testimony of Eda Jewin.
42. Shechter, *Lost Youth*, pp. 114–17.
43. Testimony of Irena Seńko.
44. Testimony of Eda Jewin.
45. Testimony of Halina Razowski.
46. Testimony of Paulina Buchenholz.
47. Testimony of Regina Rabinowicz-Landau.
48. S. Demidowicz, 'Ewakuacja', in Teodorowicz (ed.) *Nadzieja była wolność*, p. 79.
49. Romualda Stramik, ibid., p. 76.
50. Letter from Matylda Woliniewska, 19 April 1994.
51. Testimony of Felicja Blum.
52. Testimony of Henia Strelski, *We Remember*, p. 72.
53. Testimonies of Ester Netzer, Paulina Buchenholz and Eda Jewin.
54. Testimonies of Felicja Shahar and Paulina Buchenholz.
55. Heiner Lichtenstein, *Majdanek, Reportage einess Prozesses*, (Frankfurt a/M: Europäische Verlaganstalt, 1979), p. 9.
56. Testimonies of Maria Lewinger; Eda Jewin and Felicja Karay.
57. Testimony of Halina Schütz.
58. Oral testimony of Lola Adler-Grinstein; Kornblum-Rosenberger, *Neder*, p. 83.
59. Testimony of Malka Hottner.
60. Testimony of Irma Neuman.
61. Testimony of Halina Razowski.
62. Kornblum-Rosenberger, *Neder*, p. 87.
63. Testimony of Sara Fajszewicz.
64. Testimony of Irma Neuman.
65. Testimony of Dora Bek, YV, M-1/E/348/270.
66. Letter from Matylda Woliniewska, 19 April 1994.
67. Testimonies of Maria Lewinger, Eda Lewin and Felicja Karay.
68. Testimony of Sara Shalem.
69. Kornblum-Rosenberger, *Neder*, p. 89; testimonies of Luna Kaufman and Miriam Eitan.
70. Amt für Betriebsneuordnung, Leipzig, 5 March 1946, Betreff.: Hugo Schneider AG, StAL, AG Leipzig, HRB, 169.
71. See Chapter 1. Two bank managers, Gruber and Jagman, had been added to the list of members of the Board of Directors: *Hasag an das*

Hasag-Leipzig Slave Labour Camp for Women

Amtsgericht Leipzig, Leipzig, 18 February 1946, StAL, Ag HRB 169.
72. Ibid.
73. 'The managers of Hasag were tried individually in 1948 in Leipzig, but not the 'invisible' Hasag Co., itself', see Hans Frey, *Die Hölle von Kamienna unter Benutzung des amtlichen Prozessmaterials zusammengestellt von Hans Frey*, (Berlin–Potsdam: VVN Verlag, 1949), p. 7.
74. Ibid., p. 19.
75. Kamienna Trial, YV, TR-10/7.
76. Rena Taubenblatt, 'Przed wyzwoleniem', in Borwicz *et al.* (eds) *Dokumenty zbrodni i męczeństwa* (Kraków: Żydowska Komisja Historyczna, 1945), p. 103.

Conclusion

Current Third Reich historiography is witnessing the renewed popularity of the 'individualistic' school that places the blame for all the crimes of National Socialism on the shoulders of Hitler alone. This trend is apparent not only among German scholars, such as Sebastian Haffner, who regards Hitler as the prime enemy of the German people.[1] Even for non-German researchers such as Alan Bullock, the idea that Hitler and Stalin are solely responsible for all the calamities of the twentieth century is a comfortable thesis.[2]

Was Hitler also the enemy of the German concerns, ordered by him to increase their wealth? He did want property-owners to 'be stripped of independence and in a constant state of fear of worse things... to come'.[3] But reality was very different. With the declaration of the arming of Germany in the Four Year Plan (*Vierjahresplan*) in 1936, the government became dependent on heavy industry for the supply of military *matériel*, a dependency that grew even greater with the outbreak of the war. Factory-owners could now seek to influence the rate and extent of munitions acquisitions to suit their own interests.[4] Up until the very end of the Nazi regime, they also applied the policy of 'business as usual' with regard to the recruitment of manpower. The success of their efforts is attested to not only by the 135 *Aussenkommandos* of Buchenwald in existence in March 1945 but, also – and primarily – by the rise in the value of German industrial shares during the war. The citizens of the Third Reich, who benefited from this situation by being spared the ordeals of inflation, lauded the *Wehrmacht*'s victories and took full advantage of their fruits until the Allies started their campaign of heavy bombing. In their incredible 'Teutonic arrogance', German scholars and the like, hoping to cleanse the German people of their contemptible past, deliberately attempt to hide the fact that the economic might of the Third Reich and the security of its citizens were made possible also by the unpaid labour of millions of starved prisoners incarcerated in thousands of anonymous camps around Europe.

As we have seen, those who benefited the most were the industrialists, the owners of companies operating to this very day, who were undeterred by the fact that their profits came directly from the extermination of millions of human beings. As the Polish poet Tadeusz Borowski, a former inmate of Auschwitz, writes:

> We work in factories and mines. We perform the colossal work from which someone makes huge profits... The German company Lenz built us a camp, factory floors, barracks, warehouses, bunkers, furnaces... Like all the German concerns, Lenz increases its capital. It did massive business in Auschwitz and is waiting for the war to end. Wagner, Continental which built the water system in the camp, Richter which dug the wells, Siemens which supplied light and electricity, all did the same... So did the giant automobile company Union, the waste recycling plant of DAW, the owners of the mines in Gliwice and Janino, and others... They exploited our bodies as much as possible...[5]

Was Hasag any different? The facts revealed by this study show that this modest concern enjoyed certain privileges from the government even during the decline of the Third Reich. This is evidenced by the new projects that continued to receive support both from Minister of Armaments Speer and from the SS-WVHA and its officials. Was defence of the Fatherland really Hasag's prime consideration? The answer can be found in the following statement: 'The goal of the Hasag managers was not only to serve the political will of the government, *but first and foremost the desire to increase profits'*.[6] This truth remains undeniable, even if a considerable portion of those profits found their way into the public and private pockets of the SS authorities.

The bare facts reveal that half of the shares in the Hasag concern were held by Dresdner Bank. In other words, the women imprisoned in the Leipzig camp, like those in the other Hasag camps, worked for Dresdner Bank and its partners, whether active or silent. Hasag has long disappeared off the stage of history, but Dresdner Bank continues to operate and prosper, secure in the knowledge that the inviolability of banking confidentiality will prevent curious researchers from uncovering its dark secrets from the time of the Nazis. Clearly, Dresdner Bank – like other German banks – can in no way be considered just another one of Hitler's helpless victims. On the contrary, it was an active accomplice in his crimes, not only cooperating in acts of theft under the policy of 'Aryanization', but also earning substantial profits from forced labour. Every Hasag prisoner knew what many distinguished scholars seem to 'forget' today: 'We provided the corporation owners with free manpower with which they earned huge profits.'[7]

It was this fact that also determined the fate of the prisoners in the Hasag-Leipzig camp. The women did not choose to work in the munitions plants in exchange for a hot shower, the subject of one of their sarcastic ditties, but because they were terrorized in a variety of horrific ways. On the surface, it would appear that the terror tactics employed within the borders of Germany were somewhat less appalling than elsewhere, as vouched for by the testimony of numerous prisoners of all nationalities who report the fair treatment they received from their German supervisors in the factories. Without disregarding individual acts of kindness, however, there can be no doubt that the change for the better in the treatment of the inmates in general, and the Jewish women in particular, resulted from the German fear of the Allies' rapid advance. When it became apparent in April 1945 that the camp would soon have to be evacuated, the managers hastened to take their leave from the inmates, begging to be remembered kindly.

This attempt to prepare an 'alibi' in light of inevitable defeat was also behind Commandant Wolfgang Plaul's policy toward the prisoners. Only one year separated the 'Jew-hater' of Buchenwald from the 'benevolent' Commandant of Leipzig – surely too short a period to account for this metamorphosis without seeking an explanation in the imminent Allied victory and the likelihood of his being accused of war crimes. The same fear undoubtedly motivated the SS overseers, whose very function says something about their character.

As we have seen, Plaul promised equality among all the national groups in the camp, and seemingly maintained this policy in regard to the Jewish women as well. All prisoners were given the same food rations and were subject to the same roll-calls.

A close study of his regime reveals that in his final posting, Plaul chose to implement principles quite different from those typical of other concentration camps: to keep his distance as supreme commander and apply a *laissez-faire* policy in respect of the internal life of the camp. By doing so, he displayed an excellent understanding of prisoner mentality. In Buchenwald he had learned to identify the collective character of each national group, the historical conflicts between them, and the anti-Semitic sentiments of most. Thus, underlying his liberal policies was the clear intention to give them the chance to eat each other alive – without his interference.

Was this, in fact, what actually happened in Leipzig? Opinion is divided. In her *Journal*, Felicja Bannet-Schäftler places primary blame for the hostility between groups on the camp authorities. On the other hand, Albert Rohmer claims that it was not only a policy of 'divide and conquer', even a covert one, that led to the lack of multinational solidarity among the prisoners. He maintains that 'Despite the brotherhood of suffering as slaves, most of the time the national groups in the camp remained separate from each other.'[8] Matylda Woliniewska takes a contrary, positive, stand when she says: 'With regard to relations between the various national groups in Leipzig, from the perspective of time I can say that they were much better than those we now see in the free world with all its bloody conflicts.'[9]

In short, the reality of the Leipzig camp offers support for all three contentions. There can be no doubt that the organization of the camp and the choice of functionaries was dictated by a policy of 'divide and conquer'. As for solidarity, each group kept to itself, lending this virtue a thoroughly national aspect. It was, however, very strong within each group; even the Jewish prisoners stress that '*in comparison to*

Skarżysko, there was much greater solidarity among us in Leipzig'.
Several factors contributed to this closer bond: the
multinational composition of the camp population; the
example of other groups; and the anti-Semitism on all sides.
At the same time, the struggle for survival was less harsh
given the improved living conditions and the hope of an
imminent end to the war. In respect to the interaction between
the different national groups, it must be said that despite the
conflicts, relations were tolerable and there were no instances
of outright aggression. *But neither were there any structured
connections between the groups on the collective level, only
individual spontaneous associations.*

The absence of intergroup solidarity was also fostered by
the unequal policies applied by the prisoner functionaries,
who treated each of the national groups differently in their
day-to-day dealings, if not on the official level. It is no chance
that a large number of testimonies accuse the 'Polish
duchesses' of treating the Jews with contempt. On the other
hand, there are very few complaints of deliberate cruelty. Even
the women performing the most hateful functions tried,
whether consciously or unconsciously, to find a golden mean
and earn the approval of the prisoners.

Regarding relations between the Jews and the other national
groups, several successful attempts to find a common language
with the Frenchwomen stand out, while there were virtually no
such links with the Russians or Ukrainians. As for the Poles,
when I met with Matylda Woliniewska and several of her
friends in Warsaw,[10] I asked them why, despite their experiences
in Majdanek, they made no move to form social contacts with
Jews. Matylda confessed that in Leipzig, unlike Majdanek, she
felt she was not needed, since all the prisoners were more or less
in the same situation. Irena Pełka-Seńko offered a political
explanation: they were deeply affected by reports of the
behaviour of the Jews toward the Poles under the Soviet
occupation of Poland (the area of Eastern Poland in 1939–41).
She believed that most of the Poles in Leipzig held the popular
opinion that some of the Jewish women might be communists,
and that was why they refrained from initiating closer contact.

As a result of this situation of 'to each her own', *social life
was also organized by each group individually,* although it was

necessarily influenced by identical factors: official policy; the absence of men; the amount of free time; and living conditions. To these can be added the 'advantage' of experience. The uniform structure of all Nazi camps helped the prisoners adjust to life in Leipzig without undergoing the initial stage of shock, particularly given the fact that conditions were better here. The acclimatization of the Jewish inmates was also made easier because they continued to perform the same sort of tasks in the factory as in Skarżysko. Thus, for example, a woman sent to work with heavy machinery already knew what kind and how many cleaning rags she could ask the foreman for, so as to 'organize' a few for her personal use. Along with this practical knowledge, the women also brought with them habits and relationships that had a bearing on their daily routine.

The women sent from Majdanek or Ravensbrück underwent even less of a transition than the Jews, who suddenly found themselves with no men. Those who had had a husband, brother, or boyfriend at Skarżysko were forced to form some sort of female grouping, such as those previously noted. Thus, alongside actual family units (mothers and daughters, sisters, cousins, sisters-in-law), 'camp families' again emerged consisting of several girls, pairs of friends, groups of religious women, former members of the same ideological movement (such as Akiva), or circles organized for a particular purpose, like the Kraków group. The ultimate importance of these unions was that they were a means of mutual support. All other national groups displayed the very same social models, with the addition of specific alliances, such as the Polish 'Pawiaczki' and 'Bunkerkommando' or the Russian prisoners of war.[11]

The patterns of social life were also similar: a few women getting together on a bunk or in a corner of the block; larger-scale meetings in one of the administration halls, the washroom, or the bunker; and mass assemblies in the block or bunker for a special show. The content of these activities varied and might include: small-talk and gossip; bartering of goods and services; grumbling about a supervisor or overseer; nostalgic reminiscences; a lot of talk about the food they had once eaten and would some day eat again; gossip from the factory or the foremen; occasional attempts to interpret the latest news from the front (often leading to vociferous political arguments); and impressions of the last 'concert'. Indeed, these meetings were directly related to the cultural activities in the camp.

Unfortunately, the subject of Jewish cultural activity in the Nazi camps has received very little mention in the academic literature in Israel. It is addressed extensively only in *Death Comes in Yellow* with reference to Skarżysko, and in Bella Gutterman's *With Death a Toast to Life*, with reference to the slave labour camp at Janowska.[12] The difference stands out especially in the source materials: whereas the Poles and French (and perhaps we will learn the same about the Russians one day) held on to every scrap of paper and provide a rich picture of cultural activity in their memoirs (only small portions of which appear in this study), the Jews retained only a few bits of testimony, a small number of texts and – primarily – poems.

None the less, all existing sources help to create a broad diverse picture of cultural activity in the Leipzig camp. Several reasons account for its flourishing here. First are the 'liberal' policies of the Commandant, who seems to have believed that at that moment in time, on the eve of defeat, songs and recitations could serve as a most effective outlet to ensure quiet and ease tension in the camp. Second, the prisoners had tacit approval, and even a certain degree of assistance, from the internal administration. Moreover, the extent of cultural activity was unquestionably affected by the practices and experience the inmates brought with them from their previous camps, as exemplified by the Poles from Majdanek and the Jews from Skarżysko. A final significant incentive seems to have been the element of competition, both among the different nationalities and among the participants themselves, who enjoyed the status of celebrities.

Produced under similar conditions of crowding, terror and the need to operate surreptitiously, cultural activity in Leipzig took the same forms as in all other camps. These included reminiscences, stories and recitations from world and camp literature, lessons, solo and community singing, plays and 'concerts', dancing, occasional exhibitions and religious activity. The most common, and most meaningful, form was camp literature of all types: journals, sketches, *feuilletons*, narratives, nostalgic poems, religious laments, descriptions of events, songs of revenge and lyrics satirizing the functionaries and camp life. All of these were produced by the Jewish prisoners, but only a small part of them are presented here. Most were lost on the Death-March.

Each national group had its own individual aims and contents. Although the Poles also performed satirical sketches and religious plays, their shows were predominated by a national–folk–historical element. It was their goal to prove to the other groups that 'they belonged to a proud nation with a rich culture and were not sub-human'.[13] Such an attitude was in no way apparent among the French, who viewed their activities as a means of strengthening their bonds of friendship and raising their spirits. They performed Molière and ballet extracts in the supreme confidence that their entire audience would be familiar with the pieces since they represented French culture! From the little we know of Russian activities, they appear to have been dominated by patriotic songs and folk dances performed for their own enjoyment. The choice of a Chekhov play for their 'concert' undoubtedly stemmed from the assumption that the other groups would be acquainted with it.

With regard to the Jews, it must be noted that all types of cultural activity were conducted in Polish. There is no evidence whatsoever of Yiddish language or folklore, despite the fact that a goodly number of women steeped in this culture were brought to Leipzig from Skarżysko. It seems reasonable to assume that this void was largely influenced by the fear that the demonstrative performance of Yiddish songs would be greeted with contempt or outright hostility by the Polish functionaries. Furthermore, the Kraków group, who achieved hegemony in the realm of cultural activities, was remote from the Yiddish experience and sought a common language with the Poles, at least on the cultural level. As for *objectives*, there was a strong feeling that 'if the others can organize concerts and plays, we can too. They are no better than us'.[14] There is not the slightest sense of inferiority in this declaration – on the contrary.

The *content*, however, was different: devotion to Jewish tradition; support for the Zionist cause; a craving to be integrated into society; and a leaning toward cosmopolitanism. It is significant to note that while the Jewish prisoners celebrated Hanukkah in their block, reciting the heroic tales of the Maccabees and singing Hebrew songs, no nationalistic content appeared in the Grand Concert performed before a multinational audience. Unlike the other groups who chose to highlight the distinctiveness of their culture, the Jews preferred to present classical plays, American music and European dances. The poem of the robots did not refer specifically to the Jews, but to all the slave labourers in all Nazi camps. This programme was not the product of ignorance: the entire Kraków group knew Hebrew songs and could have found other material as well, had they wished to. *What was at work here was the overwhelming desire to be like everyone else, to be a part of the international community.* The obvious *conclusion* is that the content of Jewish cultural activities gave expression both to national aspirations and to a cosmopolitan outlook: a symbiosis typical of the assimilated Jewish intelligentsia throughout history.

From a broader perspective it can be said that cultural activity in general, both active and passive, played a major role not only in preserving the sanity of the prisoner and preventing her from becoming nothing more than a 'guinea pig'. It also served as the single bridge between the different national groups. Its most significant aspect was the opportunity it offered to resurrect, if only for a short while, the human values that were excised from the Nazi camps: compassion, brotherhood, mutual respect.

'What was most important,' writes Kazimierz Szwemberg, a former prisoner of Auschwitz, 'is that the expressions of "camp culture" strengthened the ties, linking the prisoners of different nationalities, reinforcing the basis of their solidarity. It is no chance that every cultural activity, regardless of the prisoners' nationalities, won the support and defence of the others (sometimes in the form of a piece of bread offered to the artist). On deeper consideration, if the attempt to force on the individual in the extermination camp the state of a vagrant in a cultural void was a failure – such an attempt will never succeed.'[15]

Some might say: 'But Leipzig wasn't an extermination camp!' True, the prisoners here were given coupons to use in the empty canteen instead of simply dying slowly of starvation, they were slapped instead of being kicked by jackboots, whipped instead of being bound to instruments of torture, wore stripes instead of grey, stood in punitive roll-calls instead of being sent directly to the gas chambers, were sent away on 'transports' instead of straight to the crematorium, got hot showers instead of gas chambers! Here they were the slaves of Hasag and not the enemies of the Third Reich. Why did they enjoy such 'benefits'? Because defeat was just around the corner, because the 'masters' were scared. Yet despite this fear, they were still made to undergo expulsion from paradise to purgatory – the Death-March...

Memorial on the former site of the Hasag-Leipzig Camp.

The inscription reads:
On this site stood an auxiliary camp of the Buchenwald and Ravensbrück concentration camps from in 1944 to 1945. Thousands of women of different nationalities were subject here to inhumane exploitation by the fascist weapon manufactory at Hasag. We honour the memory of those who suffered and lost their lives here.

Conclusion

Today people can no longer comprehend what we went through. Those responsible are trying to hide the facts and obliterate them. Their descendants will have neither the imagination, the knowledge, nor the desire to reconstruct for themselves the picture of the events of that past time (Hans Magnus Enzensberger).[16] Will that happen to us too?

Notes

1. Sebastian Haffner, *The Meaning of Hitler* (New York: Macmillan, 1979).
2. Alan Bullock, *Hitler and Stalin: Parallel Lives* (London: Harper Collins, 1991).
3. Herman Rauschning, *Sihot im Hitler* (Gespräche mit Hitler) (Hebrew), (Tel Aviv: Masada, 1941), p. 140.
4. Karay, *Death Comes in Yellow*, pp. 13–16.
5. Tadeusz Borowski, 'U nas w Auschwitzu', *Pożegnanie z Marią i inne opowiadania*, (Warsaw: Państwowy Instytut Wydawniczy, 1961), p. 115.
6. *Die Hölle* , p. 7. (Emphasis added.)
7. Testimony of Luna Kaufman.
8. Wormser-Migot and Michel (eds), *La Tragédie de la Déportation*, p. 224.
9. Letter from Matylda Woliniewska, 19 April 1994.
10. Woliniewska, Karay *et al.*
11. Cf.: Shamai Davidson, 'Mutual Human Relations and their Significance Among the Prisoners of Nazi Concentration Camps', in *The Nazi Concentration Camps*, pp. 436–37.
12. Gutterman, 'Cultural Activity', in *With Death a Toast to Life.*
13. Stramik, 'Los zakładniczki'.
14. Testimony of Maria Lewinger.
15. Z. Jagoda, S. Kłodziński, J. Masłowski, *Oświęcim nieznany*, (Kraków: Wydawnictwo Literackie, 1981), p. 134.
16. Z. Kałużyński, 'Ząbki systemu', *Polityka* (17 June 1995), p. 16.

Bibliography

Archives

Yad Vashem Central Archives (YV) Jerusalem

Collections

Wiener Library: Collection of Testimonies and Documents, London, 0–2.
Testimonies and Documents Section, 0–3.
Collection of Testimonies of Hungarian Jews, 0–15.
Jewish Historical Committee of Poland, Collection of Testimonies, 0–16.
Collection of Miscellaneous Testimonies, 0–33.
Central Historical Committee in Munich, Collection of Testimonies, M–1/E.
War Criminal Section of the Central Committee of Liberated Jews, Munich, M–21.
Indictments and Verdicts of Nazi War Criminals, TR–10.
Microfilm Collection, JM.
BD–BU, ITS–Basic documentation of Concentration Camp Buchenwald.

Additional Sources

Bannet-Schäftler, Felicja, 'Pamiętnik z obozu Hasag-Leipzig', (*Journal*) (journal from the Hasag-Leipzig Camp), 0-33/4096.
Brzosko-Mędryk, Danuta, Letters and Memoirs, 0-33/4239.
Frey, Hans, *Die Hölle von Kamienna, unter Benutzung des amtlichen Prozessmaterials zusammengestellt von Hans Frey*, (Berlin: VVN Verlag, 1949).
Margulies-Timberg, Ela (Wachtel) (Margulies-Timberg Collection), Collection of Documents, Memoirs and Poems, 0-48/47-d-3

Öffentlichen Sitzungen der Strafkammer des Landesgerichts, Kamienna Prozess 1948, TR-10/7.

Trial of the Major War Criminals before the IMT, Nuremberg, 14 November 1945–1 October 1946, Case Pohl.

Woliniewska, Matylda, Collection of Documents, Letters and Materials on the activities of the 'Bunkerkommando' in the Hasag-Leipzig Camp, 0-33/4237.

Sächsisches Staatsarchiv, Leipzig (StAL)

Die Grossunternehmen im Deutschen Reich, *Handbuch der deutschen Aktiengesellschaften*, 1943, Band 5, pp. 5259–62 (HASAG).

Verzeichnis der in der ordentlichen Hauptversammlung der Hasag vom 11 Oktober 1943 erschienenen oder vertretenen Aktionäre und der Vertreter von Aktionären, AG Leipzig, HRB 169.

HASAG, Dritte Beilage zum Deutschen Reichsanzeiger und Preussischen Staatsanzeiger, Nr.139, Berlin 1940, p. 180.

'Handelsregister', Registerakten Hugo Schneider Aktiengesellschaft Leipzig, 118 HRB 169.

Amt für Betriebsneuordnung, Leipzig 1946, Briefe, HRB 169.

Bundesarchiv Koblenz (BA)

Reichsministerium für Rüstungs und Kriegsproduktion: R3, (RmfRük) Ministerbüro Speer.

Archiv der Nationalen Mahn und Gedenkstätte Buchenwald (NMG)

Lists of the transports and other materials.

Thüringisches Hauptstaatsarchiv (ThHSA), Weimar

Konzentrationslager Buchenwald: (KZ Buchenwald) Verwaltung, Betr. die SS-Aufseherinnen im Arbeitskommando Hasag-Leipzig, NS 4 BU, Vlg. 99.

Archiwum Głównej Komisji Badania Zbrodni przeciwko Narodowi Polskiemu, Instytut Pamięci Narodowej (AGK), Warsaw

Aussenkommando Hasag-Leipzig, Zugänge, Juni 1944 – Dezember 1944, KL Buchenwald, sygn. 55.
Hans Pflaum Prozess, Zespół 'Ob', Ravensbrück, sygn. 84.
Kartoteka 1200 Żydówek z obozu Kamienna zatrudnionych w firmie 'Hasag' z dnia 4.8.1944, SWK, sygn. 217.

Archiwum Żydowskiego Instytutu Historycznego (ŻIH), Warsaw

The poems of Henryka and Ilona Karmel (Polish), sygn. 246.

Archiwum Państwowego Muzeum na Majdanku (APMM)

Sondertransport-Überstellung von Lublin (nach Ravensbrück), 21.4.1944.

Document collections

Anatomie des Krieges, Neue Dokumente über die Rolle des deutschen Monopolkapitals bei der Vorbereitung und Durchführung des zweiten Weltkrieges, hrsg. von D. Eichholtz und W. Schumann (Berlin: VEB Deutscher Verlag der Wissenschaften, 1969).
Buchenwald: Mahnung und Verpflichtung (Frankfurt a/M: Kongress Verlag, 1960).
Deutschlands Rüstung im zweiten Weltkrieg, Hitlers Konferenzen mit Albert Speer 1942–1945, hrsg. von A.W. Bölcke (Frankfurt a/M: Athenaion, 1969).
Documenta occupationis teutonicae, Vol. VI, Hitlerowskie Prawo okupacyjne w Polsce, Generalna Gubernia (Poznań: Instytut Zachodni, 1958).
Dokumenty zbrodni i męczeństwa, ed. M. Borwicz, N. Rost, J. Wulf (Kraków: Żydowska Komisja Historyczna, 1945).
SS-im Einsatz, Dokumentation (Berlin: Kongress Verlag, 1957).
Vaupel, D., *Das Aussenkommando Hess. Lichtenau des Konzentrationslager Buchenwald 1944/45*, Eine Dokumentation (Kassel: Gesamthochschule Kassel, 1984).

Memoirs and diaries

Kornblum-Rosenberger, Rut, *Neder [Vow]*, (Hebrew) (Tel Aviv: Moreshet-Sifriat Poalim, 1988).
Nadzieją była wolność, Wspomnienia, Teodorowicz, Maria (ed.), (Olsztyn: TON, 1991).
Nelken, Halina, *Pamiętnik z getta w Krakowie* (Toronto: Polish-Canadian Publishing Fund, 1987).
Shechter, Genia, *Lost Youth* (Hebrew) (Tel Aviv: Ministry of Defence, 1998).
Stendig Jacob, *Płaszów* (Hebrew) (Tel Aviv: Menora,1970).
W kraju, na Wschodzie i na Zachodzie, Wspomnienia inwalidów wojennych (Olsztyn: Zarząd Okręgowy ZIW w Olsztynie, TON 1991).
We Remember: Twenty-four Members of Kibbutz Megido Testify (Hebrew) (Tel Aviv: Moreshet-Sifriat Poalim, 1988).
Zilberberg, Towa, *Mama, Your Prayers Have Been Answered* (Hebrew) (Tel Aviv: Bney Brak, 1994).

Journal articles

Czuj, T., Kempisty, C. and Ojrzyński Z., 'Działalność hitlerowskich instytutów naukowych w świetle tajnych dokumentów Deutsche Forschungsgemeinschaft odnalezionych we Wrocławiu', *Biuletyn GKBZHwP*, 26 (1970), p. 195.
Demidowicz, S. 'List z Buchenwaldu', Gazeta Olsztyńska (26 December 1993), p. 10.
Karay, F., 'The Social and Cultural Life of the Prisoners in the Jewish Forced-Labour Camp at Skarżysko-Kamienna', *Holocaust and Genocide Studies*, 8 (1994), p.1.
Karay, F., 'The Conflict among German Authorities over Jewish Slave Labour Camps in the General Gouvernement' (Polish), *Zeszyty Majdanka*, 18 (1997), p. 27.

Books

Arndt, Ino, *Das Frauenkonzentrationslager Ravensbrück*, Schriftenreihe der Vierteljahreshefte für Zeitgeschichte, nr 21 (Stuttgart: Studien zur Geschichte der Konzentrationslager, 1970).
Ber, Marc, *Megilat Auschwitz* (Hebrew) (The Auschwitz Scroll) (Tel Aviv: Sifriat Poalim, 1978).

Bernadac, Christian, *Kommandos de femmes, Ravensbrück* (Paris: M. Lafon, 1973).

Billig, Joseph, *Les Camps de concentration dans l'economie du Reich hitlerien* (Paris: Presses Universitaires, 1973).

Borowski, Tadeusz, *Pożegnanie z Marią i inne opowiadania* (Warsaw: Państwowy Instytut Wydawniczy, 1961).

Borwicz, Michał (ed.), *Pieśń ujdzie cało* (Warsaw: Centralna Żydowska Komisja historyczna, 1947).

Brzosko-Mędryk-Danuta, *Niebo bez ptaków* (Warsaw: Min. Obrony Narodowej, 1968).

Brzosko-Mędryk-Danuta, *Matylda* (Warsaw: Min. Obrony Narodowej, 1970).

Buchmann, Erika, *Die Frauen von Ravensbrück* (Berlin: Kongress Verlag, 1960).

Bullock, Alan, *Hitler and Stalin* (London: Harper Collins, 1991).

Chojnowski, Z. (ed.), *Dla Ciebie Polsko: Wybrane utwory kombatantów,* (Olsztyn: ZBOWID, 1988).

Czarnecki, Wacław and Zonik Zygmunt, *Walczący obóz Buchenwald* (Warsaw: Książka I Wiedza, 1969).

Czech, Danuta, *Kalendarium der Ereignisse im Konzentrationslager Auschwitz Birkenau,* Hefte von Ausschwitz (Państwowe Muzeum w Oświęcimiu, 1964).

Davidson, S., 'Mutual Human Relations and their Significance among the Prisoners of Nazi Concentration Camps', in *The Nazi Concentration Camps* (Jerusalem: Yad Vashem, 1984), p. 436.

Demidowicz, S., 'Związek pięciu stworzeń', in Z. Chojnowski (ed.), *Dla Ciebie Polsko* (Olsztyn: ZBOWID, 1988), p. 49.

Dunin-Wąsowicz, Krzysztof, *Ruch oporu w hitlerowskich obozach koncentracyjnych 1933–1945* (Warsaw: Państwowy Instytut Wydawniczy, 1979).

Eichholtz, Dietrich, *Geschichte der deutschen Kriegswirtschaft 1939-1945* (Berlin: Akademie Verlag, 1971).

Eisenbach, Artur, *Hitlerowska polityka zagłady Żydów* (Warsaw: Książka i Wiedza, 1961).

Gutman, Israel (ed.), *Encyclopedia of the Holocaust,* (New York: Macmillan, 1990)

Gutterman, B., 'Cultural Activity and Spiritual Life in the Camp', *Toasting Life with Death: The Story of the Janowska Camp, 1941–1943* (Hebrew) (Tel Aviv, 1993).

Haffner, Sebastian, *The Meaning of Hitler* (New York: Macmillan, 1979).

ITS, *Catalogue of Camps and Prisons in Germany and German-occupied Territories* (Arolsen).

Jagoda, Z., Kłodziński, S. and Masłowski, J. *Oświęcim nieznany* (Kraków: Wydawnictwo Literackie, 1981).

Janssen, Gregor, *Das Ministerium Speer: Deutschlands Rüstung im Krieg* (Berlin: Verlag Ullstein, 1968).

Karay, Felicja, *Death Comes in Yellow: Skarżysko-Kamienna Slave Labour Camp* (Amsterdam: Harwood, 1996)

Karay Felicja: *To Face Death Alone – Psychological and Moral Issues of the Nazi Concentration Camps* (Hebrew), (Jerusalem: Ministry of Education ,1980).

Karay F., 'Women in the Forced-Labour Camps', in D. Ofer and L. J. Weitzman (eds), *Women in the Holocaust* (New Haven, CT: Yale University Press, 1998), p. 285.

Karmel Henryka and Karmel Ilona: *Śpiew za drutami* (New York: The Association of Friends of our Tribune, 1947).

Kiedrzyńska, Wanda, *Ravensbrück, kobiecy obóz koncentracyjny* (Warsaw: Klub Ravensbrück, 1961).

Klein H., 'The Search for Identity and Meaning among Holocaust Survivors', in *The Nazi Concentration Camps* (Jerusalem: Yad Vashem, 1984), p. 428.

Kogon, Eugen, *Der SS-Staat* (Munich: Kindler Verlag, 1974).

Kuczynski, Jürgen, *Die Geschichte der Lage der Arbeiter unter dem Kapitalismus* (Berlin: Tribune Verlag, 1964).

Landau Ludwik: *Kronika lat wojny i okupacji* (Warsaw: Państwowe Wydawnictwo Naukowe, 1962).

Les Françaises à Ravensbrück (Paris: Galliard,1965).

Madajczyk, Czesław, *Polityka III Rzeszy w okupowanej Polsce* (Warsaw: Państwowe Wydawnictwo Naukowe, 1970).

Oni pobedili smert', (Moscow: Izdat. Polit. Literatury, 1966).

Ricol-London, Lise, *La Mégère de la rue Daguerre: Souvenirs de Resistance* (Paris: Editions Du Seuil, 1995).

Ryszka, Franciszek, *Państwo stanu wyjątkowego* (Wrocław: Ossolineum, 1964).

Seeber, Eva, *Robotnicy przymusowi w faszystowskiej gospodarce wojennej* (Warsaw: Książka i Wiedza, 1972).

Sehn, Jan (ed.), *Wspomnienia Rudolfa Hössa*, (Warsaw: Wydawnictwo Prawnicze, 1960).

Speer, Albert, *Der Sklavenstaat* (Stuttgart: DVA, 1981).

Stramik, Romualda, 'Los zakładniczki', in M. Teodorowicz (ed.), *Nadzieja była wolność* (Olsztyn: TON, 1991).

Tillion, Germaine, *Ravensbrück* (Paris: Edition du Seuil, 1973).

Wińska Urszula: *Zwyciężyły wartości*, Wspomnienia z Ravensbrück (Gdańsk, 1985).

Wormser-Migot, Olga, *Le Retour des déportés*. (Paris: Editions Complexe).

Wormser-Migot, Olga and Michel, H. (eds), *La Tragédie de la déportation, 1940–1945: temoignages de survivants*, (Paris, 1955).

Journals and periodicals

Al-Hamishmar (Hebrew) (Tel Aviv).

Biuletyn Głównej Komisji Badania Zbrodni Hitlerowskich w Polsce (BGKBZHwP), (Warsaw).

Gazeta Olsztyńska, (Olsztyn).

Holocaust and Genocide Studies (Oxford).

Polityka, (Warsaw).

Ravensbrück Blätter.

Trybuna Ludu, (Warsaw).

Zeszyty Majdanka (*Hefte von Majdanek*).

Zeszyty Oświęcimia (*Hefte von Auschwitz*).

Testimonies (Yad Vashem)

Note: The name in parantheses was the woman's name in the camp and is the one usually used in the text. '**P**' deontes a Polish prisoner.)

Albirt, Sara	M-1/E/2210/2072
Asa (Gerber), Rachel	Oral testimony
Baner, Tema	M-1/E/325/228
Bar-Ilan (Siegel), Bracha	0-33/4839
Beitner, Hela	M-1/E/313/197
Bek, Dora	M-1/E/348/270
Bernat, Aranka	0-15/1289
Blezowska, Ester	M-1/E/1628/1516
Blum (Blatt), Felicja	0-33/1839

Bojer (Wolf), Sara	0-33/3268
Buchenholz (Schneider), Paulina	0-33/E/142-2-1
Buszmicz (Kelberg), Ida	0-3/2798
Cukier, Ewa	0-3/1664
Cypres (Wanderer), Rena	0-33/1857
Danziger (Wierzbicki), Rachel	Oral testimony
Debek, Danuta (P)	Oral testimony
Eitan, Miriam	0-33/2834
Ezer (Brandwejn), Hanka	0-33/3420
Fajszewicz, Sara	M-1/E/1797/1655
Faranyi, Janona	0-15/506
Fenik, Eda	0-3/1272
Fradkin, Rina (Taubenblatt, Rena)	0-16/249
Fugiel (Kołecka), Zofia (P)	0-33/4838
Gimes, Paula	0-3/1080
Goldberg (Lichtensztejn), Lilian	0-33/4837
Goldszmid, Arnona	0-15/566
Goldweiss, Pola	M-1/E/2113/1892
Granatsztajn (Finkler), Malka	0-3/3323
Grinstein (Adler), Lola	Oral testimony
Gross, Margalit	0-3/7526
Grossmitz, Bella	M-1/E/1612/1495
Harit (Thieberger), Nurit	Oral testimony
Hartman (Rotenberg), Ziuta	0-33/1851
Haubman (Ohrenstein), Regina	Oral testimony
Herling, Fela	M-1/E/1987/1810
Herstein (Zakrzewski), Bina	0-33/1796
Hertz (Fugman), Tema	0-33/3269
Hollender, Mata	0-16/1215
Hottner (Zuckerbrot), Malka	0-33/1655
Ickowicz (Kühnreich), Blanka	0-33/3421
Jewin (Lewin), Eda	0-33/1838
Jolinger, Jeta	0-33/3419
Kalman, Regina	M-1/E/2370/2445
Karay (Schächter), Felicja	0-33/1812
Katz (Budyn), Malka	0-33/3272
Kaufman (Fuss), Luna	0-33/1819
Kornfeld, Hanka	0-16/502
Kurzman (Feig), Helena	0-33/3280
Landau (Rabinowicz), Regina	Oral testimony

Landowska (Wolska), Jadwiga (**P**)	0-33/4238
Latowicz, Janina	0-3/1384
Lewinger (Schächter), Maria	0-33/1802
Meiersdorf, Gela	0-3/869
Muskatenblut (Bladberg), Lea	0-33/1801
Najberg, Riwka	M-1/E/2460/2526
Natanson (Wójtowicz), Barbara (**P**)	0-33/4241
Netzer (Nessel), Ester	0-33/650
Neuman, Irma	0-2/768
Rapp (Silberzweig), Fela	0-33/1803
Razowski (Zuckerman), Halina	0-33/3287
Reibscheid, Barbara	0-16/1911
Reich (Perlberg), Maryla (in the camp – Hanka Skowrońska)	0-33/3316
Reiser (Grünberg), Genia	0-33/3485
Rozenblum, Sabina	0-3/3572
Różycka, Eugenia	0-33/712
Schütz, Halina	0-16/329
Seńko (Pełka), Irena (**P**)	0-33/4242
Shahar (Silberstein), Felicja	0-33/3334
Shalem (Iwańska), Sara	0-33/3332
Siegman (Brand), Frania	0-3/2979
Sperling (Hofnung), Mala	0-33/4652
Sroka, Dora	M-21/4-89
Stern (Rosental), Sara	Oral testimony
Strelski (Buchman), Henia	0-33/1836
Światłowska, Sonia	M-21/4-89
Szymkiewicz, Ester	M-1/E/1210/1276
Todtleben, Teresa (**P**)	Oral testimony
Węgrzycka (Lipska), Jadwiga (**P**)	0-33/4240
Witosz, Fela	M-1/E/2487/2568
Wolański (Szklanka), Hanka	0-3/1174
Wolfe (Karmel), Henryka	0-33/1852
Woliniewska, Matylda (**P**)	0-33/4237
Zelwer (Horn), Roza	0-3/1074
Zorski (Schächter), Helena	0-33/1797
Zweig, Zacharia	0-3/2192
Żychlinski, Hanna	M-21/1-16/MAPPE/16

Index